Developing Museum Exhibitions for Lifelong Learning

Edited by Gail Durbin
on behalf of the
Group for Education
in Museums

MUSEUMS & GALLERIES
COMMISSION

GEM

London: The Stationery Office

Applications for reproduction should be made to The Stationery Office, St Crispins, Duke Street, Norwich NR3 1PD

ISBN 0 11 290552 8

British Library Cataloguing in Publication Data
A CIP catalogue record for this book is available from the British Library

To the editor's and publisher's best knowledge the appropriate permission has been granted for the reproduction of all copyright material in this book. Any errors or omissions which may be detected are unintentional and regretted.

The Stationery Office

Published by The Stationery Office and available from:

The Stationery Office
(mail, telephone and fax orders only)
PO Box 29, Norwich NR3 1GN
Telephone orders/General enquiries 0870 600 5522
Fax orders 0870 600 5533

www.itsofficial.net

The Stationery Office Bookshops
123 Kingsway, London WC2B 6PQ
020 7242 6393 Fax 020 7242 6412
68-69 Bull Street, Birmingham B4 6AD
0121 236 9696 Fax 0121 236 9699
33 Wine Street, Bristol BS1 2BQ
0117 926 4306 Fax 0117 929 4515
9-21 Princess Street, Manchester M60 8AS
0161 834 7201 Fax 0161 833 0634
16 Arthur Street, Belfast BT1 4GD
028 9023 8451 Fax 028 9023 5401
The Stationery Office Oriel Bookshop
18-19 High Street, Cardiff CF1 2BZ
029 2039 5548 Fax 029 2038 4347
71 Lothian Road, Edinburgh EH3 9AZ
0870 606 5566 Fax 0870 606 5588

The Stationery Office's Accredited Agents
(see Yellow Pages)

and through good booksellers

Contents

Preface

This book is for anyone planning a new museum gallery or exhibition who needs information at their fingertips on how to maximise the learning potential of their galleries.

Education, in its broadest sense, is at the core of all museum activity, and displays are perhaps the most important means by which museums can either inhibit or encourage learning. Of the books written about the development of museum displays, most have focused on the practicalities of the process at the expense of the educational aims and content of displays. This book sets out to restore the balance.

In recent years, a great deal of useful material has been published in scattered journals, often American, but it is not easily available to museum professionals who do not have access to large research libraries. This anthology is an attempt to gather up some of this writing in one comprehensive volume. Selected articles and extracts provide a philosophical and theoretical framework as well as practical information for gallery planners intent on providing intellectual access to their collections.

The task has not been easy: learning theories of relevance to museums may not have been applied to museum issues, and the needs of specific audiences may not have been studied in the museum context. Preference has been given to extracts which are related to museums, rather than to useful material of a more general nature, but you may still have to use imagination to understand the relevance of the content to individual museums, galleries or learners. The book is also vulnerable to the obvious disadvantage of any anthology: if no article on a burning issue has been written, then that issue cannot be addressed here.

The book deals with the planning and implementation stage of exhibition and gallery development rather than educational activities that might be run in a gallery once the exhibition is open. It omits discussion of guide books and leaflets, or of displays of a special character such as touch exhibitions.

Depending on your own needs and learning style, you may want to start this book with the theory or with the practice. Two articles introduce the book. Elaine Gurian deals, in an up-beat and direct way, with many of the thorny issues of display planning and sets an agenda for much of the rest of the book. Lisa Roberts analyses the role of educators on gallery teams. The first main section opens with a discussion of a range of learning theories that can be applied to museums. Since no exhibition can be planned without considering the various audiences who might be addressed, there is a large section defining the needs and characteristics of these distinct groups in a museum context. The section on exhibition planning includes many extracts dealing with exhibition policy, the organisation of gallery teams and some of the practical issues they face. This is followed by some exhibition case studies. Museum literature is crammed with descriptions of how people have planned and opened new galleries but this material is often parochial and self-congratulatory and makes few points of more general interest. The selection here focuses on those case studies where the methods were innovative or the problems faced are relevant to other institutions in the 1990s. The issue of museum text, always a vexed one, has been given a section to itself, running from the theoretical to the practical. The book concludes with a section on evaluation.

The Project

This is a volume produced by committee – several of them – but we hope our project has coherence, generated by pooling the experience of so many people who have had to face the issues the book addresses.

The book was conceived at the 1991 AGM of the Group for Education in Museums. Members were finding themselves on gallery teams where they had to do more than respond intuitively to proposals. If they were to represent the needs of the visitor and to argue cogently they needed access to research findings relevant to learning in museums.

And so do others, as, of course, it is not only educators who play the role of audience advocate or who will benefit from the contents of the book: this anthology has been produced with the needs of all gallery or exhibition project team members in mind.

The project has involved large numbers of GEM members who have been prepared to commit many hours to it. Gail Durbin, Head of the Schools Section at the Victoria and Albert Museum, acted as the project co-ordinator, strongly supported by a steering group made up of David Anderson, Head of Education at the Victoria and Albert Museum, John Bainbridge, Assistant County Museums Officer, Somerset County Museums Service, Mary Bryden, Head of Public Affairs at the National Museums of Scotland, Dr Eilean Hooper-Greenhill, Senior Lecturer in Museum Studies at the University of Leicester, Hazel Moffat, formerly HMI with national responsibility for museum education, now a consultant, and Dr Sheila Watson, Community Museums Officer, Norfolk Museums Service.

One of the first tasks was to make a literature search and for this we employed Dr Annette Stannett who has also rigorously checked details and sought out copyright holders. Since an important aim of the project was to provide professional development for GEM members it was decided to set up reading groups, on the main themes of the book, whose job it would be to make recommendations on content. The reading team leaders were Liz Awty, Ian Baxter, Ruth Briant, Peter Clarke, Sian Jones, Margarette Lincoln, Nancy Martin, Sandra Marwick, Gill Page, Oonagh Palmer, Anne Pennington-George, Christine Ryan, Jill Slaney, Sue Wilkinson and Sue Wright. These group leaders worked extremely hard over more than two years circulating articles, collating responses and finally making recommendations. Over 100 GEM members were involved in the reading groups and valiantly read through and commented on prodigious amounts of text. As a collaborative exercise this project was hugely successful and involved a large proportion of GEM's membership.

Once this first stage was completed, the recommendations were assembled and the steering group embarked on the task of making the final selection. Each member took two or three topics and read all the articles again, confirmed suggestions or identified a need for a further search. The sharing of expertise within the group proved to be extremely helpful. Gaps were identified and filled where possible; topics were combined; and a better structure was created until we were eventually able to see and refine the complete selection.

The literature search stopped in 1994 and, except for one piece by Douglas Worts, seen in draft at that stage, no articles after that date have been included. The introductions to each section refer to a few pieces not published in this book. Some of these were printed after 1994. Our selection will provide a thorough base from which to explore current publications. The book also includes a number of items published before 1990, where we believe that they are still significant and relevant to others working in the field.

Editorial Policy

Few of the articles included in this anthology are printed in their entirety. We have made many cuts which are clearly indicated. Our policy has been to keep only what is practically useful to members of a gallery team. In some cases descriptions of the research methodology have been omitted. Sometimes the body of the argument in a particular article has been kept, and sometimes it is only the conclusions that have been included here. For clarity we have sometimes given an extract a new title but the name of the original article or book is always recorded as well. We have retained all relevant references but have omitted other kinds of footnotes. Illustrations have been omitted where they are not essential to the argument. In all cases it is recommended that those who want further information or plan to cite these articles in their own work should consult the original works. Further references can be found in the GEM bibliography, Bosdêt M and Durbin G (1989) *Museum education bibliography 1978–1988*, and in the annual updates produced by Annette Stannett in the *Journal of Education in Museums*, all available from the Group for Education in Museums.

Guidelines on Planning a Display

Some members of the steering group have a strong predilection for checklists and this introduction is our opportunity to produce a short list of key questions and stages in the process, as a guide for anyone embarking on a new display, concerned about learning issues and wanting to put some of the material in this book to practical use.

- What is the intellectual content of your display to be? What objects do you have? What do you want to say? (not dealt with in this book)
- What kind of learning can museums and galleries enable? (see Section Two, Learning Theories)
- Who do you want to reach? (see Section Three, Audiences)
- Can you test your initial ideas? (see Section Eight, Evaluation)
- What balance will you make between content and audience? How far is your message to be determined by your audience and how far will your content determine your message? How will the learning needs of the audience affect the exhibition design? (see Section Two, Learning Theories and Section Three, Audiences)
- Who will you choose as your principal target groups? How will your target groups influence the design of the display? (see Section Three, Audiences and Section Four, Disability)
- Develop your plans, returning continuously to your message and to your target audiences and the ways in which people learn, to check that you are on course (see Section Two, Learning Theories, Section Three, Audiences, Section Four, Disability and Section Five, Exhibition Planning)
- Test if appropriate (see Section Eight, Evaluation)
- Go ahead and set up your display (see Section Five, Exhibition Planning and Section Seven, Text)

- Test to see whether you have achieved your aims. What personal meanings do your audience construct from your display? (see Section Eight, Evaluation)

- Adapt in the light of findings

These guidelines represent one of many possible approaches to exhibition and gallery display and you may not choose this model to help tackle a new display. You may prefer to work out your own approach. The questions posed, however, are some that the steering group have had to ask in planning this book and the sections that follow should go some way to providing solutions.

Acknowledgements

The Group for Education in Museums would like to thank the Museums and Galleries Commission for financial help with this volume and the employing bodies of steering group members for their support. It would also like to thank the following for permission to reproduce copyright material:

Ablex Publishing Corp. (Gardner); American Association for State and Local History (Grasso and Morrison); American Association of Museums (Borun, Cassedy, Dierking); American Museum of Natural History, Paulette McManus, Beverly Serrell and John H Falk (Falk, McManus, Serrell); Association of Manitoba Museums and M Matthew (Matthew); Athlone Press Ltd (Worts); The Barbados Museum and Historical Society (Donawa); Stephen C Bitgood (Bitgood); The Carnegie United Kingdom Trust and the Centre on Environment for the Handicapped (Pearson); Cassell Academic (Coxall, McManus); Centre for Environmental Interpretation (Binks and Uzzell, Carter); ECSITE Newsletter (Hein); Group for Education in Museums and Helen Coxall, Steve Hemming and Richard Wood (Coxall, Hemming, Wood); the Controller of HMSO (Runyard); ICOM and George Hein (Hein); Journal of Museum Education and Lisa Roberts (Roberts); Museum Association of Aotearoa New Zealand Te Ropu Hanga Kaupapa Taonga (Cassels); Museum Management and Curatorship, Elsevier Science Ltd, (Anderson, Macdonald, Phillips); Museums and Galleries Commission (Davies); Museums Association and Rebecca McGinnis, John Andrew Millard (McGinnis and Millard); National Association for the Education of Young Children and Stewart Cohen (Cohen); National Endowment for the Arts (anon); NIACE (Brisenden); National Maritime Museum (Kentley and Negus); Routledge (Hooper-Greenhill, Thomas, Dean); The Trustees of the Science Museum (Bicknell and Mann, Serrell, Hilke); Scottish Museums Council and Paisley Museum and Art Galleries (Carnegie); C G Screven (Hirschi, Screven); Smithsonian Institution Press (Gurian); and Taylor & Francis and John Stevenson (Stevenson).

Section One   Introduction

1 Noodling Around with Exhibition Opportunities

Elaine Heumann Gurian

Extracted from an article in *Exhibiting cultures: the poetics and politics of museum display*, Karp, I and Lavine, S P (eds), Smithsonian Institution Press, 1991, pp.176–190.

Museum visitors receive far more from exhibitions than just information about the objects displayed. Let me suggest that visitors can deduce from their experience what we, the producers of exhibitions, think and feel about them – even if we have not fully articulated those thoughts to ourselves.

I will explore the notion that we, consciously or unconsciously, impose learning impediments in our exhibitions for some members of our current and potential audiences. We do so because we possess unexamined beliefs about our visitors' capacity to learn and because we want them to act in a style that reinforces our notion of appropriate audience behaviour. We continue to do so regardless of our exposure to countervailing theories about learning or examples of experimentation in exhibitions. We design evaluation tools that measure only those things we wish the audience to learn rather than those the audience is actually learning. We espouse the goal of enlarging our audiences to include underserved populations and novice learners, and yet we continue not to accommodate them: we demand that they accommodate us and then wonder why they do not visit our galleries.

I will argue that it is not content that predetermines the exhibition design, strategies, and installations we use; rather, exhibition content and presentation are separable. While much has been written about the choice of content (and there is still much to explore), very little has been written about choice of style as an expression of intention. Regardless of exhibition content, producers can choose strategies that can make some portion of the public feel either empowered or isolated. If the audience, or some segment thereof, feels alienated, unworthy, or out of place, I contend it is because we want them to feel that way.

It could also be suggested that we, the staff, are partly in collusion with a segment of our audience that wants exhibition presentation to reinforce the aspirations and expectations they have for themselves. This audience of traditional museum consumers does not wish to have others join their company, as that would disrupt their notion of their own superiority and their right to an exclusive domain. Pierre Bourdieu, in the introduction to his book *Distinction: a social critique of the judgement of taste* (1984) [writes]:

> A work of art has meaning and interest only for someone who possesses the cultural competence, that is, the code, into which it is encoded . . . A beholder who lacks the specific code feels lost in a chaos of sounds and rhythms, colours and lines, without rhyme or reason . . . Thus, the encounter with a work of art is not love at first sight as is generally supposed.

The question we as producers of exhibitions must ask is why do we participate in this collusion, and what can we do to change if we so desire?

An opportunity for change is provided by the way disciplines such as anthropology, art history, and history are re-examining their foundations and acknowledging that previously held beliefs about the objectivity of research and the impartiality of the investigator were never realistic. By applying these same techniques of self-examination to ourselves as museum professionals, we may gain insights that will enable us to approach our exhibitions – and their audiences – in new, fruitful ways . . .

Museums and their Audiences: Identity, Politics and Equality

. . . Historically, it can be argued that museums have been created to promote the aspirations of their creators. Art museums have been created by wealthy patrons and collectors to reinforce their status and aesthetic, while science-and-technology centres have been created by wealthy merchants to enlist the public's concurrence about the progress and future of industry. Historical societies have been founded by people who wanted their personal and class histories preserved, and children's museums have been founded by parents and educators who were emboldened by the education theories of Dewey. Finally, counter-culture museums have been created by people of all classes who want to preserve a particular viewpoint that has not been expressed in other museums . . .

Some Parameters of Learning in a Museum

Chandler Screven, a long-time museum exhibition evaluator, writes, 'Museum learning is self-paced, self-directed, non-linear, and visually oriented' (1987). This statement points out some of the ways in which exhibitions actually work. Museum exhibitions are certainly not school classrooms, which enforce incremental, cumulative learning through authoritarian leadership over rigidly defined, constant social units. Except for school groups, museum audiences are composed of unrelated social units who remain anonymous and display uneven previous knowledge about the subject matter. Exhibitions are places of free choice. Try as we might, the public continually thwarts our attempts to teach incrementally in an exhibition. They come when they want, leave when they want, and look at what they want while they are there. Therefore, linear installations often feel like forced marches.

Exhibition content can be understood by the audience immediately, can be reassessed and integrated at some later date, or both. The visitor receives an impressionistic, sometimes indelible, sense of the topic, and in addition creates a mental inventory of items that he or she can bank for later consideration. The one-time, indelible impression to which all subsequent exposures will be referenced has been described by Michael Spock and others as 'landmark learning'. The long-term integration often comes as an 'aha phenomenon' when a second trigger is presented that makes the stored items understood in a satisfying way.

Good exhibitions are often conceptually simple. The more complex the verbal message becomes, the less understandable the exhibition turns out to be, since exhibitions are basically non-verbal enterprises. What can be displayed best are tangible materials that can be seen, sometimes touched, and often fantasised about. Exhibition topics deal with both concrete things and abstractions; we display objects that are simultaneously real and emblematic.

Objects in exhibitions can elicit emotional responses. The presence of certain artefacts can evoke memories and feelings. Mihaly Csikszentmihalyi and Eugene

Rochberg-Halton's book *The meaning of things* (1981) suggests that it is the emotional overlay we place upon impersonal objects that transforms them into objects of meaning. If we are interested in changing our exhibitions into exhibitions of meaning, we will have to be prepared to include frankly emotional strategies.

Imposed Limits to Learning

But we, the producers of exhibitions, have not fully exploited all exhibition tactics suggested by the parameters outlined above. Could this be because we are not entirely comfortable with what certain modes of exhibition might reveal about us? It is not only what we think about our audience that determines the exhibition designs we use; they are also determined by what we want the audience and our colleagues to think about us. Styles of exhibiting that enhance learning but are sensual and emotive may embarrass us and not conform with our descriptions of ourselves as erudite, intellectual, and respectable.

I believe that somewhere in the history of exhibitions, certain non-rational strategies were deemed theatrical. Being in the theatre is still not wholly respectable. Museum professionals do not want to be in show business; we want to be in academia. And yet, like it or not, exhibitions are in part public entertainment . . .

Another reason we have not fully exploited the sensory possibilities and opportunities that displaying objects can offer us may be that we have internalised certain cultural preferences for some modes of learning over others. For example, we have been taught that one mark of the civilised person is verbal ability, and so when explicating objects in, say, science or cultural-history museums, we concentrate on producing textual labels. Many of us also believe that in exhibitions focusing on aesthetics, the 'visually literate' person should know how to use the visual cues provided by the objects without any additional assistance from us, and so we often do not write explanatory labels in art galleries and rarely use auditory, olfactory, or tactile techniques there. Worst of all, appealing directly to the emotions is considered pandering to the mob, so we do not dare to appear enthusiastic. As a result of these internalised preferences, then, exhibitions often become places in which we, the exhibition makers, use certain styles of exhibiting to demonstrate our own mastery of these modes of learning, not only to ourselves but also to our colleagues and our audiences.

Nor do we want to appear friendly, because we believe that informality would reduce the importance of our work. If the audience is having fun, we may be accused of providing a circus and not behaving in a sufficiently reverential manner. If we have a Calvinistic view of our purpose, we will not permit ourselves to be informal. But if we as exhibition producers begin to think that playfulness is a permissible part of learning (as learning theorists would have us believe), different exhibition strategies may take over. For example, collections may be placed so that they are not immediately apparent, or objects may be installed in a way that reveals visual jokes. The label will reveal that there is a task of interpretation in the very act of looking. Such an attitude may also make more apparent the humour of artists or cultures, which is often omitted because humour is considered frivolous.

Accommodating Different Styles and Levels of Learning

In *Frames of mind*, Howard Gardner (1983) suggests that, regardless of our social history, every individual has his or her own set of gifts or talents, and a corresponding set of preferred learning styles. He suggests that there are many forms of learning, which can be divided roughly into seven categories: linguistic, musical, logical-mathematical, spatial, bodily-kinesthetic, interpersonal and intrapersonal. These categories are not hierarchical but rather are parallel and have equal value. Most important for exhibition producers, one form of learning is not necessarily translatable into another; thus, tactile comprehension does not necessarily translate into verbal understanding.

Since, as Howard Gardner suggests, each individual in our audience has a different learning pattern, multisensory exhibition experiences that offer many entry points could facilitate a range of learning experiences, without prejudice. It follows, then, that should we wish all visitors to learn and understand, we must construct a wide palette of exhibition opportunities that utilises all the senses. There are materials visitors long to touch. There are many objects that could be better understood if the audience has a chance to participate in a process or an experiment.

In addition to preferred learning styles, everyone is a novice about every subject at some time in his or her life. It is safe to assume that every exhibition will have novice learners in its audience, and yet most adults do not like to admit publicly their beginner status. It is much kinder for the exhibition producer to accommodate the novice than to assume that the exhibition should work only for the exhibit creator and his or her knowledgeable colleagues. The assumption that novice visitors need to feel welcome suggests the following (not exhaustive) list of obligatory strategies: defining all terms when used, providing an introduction to the social context for all exhibitions, locating all geographical references, and allowing all processes of art production to be understood.

Strategies [are being developed] for including the novice learner in an art museum setting.

> Novices have very mixed feelings, about hearing what experts think about art objects. While they acknowledge that the experts know something that might be useful to them in looking, novices are quite adamant that they don't want anyone to decide for them what is good or bad. They don't want someone to tell them that something they really like isn't 'good' . . . They also don't want to be talked down to . . . Novices also perceive experts as looking at objects in a very intellectual, unfeeling way . . . As novices they tend to have their most pleasurable experience with art when they look at it in a very emotional, feeling-laden way (McDermott, 1987).

If we, the creators of exhibitions, think that viewers are inherently smart (though not necessarily well-educated or familiar with the subject matter) and that they are entitled to ask questions and receive answers, then we will address questions the audience has rather than tell them what we think they should know. It is logical, then, that the author will have to consult with the public before writing final copy. This implies the time-consuming task of audience interviews before the final installation is done.

Label Copy

Even for the writing of label copy there are techniques that can promote inclusion or exclusion. If the label writer believes the audience is composed of receptive students, and the information he or she wants to pass on is genuinely good for them, then the label writer will assume the role of a teacher transmitting information. The audience will be viewed as a passive but obedient recipient. The audience's only choice then is whether to read or not to read, to be willing or to be recalcitrant. However, failure to read labels is often perceived by the audience as something 'naughty'; consequently, they feel guilty.

The role of teacher is not the label writer's only possible stance. He or she can choose instead to be co-conspirator, colleague, preacher, or even gossip columnist. Altering these assumptions about the label writer's role might cause the audience to change their behaviour as well. For example, if the writer sees the audience as a partner, then perhaps the audience might participate like a partner. There are also label-writing strategies that encourage interaction both between the viewer and the object and between the viewer and members of his or her party . . .

[Other] strategies . . . encourage the *audience* to become the teacher. These strategies, like Spock's 'talk-back boards' identify the visitor as a resource in addition to the curator and the institution. This allows ownership of the exhibition to extend beyond the staff . . .

Additional Sources of Information

Some novice members of our audiences will become intermediate or even advanced learners within a single museum visit. An object that intrigues the visitor brings out the instantaneous need for more information. Adding information to an exhibition is always a problem, because we are mindful of detracting from the object and cluttering up the exhibit. We understand that not everyone wants the same additional information, but the individual who does want more information wants it then and there. Immediate access to information is satisfying to the audience; therefore, the task is to provide information in the exhibition in a manner such that the audience knows it is available without its being intrusive. Putting the catalogue in the gallery is one way to allow the visitor immediate access to more information about the subject to hand. Other strategies include installing computers and interactive videodiscs with branching programs, which have the capacity to hold additional information without cluttering the walls. Embedding a resource centre within or next to the exhibition space has been used by many museums, including the M H de Young Memorial Museum in San Francisco.

Blurring the distinctions between kinds of museums works to the benefit of the audience as well. For the visitor, an object of interest provokes many questions that are cross-disciplinary; he or she is probably not interested in our museological territorial boundaries . . .

Identifying the Exhibition Creator

An alternative exhibition strategy that also allows the visitor to feel included involves creating an exhibition in which each object has been personally selected by an identifiable source, who self-consciously reveals the decisions surrounding the inclusion of each item. This strategy of making the curator the narrator invites the visitor to become a fellow traveller . . . An exhibition that is signed, uses the first person in the label copy, and/or reveals the personality of the artist is a personal, creative act analogous to a signed work of art, and intentionally becomes an autobiographical exhibition. While visitors expect to see the authors of works of art, music, and fiction identified, they are not used to perceiving exhibitions as the personal work of identifiable individuals. Unsigned exhibitions reinforce the notion that there is a godlike voice of authority behind the selection of objects. But presenting a curator as an individual usefully demonstrates that exhibitions are in reality like signed columns rather than news releases and that each producer, like each columnist, has a point of view . . .

The Museum as Gathering Place

Ellen Posner (1988) writes in the *Atlantic*:

> . . . museums stand at the centre of social life. And the buildings themselves are expected to attract and seduce the casual passerby, to deliver glamour, panache, and chic and to promise a good time to be had by all.

This point is reinforced by John Falk's work (1985), which has demonstrated that people visiting any exhibition spend a considerable amount of time interacting with the people they came with and watching strangers. The need to be in a congregative setting is perhaps much more important than we in the museum business commonly acknowledge. Exhibitions need to support both individual learning and social interactions. Many people do not want to display their ignorance in front of strangers, and so learning opportunities will need to be designed that simultaneously encourage social interaction among members of the visiting party and private contemplation. If we begin to feel that it is within our mission to support sociability, then we will feel more comfortable about promoting seating arrangements that, quite frankly, reinforce social interaction as well as interaction with the objects. For example, despite the conservation problems, cafés in the middle of exhibition spaces, surrounded by the objects, might enhance learning better than cafés separated from these areas.

Conclusions

While we may be reluctant to admit it, the production of an exhibition is more akin to the production of a theatre piece than any other form. Like theatre, exhibitions are formed by a group of people who have highly individualised visions and styles, in a process in which compromise is the order of the day. The relationship among values expressed in the exhibition, content, and style has to be broadly agreed upon, or else the team must be autocratically ruled in order to avoid a cacophony of ideas.

The process of exhibition production and the loci of power within the exhibition team are interesting topics in themselves and deserve further study. For the purposes of this paper, however, I suggest that the resultant product – the exhibition – must have embedded within it either agreed-upon assumptions about the audience or a coherent view of the audience as articulated by a single prevailing power source.

In current practice, however, during production of an exhibition the team members rarely force themselves to reveal and share their views of the visitor. Of course, we can continue to keep our views of the audience hidden even from ourselves, but doing that reinforces messages that I am sure we would be too embarrassed to acknowledge. It follows that if, as part of the initial stages of exhibition formation, we develop tools to allow all of us to articulate our individual assumptions instead, we might be more willing to include strategies that reinforce what we would *like* to think about our visitors. Then exhibitions may be created that work for the audience – not because we necessarily inherently care about the audience, but because we *want* to care about the audience and will adjust our behaviour accordingly.

As Stephen E Weil (1989), deputy director of the Smithsonian Institution's Hirshhorn Museum and Sculpture Garden, writes:

> The real issue, I think, is not how to purge the museum of values – that, in all likelihood, would be an impossible task – but how to make those values manifest, how to bring them up to consciousness for both ourselves and our visitors. We delude ourselves when we think of the museum as a clear and transparent medium through which only our objects transmit messages. We transmit messages too – as a medium we are also a message – and it seems to me vital that we understand better just what those messages are.

References

Bourdieu, P (1984). *Distinction: a social critique of the judgement of taste*, Cambridge, Massachusetts, Harvard University Press, pp. 2–3.

Csikszentmihalyi, M and Rochberg-Halton, E (1981). *The meaning of things*, Cambridge, Cambridge University Press.

Falk, J et al. (1985). 'Predicting visitor behavior', *Curator* 28(4), pp. 249–257.

Gardner, H (1983). *Frames of mind: the theory of multiple intelligences*, New York, Basic Books.

McDermott, M (1987). 'Through these eyes: what novices value in art experience', preliminary draft of report prepared for the American Association of Museums Program Sourcebook. [photocopy]

Posner, E (1988). 'The museum as bazaar', *Atlantic* 262(2), p. 68.

Screven, C (1987). 'Museum learning and the casual visitor: what are the limits?' Paper presented at the University of Toronto.

Weil, S E (1989). 'The proper business of the museum: ideas or things?', *Muse* 12(1), p. 31.

2 Educators on Exhibit Teams: a New Role, a New Era

Lisa C Roberts

Extracted from an article in *Journal of Museum Education*, Fall 1994, pp. 6–9.

In the early 1980s, for the first time in any systematic fashion, educators began to be invited to sit at the exhibit development table. This noteworthy occurrence marked the beginning of an approach to exhibit development that took into account curatorial design and new educational perspectives. 'The team approach to exhibit design' – it rang of democracy, fellowship and collaboration. During the next decade museums throughout the country would jump on the exhibit team bandwagon, part of a growing national conscientiousness about museums' public dimension.

It has not all been smooth sailing however. Exhibit teams have been dogged by problems that range from establishing priorities to achieving consensus. And no wonder. The inclusion of educators on exhibit teams has introduced new interests, criteria and influence into the process of exhibit making. Change on this scale can hardly happen overnight. Role definition has been especially problematic because on the surface it has appeared so straightforward: curators are responsible for an exhibit's content, designers are responsible for its look, and educators are responsible for the visitors – as well as for other potential audiences, and pedagogical soundness, and communication and supplementary programming to enhance the exhibit.

Well, it *seemed* straightforward anyway. At the very least, it is safe to say that educators are in some sense responsible for assuring that an exhibit is intelligible to viewers. Exactly what that means – to make an exhibit 'intelligible' – is the subject of this article. Educators' role in the exhibit development process has never been clear-cut. It is relatively new, after all, and it is still evolving. Broadened notions of learning, growing knowledge about visitors, new complexities in interpretation, and expanded responsibilities – all continue to influence the role educators are expected to play.

Just as this role has been subject to change and refinement, so are these attempts to define it. This article is meant to be not prescriptive, but descriptive. I hope to begin to lay out some common guidelines for understanding precisely what educators are responsible for on exhibit development teams. I will also consider the consequences of that responsibility for the exhibits visitors now encounter: how have exhibits changed as a result of educators' involvement? And what are the implications of these changes for the museum as an institution?

An Evolving Role

The Children's Museum in Boston and Field Museum of Natural History in Chicago are widely credited with originating the models that led to what we now call the team approach to exhibit design. Realising that this approach was the wave of the future, Field Museum presented a series of workshops between

1982 and 1987 on the team approach: they were attended by some 300 educators and designers from 105 museums throughout the country. These workshops mark one of the first concerted efforts to define team members' roles in the exhibit development process. Over the course of five years and as many workshops, definitions for the three perspectives emerged:

Curator: The curator provides the scholarly expertise based on knowledge of the collection. As subject matter specialist the curator is responsible for establishing the overall concept of the exhibit.

Designer: The designer is responsible for the visual appearance and coherence of the exhibit. The designer's expertise assures that the exhibit material is set out in an appealing, understandable and attractive manner.

Educator: The educator establishes the link between the content of the exhibit and the museum audience. The educator is a communication specialist who understands the ways people learn, the needs that museum audiences have and the relationship between the museum's programme and the activities of other educational institutions including schools. The educator plans evaluation activities that will examine the exhibit's success in meeting its intended objectives and communicating with visitors (Munley, 1986).

Such clear-cut definitions did not always translate so neatly into the realities of the job. In actual practice, exhibit teams might comprise any number of staff representing these or other museum occupations, and some museums developed their own nomenclatures to describe the roles of team members. Teams have had to tinker with process-related issues like defining task stages and determining team leadership. But the essence of the team idea was that the three types of expertise outlined above – subject matter, design and communication – needed in some way to be represented.

As newcomers to exhibit development, educators have found that their role on the team has remained the murkiest. It has not always been clear just what they are expected to *do*: and in some cases their responsibilities seemed to overlap those of other team members. Herein, then, is the beginning of a primer for educators serving on exhibit teams.

Areas of Responsibility and Expertise

At this point in time, it is safe to say that educators' responsibilities embrace at least seven general areas:

Audience Advocacy

As advocates for museum audiences, educators must represent the interests of the variety of visitors an exhibit will potentially serve. Youth, families, seniors, disabled people, schoolchildren and multicultural groups are common visitor types. Each has characteristic needs and interests that it is the responsibility of the educator to know and represent. Information about some of these groups is readily available in visitor studies literature. More specialised resources may be found elsewhere. In the case of school groups, for example, educators need to be familiar with state goals for learning and school curriculums that an exhibit might support. For people with disabilities, educators must be able to speak to the accessibility requirements of the Americans with Disabilities Act.

When knowledge about target audiences is lacking or when exhibit developers have specific questions about visitors' interest or knowledge levels in some subject, it is incumbent on the educator to conduct front-end studies to find out this information. This responsibility leads directly to the next.

Evaluation

In the ideal world, there is an evaluator at the exhibit development table who is responsible for conducting visitor studies that will improve an exhibit's effectiveness. Indeed, many museums are beginning to employ professional evaluators to fill this need. Until they become a permanent presence, however, the responsibility must fall to educators.

Two types of evaluation studies are central to the development process. Front-end studies occur at the beginning and are designed to investigate visitors' knowledge, assumptions, attitudes or expectations about some topic. Formative studies occur during the course of exhibit development and consist of prototyping exhibit elements to assess their effectiveness with visitors before going into final production.

Evaluation can be as quick and dirty or as thorough and costly as one makes it. While one need not be a professional evaluator to conduct evaluation studies, the achievement of accurate, usable results does require knowledge about some basic principles of study design and sample selection.

Learning Theory

It has long been held that educators should have expertise in how people learn. It has also been said that educators should be conversant in philosophy of education, developmental psychology, communication theory, cognition research and perception studies. Exactly how informed educators need to be about these fields is arguable. Not all of this knowledge translates well into the informal learning setting of a museum. Yet these disciplines do constitute a base of knowledge from which educators can draw when determining the best way to present exhibit messages.

At the very least, educators must have a good grasp of those elements that contribute to effective learning experiences in museums (intrinsic motivation, reinforcement, and so on). Educators should also be abreast of current visitor research. A great many studies that deal with various aspects of the visitor experience are now available. Familiarity with this research or at least knowledge of where to find it can help take much of the guesswork out of decisions related to communicating effectively.

Finally, educators must be able to speak to that most basic of questions. What is learning? While the word 'learning' continues to connote information transfer and cognitive engagement in museums it has come to refer broadly to a whole range of experiences that describe different ways of connecting people to the collections. Learning in museums includes emotional, social, contemplative, recreational and attitudinal aspects, all of which have been documented by researchers seeking to characterise the nature of the visitor experience. An understanding of these aspects is essential to developing exhibits that reach learners in ways meaningful to them.

Communication

Effective communication is key to producing visitor-friendly exhibits. What is an exhibit about? What are the three most important messages? Are they comprehensible? Are they interesting? Communication is hardly limited to the words on the wall and yet words are the primary means through which exhibit messages are conveyed.

While the task of writing exhibit copy may not fall to the educator, the responsibility of assuring its comprehensibility does. Good writing is both an art and a science: an art, because it still takes a voice to make a narrative come alive; and a science, because it follows principles of good narrative construction. Educators must be sensitive to a whole range of factors embedded in a text to which visitors might respond. Prior knowledge and assumptions, personal relevance and age appropriateness all relate importantly to how messages are crafted.

To the extent that the medium is the message, educators may also be called upon to help conceptualise how messages are conveyed. Particularly with the growing use of interactives, the effectiveness of a message is linked to the manner in which it is presented. To this end, educators must be able to draw on teaching skills – the one area of expertise with which they have always been associated. Good teaching is, at bottom, about good communication, and educators need to be able to recognise how effective teaching methods can be adapted to the communication needs of exhibits.

Finally, as experts in communication, educators must recognise when exhibit messages might more appropriately be conveyed by other means. First-person interpretation, written handouts, and programme curricula all present alternative options for conveying information. Familiarity with supplementary media will help educators advise on the shaping of exhibit messages.

Interpretation

Interpretation is the single most basic purpose of an exhibit. Whether implicit or explicit, interpretation is embedded in the act of display – in how a thing looks, in what surrounds it, in what is said or not said about it. As such, interpretation is the business of every member of the team.

As content specialist the curator has traditionally been responsible for shaping an interpretation. With the advent of exhibit teams, educators may now have a hand in determining interpretive messages. This responsibility goes beyond how well exhibits communicate to what they communicate. Does this musket represent the bravery of American frontiersmen or the conquest of native people? To the extent that educators serve as audience advocates, it is their responsibility to present to the team views about the meaning of collections that will resonate with museum audiences.

Furthermore, it is the educators' responsibility to assure that visitors understand something about decisions behind an interpretation. Why is this an important or valued story? Whose story is it? Too often museums present an anonymous, authoritative view that bears no relation to the interests or meanings important to visitors. Interpretation is in part an act of negotiation – between the values and knowledges upheld by museums and those that are brought in by visitors (Rice, 1987, 1993).

Subject Matter

Although it is generally the responsibility of the curator to provide subject matter expertise, educators will function more effectively on the team if they hold some knowledge about the subject under development. Not only will they be better equipped to participate in exhibit discussions, but they will be able to speak to alternative visitor-centred approaches from a more informed position. Exactly how knowledgeable educators need to be is hard to say and probably depends on the particular situation. But the more familiar with a subject they are the more weight their views will carry.

Flexibility and Respect

As the preceding discussions make clear, some of the responsibilities delegated to educators overlap those that fall to designers and curators. Many designers, for example, describe their role less in terms of aesthetics than in terms of service to visitors. For them, good design is as much a matter of function as it is of looks. Likewise, curators now find themselves sharing their interpretive role with educators who are versed in visitors' perspectives. However clearly articulated team members' roles and responsibilities, there will always be shades of grey. Educators along with every other team member need to be cognisant of this fact and exercise flexibility and respect as they are required.

The Educative Museum

So educators have finally made it on to exhibit teams. What effect have they had on the face of exhibits and museums? Have they had an effect?

There is no question that exhibits produced in the last 15 years have been increasingly sensitive to the viewing public. Legibility has improved, evaluation techniques and advisory groups are being more widely employed and exhibit content better reflects visitors' knowledge and interest levels. In some museums these changes are the direct result of educators' involvement. In others, they reflect a growing sensitivity among staff as a whole toward museums' public dimension.

How these changes have improved visitors' experience varies widely. While overall visitor satisfaction seems to be on the upswing, many exhibit teams still need practice in making exhibits that are truly visitor centred. And the challenge remains of balancing the needs of the visitor against the interests of the scholar. As more space has been given over to interpretation, less is made available for objects: and in some minds, the collections – for which many museums were even founded – are being given short shrift. How this balancing act will play out in the future remains to be seen.

Outwardly, then, educators – or at least educational perspectives – have had a considerable impact on the way exhibits are made. The significance of this impact, however, goes beyond the physical façade. Educational interests strike at the heart of what it means to be a museum. Long-standing assumptions about the purposes of museum collections, the meanings they hold, and the authors of those meanings have been upended by educators' insistence on more broadly shared authority over collections and what they represent.

These changes mark the occurrence in museums of a much wider epistemological shift, one that has touched nearly everyone in the business of knowledge. This shift has seen traditional views in which knowledge is objective and absolute overturned by the notion that knowledge is socially constructed, shaped by the interests and values of the knower. Museum educators, with their concern for audience, diversity and multiple meanings, have been at the forefront of this shift in museums.

This shift in definitions of knowledge and knowledge derivation first took place in the practices of academicians – many of whom surely counted curators among their numbers. Historians, for example, became increasingly conscious of the extent to which their questions and approaches to the past are shaped by the character of the historical moment in which they work. Similarly, anthropologists began paying closer attention to the cultural biases in their studies and the racist undercurrents often embedded in their depictions of other cultures. Fields like art and literary criticism tested their own boundaries by demonstrating how social forces ultimately shape definitions of art, beauty, and quality. The development of psychoanalytic theory turned attention within, to the repressions and desires of individual human consciousness as the ultimate shaper of thought and perception.

History, culture, society, personality – while each variable represents a distinct set of influences, all are united by one thing: they describe conditions that shape what we think we know. Whatever the object, whatever the analytical method, knowledge exists in reference to a wider context of interests and values. To speak of a historical event or an artistic masterpiece, in other words, is also to speak of criteria of tastes and value by which they are judged to be important. Knowledge, then, may be understood to be linked inextricably to the context of its production, for it is the prevailing interests, values, social mores and beliefs that prescribe the standards of quality and criteria of truth according to which it is defined.

As practising scientists and historians, curators cannot have been untouched by these developments. With but a few exceptions, however, they have failed to consider the implications for exhibits. Educators are the ones who have sounded the cry for more inclusive exhibits that take into account how others might view the collections. While educators can hardly lay claim to the new scholarship and interpretations that have come out of making exhibits more inclusive, they can be credited with taking an activist role in insisting that such interpretations be considered.

It is here that the real significance of the inclusion of educators on exhibit teams becomes clear. When educators represent the views of exhibit audiences, when they argue for more diverse messages, they are bucking traditional ways of knowing and treating objects. As such they have been the catalysts in museums for the wider shift to a more context-based definition of knowledge. Their concerns raise questions – about the authority of curators and the primacy of their knowledge – that not only break with traditional, absolutist views of knowledge, but that touch on the very purposes of collections display. What do objects mean? Who are they for? Museums have throughout history struggled with questions such as these. Educators have now brought the discussion to a new level of meaning . . .

References

Munley, M E (1986). *Catalysts for change: the Kellogg Projects in museum education*, Kellogg Projects in Museum Education, Washington, Chicago and San Francisco, p. 31.

Rice, D (1987). 'On the ethics of museum education', *Museum News* 65(5), pp. 13–19.

Rice, D (1993). 'The cross-cultural mediator', *Museum News* 72(1), pp. 38–41.

Section Two   Learning Theories

Introduction

It is significant that the first four articles in this section are written by Americans, and the fifth concerns work developed in America. The debt owed by the profession to American research on learning theory is immediately apparent. It is also significant that the learning theories described here have all been developed by people working outside museums. This is a reflection of the current state of research on learning theory in museums in general, and UK museums in particular. The profession relies heavily upon theoretical work developed outside the museum sector, and very little research is done on the learning process in exhibitions and galleries by museum staff in this country. It is hard to escape the conclusion that, despite the widespread acceptance by museum staff that education is a core function of museums and research is one of their fundamental responsibilities, in practice the learning process is a low priority.

At the heart of the debate is the question 'Of what does the learning process consist?'. It is conventional, at least within museums, to separate learning theory from the subject of the learning (the collections and the disciplines they represent). In many institutions, research activities are conceived of, and written about, in terms of a hierarchical, sequential research process, in which the first and main focus is on the collections, and learning research is a branch of applied research whose function is to make the latest research discoveries available, accessible and comprehensible to a non-specialist audience.

The articles in this section present a challenge to such models of gallery and exhibition learning, and the theoretical assumptions which underlie them. Lynn Dierking, in her exceptionally wide ranging and lucid articles 'Historical survey of theories of learning' and 'Contemporary theories of learning', questions the view that learning is only concerned with the acquisition of a greater amount of knowledge (or feeling, or kinesthetic ability) and suggests that it may be as much to do with the way we think about something or do something. She also points out that there are fundamental differences in the way learners perceive and process information which make it difficult to create predictive models of learning.

George Hein, in 'Constructivist learning theory', explores the idea that learners individually (and socially) construct meaning for themselves. He points out that this means that there is no such thing as knowledge 'out there' independent of the learner, or community of learners. As Hein is aware, constructivist theory presents a fundamental challenge to the concept of hierarchical production and communication of meaning from specialists to non-specialists that most museum staff still hold to as an article of faith.

Howard Gardner's theory of multiple intelligences (described in 'Developing the spectrum of human intelligences') and Bernice McCarthy's 4MAT system (outlined in Richard Cassels' 'Mind, heart and soul: towards better learning in heritage parks') offer alternative approaches to identifying these individual differences. McCarthy's system, which draws heavily on the work of David Kolb on individual learning styles, distinguishes four types of learner (imaginative, analytical, common-sense problem-solver, and dynamic) and relates these to research on the functions of the left and right sides of the brain (see Bernice McCarthy, *The 4MAT system: teaching to learning styles with right/left mode techniques* Chicago: Excel, 1980). Another useful summary of McCarthy's work is provided by Elizabeth Rees Gilbert in a recent article in the US *Journal of Museum Education* 'Using the learning style inventory', 16(1), 1991, pp. 7–9, not included in this volume.

Howard Gardner's work on multiple intelligences offers an analysis of the seven intelligences he has identified (linguistic, musical, logical-mathematical, spatial, bodily-kinesthetic, interpersonal and intrapersonal). These are described in more detail in his seminal book, *Frames of mind: the theory of multiple intelligences* (Basic Books, New York, 1983) and their application to museums is explored in his subsequent book, *The unschooled mind* (Basic Books, New York, 1991).

Just as important as his work on individual differences are the implications they have for the relationship between the learning and the nature and processes of the disciplines being learned. Each of the conventional museum disciplines (history, fine art, decorative art, science or technology, for example) relates in a different way to the spectrum of Gardner's intelligences. The separation of collections research from learning research is, then, no longer sustainable, either theoretically or practically. The articles in this section are first steps towards the development of alternative theoretical models.

3 Historical Survey of Theories of Learning

Lynn D Dierking

This article appeared in *The audience in exhibition development*, American Association of Museums, 1992, pp. 24–28.

[There are] some major schools of thought on learning: behaviourism, developmentalism, and cognitive science. We will . . . talk about some of the implications of these schools of thought for organising an exhibit. Historically, we can trace attempts to understand the learning process to Aristotle and other early philosophers. They were very interested in cognition and thinking, and in fact their writings reflect their attempts to deal with the important part that cognitive capability plays in being human.

Behaviourists were among the first contemporary psychologists to address learning. The behaviourists turned interest in learning into a science. They were influenced by the early German experimentalists who were trying to understand human phenomena such as reflexes and attention. The behaviourists developed an associational notion of learning: there is a stimulus that the learner perceives, and then over a series of associations with that stimulus and a certain response, the material, concept, or fact is learned. Probably the most famous example of behaviourist learning is Pavlov's dogs, who learned to salivate at the sound of a bell because of an earlier association of that bell with meat powder, which caused salivation. Over time, the bell became associated with the meat powder, so merely hearing the bell was sufficient to elicit a salivation response. That is a simple demonstration of a behaviourist's perspective on how learning might occur.

It is easier to understand behaviourism as a guiding force if you are thinking about simple concepts and facts. Over the years, however, behaviourists have struggled with trying to explain more complex types of learning. R M Gagné (1968), for example, developed a plan that he called 'cumulative learning', in which a series of associations are put together. He described a process of building more and more complex connections between simple stimulus-response associations as a mechanism for describing more complex types of learning.

Behaviourist theory suggests that we can take the body of information that we are trying to teach the learner and break it down into a hierarchy of sub-skills and subconcepts. Behaviourism allows little or no room for individual differences within these hierarchies. In other words, behaviourist theory for the most part does not recognise that there may be many ways to 'know' something and that individual differences strongly influence learning. Behaviourism does acknowledge that perhaps someone does not learn as much or was not able to learn something because he or she did not learn the subinformation, but there is no sense that a learner might need the information organised in a different manner or even that there might be different ways of organising information. There is no real appreciation that people have different ways of perceiving and processing information or that the learner's response is very much shaped by the way the information is put together.

Although most people respond in a negative fashion to descriptions of behaviourist theory, it is a model that is widely used in our society. Much of advertising, for example, is based on behaviourist notions. If we look at the models that have guided our thinking about exhibits, often they, too, represent behaviourist models. We have incorporated the behaviourist influence for a number of reasons. At the time we in museums became interested in determining what makes an effective exhibit, Skinner's models were prevalent and we focused on the exhibit as stimulus. We paid little attention to the physical context in which the exhibit would be placed or to the social milieu it created. For the most part, the museum field continued to approach exhibit design as an attempt to create an ever more improved stimulus (the exhibit); the notions of 'attracting power' and 'holding power' that have dominated museum exhibit design principles are essentially behaviourist notions. In those early studies there was not a great deal of effort to get inside the head of the visitor. Instead we were concerned with what colour to use, or how large to make the type on the labels, or how to enhance learning by creating a space that focused attention on an object. Only recently have we thought of the museum experience as encompassing more than the exhibit. There is a real understanding of how different social configurations shape the experience and what the physical context adds to or detracts from the exhibit. I have found it really provocative to think first about the experiences we want the visitor to have and then try to create an exhibit or a space that will allow those experiences to happen.

Next, I would like to discuss developmental psychology, which has been widely used in the museum field. When I was training docents to work with schoolchildren, it was very useful to be able to describe certain learning characteristics for different ages of children. Developmental psychology had a great influence on the notion of hands-on learning, not only in museums but in the whole educational field, because it advances the notion that learning must be an active process for the learner.

Perhaps the most famous developmental psychologist was Jean Piaget (Bybee and Sund, 1976), who described the learning process as the perception and processing of information into organising frameworks, or schemata. In Piaget's view, as we learn, branch-like connections are constructed inside our heads. When I first studied developmental psychology, it was believed that as one developed, more branches were created and then connected. Researchers are beginning to believe, however, that infants are born with many existing branches and that learning may actually be the connection of those branches. The branches are not created as one interacts with the environment – which is Piaget's notion – but instead as learning occurs connections are made between these existing branches.

Piaget described four stages of cognitive development: the sensorimotor stage (ages 0–2), the preoperational stage (ages 2–7), the concrete operational stage (ages 7–11), and the formal operational stage (ages 11–14). Sund describes (Sund, 1976) these stages in greater detail. Piaget believed that all children progressed through these stages in succession; he did concede that the average age at which children go through each stage could vary. Piaget's stage theory, as it is called, does provide a rough framework for thinking about children at various ages, and I think its simplicity and descriptiveness are the reasons the theory was easily put into practice.

Piaget felt strongly, as do other developmental psychologists, that the learner must interact – either mentally or physically – with the material to be learned. Individuals interact with each other, with objects and events in their environment, actively constructing meaning for these and creating movement from one stage of development to the next.

Early on, Piaget was interested in social interaction and its role in mediating learning. But unfortunately, as he began refining his developmental stages he began to do his research in laboratories. He worked with children independently and got them to perform the tasks he had developed to determine their developmental stages. The behaviourists' studies, too, were largely honed and refined in laboratories, usually with individuals, sometimes with pairs of individuals. Generally, there has been little effort by researchers to understand what is going on in naturalistic settings because they can't control the variables. But good psychologists these days, even behaviourists and developmentalists, are appreciating the need to do more ecologically valid research by conducting studies in naturalistic settings as well as in laboratories.

The major criticism of developmental theories has revolved around the issue of predictability. The theories are descriptive, but they do not seem to hold true for all individuals in all areas of learning. Another criticism focuses on the belief that all people move through the stages in a set pattern. Many of us can probably think of adults who may be very formal-operational in particular disciplines but very concrete and perhaps even sensorimotor in others. Developmental psychologists are also criticised for their failure to describe what 'meaningful interaction' is about. There may be different ways of designing or thinking about experiences that are better for certain children. The other interesting criticism, which has primarily come from Howard Gardner (1983), is that Piaget's training as a scientist led him to create developmental tasks that involve mathematical and logical reasoning. He created a model for logical-mathematical thinking, but he neglected other forms of intellectual development, such as artistic or linguistic.

Like developmental theory, cognitive theories of learning focused a great deal on the process of learning. Early cognitive theories modelled learning as a series of sequential operations referred to as information processing. Information processing models identified critical steps in the learning process: perception, attention, encoding, retrieval and transfer, and short- and long-term memory.

The cognitive science school grew out of behaviourism. A group of research scientists were concerned that there had not been an effort to understand the internal nature of learning as defined by behaviourism. At the time these behaviourists were becoming interested in learning, the computer age was beginning. They saw computers as an ideal tool to help us understand human learning. That gives you a great deal of insight into early cognitive science: it is very much a linear, input-output model.

Like the developmentalists, cognitive scientists view learning as an active process requiring the construction of schemata and the active retrieval, transfer, and reorganisation of information. But rather than explaining the learning process as a series of stages found at different ages, the cognitive scientist also tries to describe in greater detail all the steps a given child uses to solve a particular problem. The ultimate goal of information-processing psychology is to describe the steps so exhaustively and carefully that an individual's performance can be simulated on a computer in an attempt to model possible information-processing sequences. This research area is also referred to as artificial intelligence research. Unfortunately, the early emphasis on computer modelling resulted in a model that did not account for the complexity of much of human learning. The research cognitive scientists are now conducting is attempting to develop more complex computer programs that branch and use a variety of data bases to better simulate the complexity of human learning.

Cognitive science also emphasises that prior knowledge and experience in the cognitive domain are the most important factors predicting how much a person will learn. But cognitive scientists have neglected the important role that prior attitudes and beliefs might play in shaping what and how we learn. Another concept important to cognitive science is the distinction made between cognition and metacognition, that is, the process of an individual reflecting on how he or she thinks and learns. Museum educators are teaching visitors metacognitive strategies for dealing with museums when they teach visitors how to look at art, how to 'read' an object, or how to 'use a museum'.

Even though there has been a great deal of research and theorising about learning, there is still no consistent, functional, 'scientific' description of what learning is or how it functions. Each theory I have described is based on assumptions about the nature of the learning process. All three approaches – the associational approach of behaviourism, the interactionist nature of developmental psychology, and the focus on sequential logical problem-solving of cognitive science – seem at times disparate with the rich experience encountered in a museum. All three theories have contributed greatly to our understanding of learning and do account for some of what goes on in the museum setting. But the conditions under which they were developed and the assumptions underlying their development have resulted in theories that are very narrow, neglect the important role of social and physical context in learning, and focus on the learning of facts and concepts to the exclusion of other types of learning.

The narrowness of these theories is not only being argued by those interested in learning in museums but is beginning to be voiced by more traditional learning theorists as well, who are beginning to advocate stronger roles for social mediation, affective factors such as motivation and attitude, and the influence of the physical context on learning.

References

Gagné, R M (1968). 'Learning hierarchies', *Educational Psychologist* 6(1), pp. 1, 3–6, 9.

Gardner, H (1983). 'Intelligence: earlier views', in H Gardner, *Frames of mind: the theory of multiple intelligences*, New York, Basic Books.

Sund, R B (1976). 'Piaget's theory of cognitive development' in R W Bybee and R B Sund (eds), *Piaget for educators*, Columbus, Ohio, Merrill Publishing.

4 Contemporary Theories of Learning

Lynn D Dierking

This article appeared in *The audience in exhibition development*, American Association of Museums, 1992, pp. 30–34.

It is likely that [having read] the overview of traditional learning theory . . . you [are] still wondering, What is this thing called learning? Each of the traditional schools of thought – behaviourism, developmentalism, and cognitive science – define learning differently. For those of us who try to put traditional learning theory into practice, the result is often a great deal of confusion.

A major source of the confusion is the assumptions the various theories make about what learning is. The first assumption underlying traditional learning theories is that learning is synonymous with education, which is in turn synonymous with schooling. Much of the research was developed in laboratories under controlled conditions with little connection to 'real world' learning. This assumption drives a second assumption – that learning involves acquiring factual and conceptual information. Traditional learning theories do not consider a broader view that includes affective aspects such as feelings, attitudes, and kinesthetic information. A third assumption involves a focus on quantitative rather than qualitative learning. I often talk about the old view of learning as the 'gas tank model'. You fill the container up and what makes the difference in how much someone learns is the size of the container, not necessarily the individual differences among the containers. But is learning a greater amount of knowledge? a greater amount of feeling? a greater amount of some kinesthetic ability? Or is it a change in the way we think about something or do something?

Traditional learning theories are often difficult to relate to the learning that takes place in museums. They provide us with an interesting perspective on thinking about learning, but at times they are inadequate when it comes to contemplating the rich museum experience that we are struggling to create. Some exciting work is going on right now in the learning field, as even traditional learning theorists are beginning to challenge assumptions they have made about important aspects of learning.

Understanding these assumptions and seeking a definition of learning that builds on traditional learning theories has some provocative implications for those of us who work in museum settings. The big issue is how you can expect to teach visitors something when they are only with you for short periods. It makes sense for us to think about learning as more qualitative than quantitative, because we have an opportunity to create a context for objects and ideas, to create a mood. Perhaps in the short period that a person is in the museum, we can help him or her see something a little bit differently, in a context that maybe he or she had not thought about before.

Let me share with you some notions that psychologists across the board are now accepting as part of the learning process. If we look at these generalisations, we will be able to pull together a view of what learning is. Let's begin with this fundamental statement: learning is an active process of assimilating and accommodating information within a social, physical, and psychological context. The first prerequisite for learning is that we perceive something and pay attention to it. People have different ways of perceiving and paying attention to an object or an idea. Some of us need to touch it. Some need to hear it. Some need to see it and think about it. Some of us think quickly, some more slowly. It is extremely evident that learning is active. But learning is not only the activity of perceiving; there is a great deal of evidence that what goes on internally for the learner is active as well. Even the staunch behaviourists are appreciating that learning involves something substantive that goes on inside of us.

The next prerequisites for learning are processing and memory. All psychologists seem to agree that learning is somehow related to the processing and storage of information over a period of time. We process information by accessing it from different places in our brain. We actively perceive something and then try to organise it in a way that makes sense to us. This notion has profound implications for how we design exhibits. We often organise exhibit information in a way that makes sense to us, and sometimes the 'us' are scholars and experts who may organise information in a way that may not make as much sense to someone who is not well versed in the subject. One of the things we must consider is more creative ways of organising information within museum exhibits. For example, although the learning that takes place in museums does not appear always to be sequential, think about how much we all worry about the sequence of a person's visit. Actually, if you follow visitors around in museums, you find that often they do not follow the sequence anyway. By trying to make our exhibits sequential, in some ways we are fighting a battle that we are likely to lose.

It is clear that memory is a very important part of learning. What seems to make something learned is that it does have lasting power. It persists over time. Like perception, a key aspect of memory is that it is an active process involving the connection of past experiences to recent ones. Memories are then consolidated, or lost, over a relatively long period of time. A shortcoming of memory research has been its emphasis on the study of short-term memory, with research often conducted in laboratories. Increasingly, there has been an effort to study more long-term memory. Most museum professionals will probably be interested in long-term rather than short-term memory – that is, information that can be recalled at least one day or more after a visit. Although it may be interesting to know what aspects of the museum a visitor can describe as he or she exits, it would seem that what is really important is which of these recollections will persist in memory long enough to be used another day.

There have been lots of studies in which people have been asked to write down all the things they saw in an exhibit, shown pictures and asked what they remember from the exhibit, or given a sheet of words and asked which ones they remember seeing in the exhibit. I am not suggesting this type of study is not important, but it is just one piece of the picture. Museums would be wonderful environments for learning research if we tried to track our visitors down the next day to see what they remembered.

Retrieval and transfer are terms used by most psychologists to describe the most basic of all learning attributes: the ability to use the information we have processed and stored in order to solve problems, answer questions, recount a story, or recall a visual picture or steps to a dance. Recollection, like perception and memory, is an active and individualised process. Humans encode generalised, highly contextualised messages. If we can understand how information is contextualised and under what circumstances – something learning research is just beginning to attempt – we will be far closer to understanding the complexity of human learning.

Motivation is also a key determinant of learning. The role of motivation has been dealt with only superficially by traditional learning researchers other than the humanists. In the 1950s, due in part to dissatisfaction with behaviourism, two individuals – Abraham Maslow and Carl Rogers – began exploring issues related to motivation and the social aspects of learning. Their research led to the development of a learning theory called humanism, which was extremely popular during the 1960s and 1970s although it had only a slight impact on traditional learning theory.

Maslow, a psychologist, developed a theory of human motivation centring around a hierarchy of basic needs. His theory has tremendous implications for learning in museums because it suggests that there are a variety of needs that must be met before anyone will be able to learn effectively in any environment. Rogers, a psychotherapist, proposed that individuals should be free to learn at their own pace and formulated a client-centred theory of personality and behaviour. His theory gave rise to andragogy, a theory of adult learning, which assumes that as individuals mature their learning styles may differ from those of children and the role of intrinsic motivation may play a far greater role in what they learn.

The notion of individual differences in the learning process is another factor that affects learning. This notion has deep implications, not just for museums. The 'gas tank' model that I described earlier has been very persistent in our society. Now the acknowledgement of individual differences is profoundly changing our thinking about learning. You open a can of worms as a scientist if you are trying to deal with individual differences. If there are no commonalities, it is really tough to create a predictive model. But finally there is acceptance that there is not necessarily something wrong with the learner; the learner may simply have a different way of perceiving and processing information. We still have a long way to go to be able to translate these notions of individual differences into practice. In the museum field, no longer are we trying to design an exhibit for the average visitor. We feel the need to think about multicultural audiences, about people with disabilities, about people who need to hear information as opposed to seeing it or feeling it. The notion of individual differences adds to the complexity of trying to create models of learning, but it is a positive direction to be moving in.

Context is yet another component of learning. All learning occurs within a physical and social context, and these contexts ultimately become important in determining what information is perceived, how it is stored, and when and how it is recalled. It is critical for museums to learn more about the effects of physical space and social interaction on learning. When we watch family groups, school groups, or other groups of visitors, for example, we appreciate that the meaning being made of the major messages of our exhibit is being filtered and mediated by people in the group. A lot of us have shuddered at the mediation that we see or hear, but it is important for us to think about our exhibits as places where groups interact. Our view of exhibits is sometimes centred too much on thinking of one person, maybe two people, but not five or six or ten people standing in front of an exhibit.

Several researchers have addressed the idea of context. William Damon (1981) speaks to the notion of how much the social nature of learning has been ignored. It is a real challenge to figure out how we in museums can meet the agenda of groups, especially families. We must consider how we can create a space and communicate a message that a family can experience together in an interactive way – which is a slightly different way of thinking about designing exhibits.

The work of Sylvia Scribner (1986), an anthropologist, has implications for the issue of context. She did a study in a dairy where she observed the strategies of people who loaded the orders for milk trucks. She discovered that people who had been loading orders for years could tell just by looking at a carton that there were 16 half gallons of milk in it. They did not have to count. They could also decide on the spot which cartons to put together to fill a particular order. She also observed some people who were familiar with dairy operations but did not fill milk truck orders, and she found that these people had to count the half gallons. This study was an effort to replicate expert-novice studies in a naturalistic setting.

One implication of this notion of context for museums is that perhaps one way we can engage groups of visitors in exhibits is by presenting them with problem-solving situations. We may have more ability to communicate abstract notions to people if we engage them in decision-making. Rather than simply telling them about environmental problems, for example, we could involve them in a simulation and give them a chance to be a decision-maker. Context, in summary, is probably the essence of what learning is all about. John Bransford (1979) is one psychologist who has attempted to study context systematically. His book *Learning, memory, and understanding* is a classic cognitive psychology text.

One of the ideas that John Falk and I have been exploring is what we call the interactive experience model, a way of understanding the museum visitor's experience. We are trying to identify important means by which the museum visitor contextualises information. We envision a three-dimensional model that has four spheres. One sphere represents personal context, the context the individual brings to the learning situation. Within the personal context are variables such as how one processes information, how one perceives objects or ideas, what one's learning style is, one's prior knowledge and experience, one's feelings, one's attitudes. The second sphere represents social context. We come most often with other people to a museum. Are we with a family or friends? How old are the children in the family? Will we be managers or will we be able to explore together? The third sphere represents physical context, which is not only the exhibit, but the exhibit within its spatial environment. Where is the exhibit in the general path of most visitors? What is the architecture of the building and how might it influence the visitor's museum experience? What is the lighting like? Are there places to sit? The final context is the one most of us have tended to focus on – the immediate activity context. This context is what visitors do at the moment they are at the exhibit. Is it an interactive exhibit? Are they interacting or are they standing and looking? Are they talking together? We are just beginning to explore and deal with this model, but we have been using it a great deal as we look at some of our research and also as we walk through museums, and so far it seems to be a useful way to think about the museum experience.

Museums in general – and exhibits in particular – have the potential to enlarge, expand, and reshape visitors' conceptual frameworks. Visitors assimilate a great deal of new information. They must accommodate their previous ideas to fit perceived realities. They use the objects they encounter to extend their pre-existing mental constructs. This may be the very essence of learning.

References

Bransford, J (1979). *Learning, memory, and understanding*, Belmont, California, Wadsworth Publishing Co.

Damon, W (1981). 'Exploring children's social cognition on two fronts', in J H Flavell and L Ross (eds), *Social cognitive development: frontiers and possible futures*, Cambridge, Cambridge University Press.

Scribner, S (1986). 'Thinking in action: some characteristics of practical thought', in R J Sternberg and R K Wagner (eds), *Practical intelligence: nature and origins of competence in the everyday world*, Cambridge, Cambridge University Press.

5 Constructivist Learning Theory

George E Hein
Extracted from an article in *Proceedings of ICOM/CECA annual conference, Jerusalem 1991*, ICOM, 1992, pp. 89–94.

Constructivism

What is meant by constructivism? The term refers to the idea that learners construct knowledge for themselves – each learner individually (and socially) constructs meaning – as he or she learns. Constructing meaning is learning: there is no other kind. The dramatic consequences of this view are twofold:

1 we have to focus on the learner in thinking about learning (not on the subject/lesson to be taught);
2 there is no knowledge independent of the meaning attributed to experience (constructed) by the learner, or community of learners.

Let me discuss the second point first because, although it appears radical on an everyday level, it is a position which has been frequently adopted ever since people began to ponder epistemology. If we accept constructivist theory (which means we are willing to follow in the path of Dewey, Piaget and Vigotsky among others), then we have to give up Platonic and all subsequent realistic views of epistemology. We have to recognise that there is no such thing as knowledge 'out there' independent of the knower, but only knowledge we construct for ourselves as we learn (Dewey, 1938). Learning is not understanding the 'true' nature of things, nor is it (as Plato suggested) remembering dimly perceived perfect ideas, but rather a personal and social construction of meaning out of the bewildering array of sensations which have no order or structure besides the explanations (and I stress the plural) which we fabricate for them . . .

The great triumph of Western intellectual history from the Enlightenment until the beginning of the twentieth century rested on its ability to organise the knowledge of the world in a rational way independent of the learner, determined by some structure of the subject. Disciplines were developed, taxonomic schemes established, and all these categories were viewed as components of a vast mechanical machine in which the parts could be explained in terms of their relationship to each other, and each part contributed to making the whole function smoothly. Nowhere in this description does the learner appear. The task of the teacher was to make clear to the learner the working of this machine and any accommodation to the learner was only to account for different appropriate entry points for different learners.

However, as I have indicated above, constructivist theory requires that we turn our attention by 180°: we must turn our back on any idea of an all-encompassing machine which describes nature and instead look towards all those wonderful, individual living beings – the learners – each of whom creates his or her own model to explain nature. If we accept the constructivist position, we are inevitably required to follow a pedagogy which argues that we must provide learners with the opportunity to: (a) interact with sensory data, and (b) construct their own world.

This second point is a little harder for us to swallow, and most of us constantly vacillate between faith that our learners will indeed construct meaning which we will find acceptable (whatever we mean by that) and our need to construct meaning for them; that is, to structure situations that are not free for learners to carry out their own mental actions, but 'learning' situations which channel them into our ideas about the meaning of experience . . . It is this tension between our desire as teachers to teach the truth, to present the world 'as it really is', and our desire to let learners construct their own world which requires us to think seriously about epistemology, and pedagogy.

Principles of Learning

What are some guiding principles of constructivist thinking that we must keep in mind when we consider our role as educators? I will outline a few ideas, all predicated on the belief that learning consists of individuals' constructed meanings, and then indicate how they influence museum education.

1   Learning is an active process in which the learner uses sensory input and constructs meaning out of it. The more traditional formulation of this idea involves the terminology of the active learner (Dewey's term) stressing that the learner needs to do something; that learning is not the passive acceptance of knowledge which exists 'out there' but that learning involves the learner's engaging with the world (Dewey, 1916).
2   People learn to learn as they learn: learning consists both of constructing meaning and constructing systems of meaning. For example, if we learn the chronology of dates of a series of historical events, we are simultaneously learning the meaning of a chronology. Each meaning we construct makes us better able to give meaning to other sensations which can fit a similar pattern.
3   The crucial action of constructing meaning is mental: it happens in the mind. Physical actions, hands-on experience may be necessary for learning, especially for children, but it is not sufficient; we need to provide activities which engage the mind as well as the hands (Henriques, 1990). (Dewey called this reflective activity.)
4   Learning involves language: the language we use influences learning. On the empirical level, researchers have noted that people talk to themselves as they learn. On a more general level, there is a collection of arguments, presented most forcefully by Vigotsky (1962), that language and learning are inextricably intertwined . . .
5   Learning is a social activity: our learning is intimately associated with our connection with other human beings, our teachers, our peers, our family as well as casual acquaintances, including the people before us or next to us at the exhibit. We are more likely to be successful in our efforts to educate if we recognise this principle rather than try to avoid it. Much of traditional education, as Dewey pointed out, is directed towards isolating the learner from all social interaction, and towards seeing education as a one-on-one relationship between the learner and the objective material to be learned. In contrast, progressive education (to continue to use Dewey's formulation) recognises the social aspect of learning and uses conversation, interaction

with others, and the application of knowledge as an integral aspect of learning.

6 Learning is contextual: we do not learn isolated facts and theories in some abstract ethereal land of the mind separate from the rest of our lives; we learn in relationship to what else we know, what we believe, our prejudices and our fears. On reflection, it becomes clear that this point is actually a corollary of the idea that learning is active and social. We cannot divorce our learning from our lives.

7 One needs knowledge to learn: it is not possible to assimilate new knowledge without having some structure developed from previous knowledge to build on. The more we know, the more we can learn. Therefore any effort to teach must be connected to the state of the learner, must provide a path into the subject for the learner based on that learner's previous knowledge.

8 It takes time to learn: learning is not instantaneous. For significant learning we need to revisit ideas, ponder them, try them out, play with them and use them. This cannot happen in the 5–10 minutes usually spent in a gallery (and certainly not in the few seconds usually spent contemplating a single museum object). If you reflect on anything you have learned, you soon realise that it is the product of repeated exposure and thought. Even, or especially, moments of profound insight, can be traced back to longer periods of preparation.

9 Motivation is a key component in learning. Not only is it the case that motivation helps learning, it is essential for learning. This idea of motivation as described here is broadly conceived to include an understanding of ways in which the knowledge can be used. Unless we know 'the reasons why', we may not be very involved in using the knowledge that may be instilled in us, even by the most severe and direct teaching.

The Meaning of Constructivism for Museums

Having suggested these principles, I want to reflect on what they may mean for our specific day-to-day work both in mounting exhibits and in developing educational programmes.

Points 1 and 3

Most museum educators have accepted the idea that learners need to be active, that in order to participate in learning we need to engage the learner in doing something, in hands-on involvement, in participatory exhibits and programmes. But the more important point, I believe, is the idea that the actions which we develop for our audience engage the mind as well as the hand. Not all experiences are educative, as Dewey (1938) pointed out in *Experience and education*. This does not mean that they necessarily have to be complex – but they do need to allow the participants to think as they act . . .

Physical involvement is a necessary condition for learning for children, and highly desirable for adults in many situations, but it is not sufficient. All hands-on activities must also pass the test of being minds-on – they must provide something to think about as well as something to touch.

Point 2

The idea that we learn to learn as we learn, that we begin to understand organising principles as we use them, is not terribly radical to most of us, but I believe that there is an important manner of formulating it that can help us, which sometimes eludes us: what are we assuming about our visitors' ability to learn (to organise knowledge) when we present exhibits to them? what organising schemes do we attribute to them, that may or may not be available to them? Let me give you an example. During the last year we have been observing visitors at the Boston Museum of Science interacting with a series of exhibits developed originally at the Exploratorium in San Francisco. We asked them what they thought of the exhibits. Some visitors did not have the tools they needed to grasp the concept of the exhibit. I don't mean that they did not understand the concept (that will be my next point) but that they did not have the organising principles, and thus the learning tools.

For example, there are exhibits which require visitors to turn knobs which will cause a component of the exhibit to move or change. Not all visitors are clear about the relationship between the knob and what it does. The exhibit is intended to explain a causal relationship between two variables in nature; one variable is altered by turning the knob, and that change then causes the other variable to respond and vary. But if the visitor does not understand about knobs and what they do, then the message of the exhibit cannot possibly be understood.

A similar issue concerns chronologies and time lines, which are common devices in history museums. Do we know that our visitors understand chronology? Are we positive that our visitors can appreciate a time line, for example, and can recognise that the distribution of dates in linear space may be intended to approximate their distribution in chronological time? There is considerable evidence that at least some visitors (i.e. children) cannot follow such reasoning; there is less evidence that any significant number of visitors can [do so].

Points 4 and 5

Learning is a social activity. To what extent do we recognise that people learn as they speak and interact with each other? In evaluating an interactive exhibit at the Boston Museum of Science in which people could get information through a variety of modalities – they could read labels, listen to tapes, smell animal smells, touch animal mounts and manipulate interactive exhibit components – we noted that individual visitors preferred different learning modes. In family groups, the conversations became more democratic, and involved more members after all these modalities were installed, as family members shared, discussed and confirmed what each had learned while perusing his or her preferred modality.

We need to ask what we have built into the exhibit that encourages visitors to discuss, to share, to find out together. Has the architecture and exhibit arrangement encouraged discussion? Some art museums have a quiet air like a church, discouraging active debate and verbal interaction. The quiet may be appropriate for individual contemplation of pictures, but perhaps these museums could provide other rooms, close to the galleries, and fitted out with reproductions, reference materials or other reminders of the paintings, which would encourage dialogue.

Point 6

This is really an elaboration of the point made previously about learning to learn as one learns. Our visitors need 'hooks' – connections – in exhibits to help them understand the messages intended. An experienced museum-goer or a person knowledgeable on a given subject can be enlightened easily. But what does it mean for a naïve visitor to be confronted with a whole case containing many objects? Of what value is it to the naïve visitor to be invited to push this button or read a sophisticated label?

It is important for exhibits to provide different kinds of entry points, using various sensory modes, different kinds of stimuli, to attract a wide range of learners . . .

Point 7

Perhaps no other issue in constructivism raises more questions than the concern with finding the right level at which to engage the learner. Vigotsky (1978) spoke of the 'zone of proximal development', an unfortunately cumbersome term which refers to a level of understanding that is possible when a learner engages in a task with the help of a more expert peer (i.e. a teacher). People learn as they are stretched beyond their own knowledge but only within a range that is within their grasp given what knowledge and skills they bring to a task.

Point 8

Finally there is the issue of time to learn, time to reflect and time to revisit an idea. Museum educators have grappled with this problem and find it a particularly challenging one, since our audiences are free to come and go, and large fractions of them are tourists who may never return. Museum galleries are not designed as places to linger, despite our desire to have visitors spend more time there . . . What do we do for the visitors who wish to stay with a topic longer? How have we organised our museums to accommodate them? To what extent have we provided additional resources (in addition to items which we are eager to sell to them in the nearby shop) that can satisfy the interested visitors' concerns that arise on the next day or a week after the visit? . . .

References

Dewey, J (1916). *Democracy and education*, New York, Macmillan.

Dewey, J (1938). *Experience and education*, New York, Kappa Delta Pi/ Collier Books.

Henriques, A (1990). 'Experiments in teaching', in Duckworth, E et al., *Science education: a minds on approach to the elementary years*, New Jersey, Erlbaum Associates.

Vigotsky, L (1962). *Thought and language*, Cambridge, Massachusetts, MIT Press.

Vigotsky, L (1978). *Mind and society*, Cambridge, Massachusetts, Harvard University Press.

6 Multiple Intelligences

Howard Gardner

Extracted from *Cognition, curriculum and literacy*, Hedley, C
et al. (eds), Norwood, New Jersey, Ablex Publishing Corp.,
1990, pp. 13–15.

Dissatisfaction with the concept of IQ and with unitary views of intelligence is
fairly widespread. One thinks for instance, of the work of L L Thurstone,
J P Guilford, and other critics. From my point of view however, these criticisms
do not suffice. The whole concept has to be challenged; in fact, it has to be
replaced.

I believe that we should get away altogether from tests and correlations
among tests, and look instead at more naturalistic sources of information about
how peoples around the world develop skills important to their way of life.
Think, for example, of sailors in the South Seas who find their way around hundreds or even thousands of islands by looking at the constellations of stars in
the sky, feeling the way a boat passes over the water, and noticing a few scattered landmarks. A word for intelligence in a society of these sailors would
probably refer to that kind of navigational ability. Think of surgeons and
engineers, hunters and fishermen, dancers and choreographers, athletes and
athletic coaches, tribal chiefs and sorcerers. All of these different roles need to
be taken into account if we accept the way I define intelligence – that is, as the
ability to solve problems, or to fashion products that are valued in one or more
cultural settings. For the moment I am saying nothing about whether there is
one dimension or more than one dimension of intelligence; nothing about
whether intelligence is inborn or developed. Instead I emphasise the ability to
solve problems and to fashion products. In my work I seek the building blocks
of the intelligences used by the aforementioned sailors, surgeons, and sorcerers.

The science in this enterprise, to the extent that it exists, involves an attempt
to discover the right description of the intelligences. What is an intelligence? To
try to answer this question, I have, with my colleagues, surveyed a wide set of
sources which, to my knowledge, have never been considered together before.
One source is what we already know of the development of different kinds of
skills in normal children. Another source, and a very important one, is information on the ways that these abilities break down under conditions of brain
damage. When one suffers a stroke or some other kind of brain damage, various
abilities can be destroyed, or spared, in isolation from other abilities. This
research with brain-damaged patients yields a very powerful kind of evidence,
because it seems to reflect the way the nervous system has evolved over the mil-
lennia to yield certain discrete kinds of intelligence.

My research group looks at other special populations as well: prodigies, idiot
savants, autistic children, children with learning disabilities, all of whom exhibit
very jagged cognitive profiles – profiles that are extremely difficult to explain in
terms of a unitary view of intelligence. We examine cognition in diverse animal
species and in dramatically different cultures. Finally, we consider two kinds of
psychological evidence: correlations among psychological tests of the sort
yielded by a factor analysis of a test battery, and the result of efforts of skill

training. When you train a person in skill A, for example, does that training transfer to skill B? Therefore, does training in mathematics enhance one's musical abilities, or vice versa?

Obviously, through looking at all these sources – information on development, on breakdowns, on special populations, and the like – we end up with a cornucopia of information. Optimally, we would perform a factor analysis, feeding all the data into a computer and noting the kinds of factors or intelligences that are extracted. Alas, this kind of material didn't exist in a form that was susceptible to computation, and so we had to perform a more subjective factor analysis. In truth, we simply studied the results as best we could, and tried to organise them in a way that made sense to us, and we hope, to critical readers as well. My resulting list of seven intelligences is a preliminary attempt to organise this mass of information.

I want now to mention briefly the seven intelligences we have located and to cite one or two examples of each intelligence. Linguistic intelligence is the kind of ability exhibited in its fullest form, perhaps by poets. Logical-mathematical intelligence, as the name implies, is logical and mathematical ability, as well as scientific ability. Jean Piaget, the great developmental psychologist, thought he was studying *all* intelligence, but I believe he was studying the development of logical-mathematical intelligence. Although I name the linguistic and logical-mathematical intelligences first, it is not because I think they are the most important; in fact, I think all seven of the intelligences have equal claim to priority. In our society however, we have put linguistic and logical-mathematical intelligences, figuratively speaking, on a pedestal. Much of our testing is based on this high valuation of verbal and mathematical skills. If you do well in language and logic, you will do well in IQ tests and SATs, and you may well get into a prestigious college. Whether you do well once you leave is probably going to depend on the extent to which you possess and use the other intelligences. It is to those that I want to give equal attention.

Spatial intelligence is the ability to form a mental model of a spatial world and to be able to manoeuvre and operate using that model. Sailors, engineers, surgeons, sculptors, and painters – to name just a few examples – all have highly developed spatial intelligence. Musical intelligence is the fourth category of ability we have identified; Leonard Bernstein had lots of it; Mozart, presumably, had even more. Bodily-kinesthetic intelligence is the ability to solve problems or to fashion products using one's whole body, or parts of the body. Dancers, athletes, surgeons, and craftspeople all exhibit highly developed bodily-kinesthetic intelligence.

Finally, I propose two forms of personal intelligence – not well understood, elusive to study but immensely important. Interpersonal intelligence is the ability to understand other people: what motivates them, how they work, how to work co-operatively with them. Successful sales-people, politicians, teachers, clinicians, and religious leaders are all likely to be individuals with high degrees of interpersonal intelligence. Intrapersonal intelligence, a seventh kind of intelligence, is a correlative ability, turned inward. It is a capacity to form an accurate, veridical model of oneself and to be able to use that model to operate effectively in life.

These, then, are the seven intelligences that we have described in our research. This can be subdivided, or the list can be re-arranged. The real point here is to make the case for the plurality of intellect. Also, we believe that individuals may differ in the particular intelligence profiles with which they are born, and that certainly they differ in the profiles with which they end up.

I think of the intelligences as raw, biological potentials, which can be seen in pure form only in individuals who are, in the technical sense, freaks. In almost everybody else the intelligences work together to solve problems, to yield various kinds of cultural endstates – vocations, avocations, and the like.

This is my theory of multiple intelligence in capsule form. In my view, the purpose of school should be to develop intelligences and to help people reach vocational and avocational goals that are appropriate to their particular spectrum of intelligences. People who are helped to do so, I believe, feel more engaged and competent, and therefore more inclined to serve society in a constructive way.

7 Learning Styles

Richard Cassels

This article 'Mind, heart and soul: towards better learning in heritage parks' appeared in *New Zealand Museums Journal* 22(2), 1992, pp. 12–17.

For many heritage parks, and indeed 'indoor' museums, 'learning' can seem to be something of a luxury when you are battling with the desperate need to increase visitor numbers, to attract funds and, at the same time, simply maintain large collections of large trams at Ferrymead or a small township of wooden buildings in South Auckland.

But learning is at the root of everything we do and stand for. It was 'to learn' that our founders chose to preserve items for posterity: the fundamental decisions about what to preserve and collect was based on assumptions, possibly unwritten and perhaps even unchallenged, about what would be of value and interest to future generations.

Learning is also at the core of good communication and good marketing, and the 'money-people' in your organisation instinctively know that this is a very important part of your business.

Learning is also what distinguishes a museum or heritage park from a fun-fair; and it is the ultimate justification for any kind of public funding.

So what is learning? Of course it has probably very little to do with schools. What were the really important things you have learned in your life, and did you learn them from a school teacher?

For convenience I would define learning as an activity that enriches an individual's experience in such a way that, for some time afterwards, he or she has more options in life.

So how do you set about enlarging people's options or enriching their lives?

Better Learning

As a museum director, I have a checklist of criteria for good displays which I apply to exhibition proposals that staff bring to me. They include a requirement for some kind of audience research and a requirement for some kind of ongoing evaluation.

But here I would like to spend time on two schemes that I have found particularly helpful. Both were presented at the MEANZ Conference in Wellington earlier this year: one was set out in a lecture by Bonnie Pitman of the University Art Museum of Berkeley, California and another comes from the work of Joseph Cornell, a famous American 'Nature Educator'.

Four Types of Learner

Bonnie Pitman described the work of Bernice McCarthy on different learning styles and I will attempt to summarise what she said.

In figure 7.1 you can see that the different types of learners are arranged around 2 'axes' or dimensions: the vertical dimension in the diagram

Figure 7.1   Types of learning
Source: McCarthy and Pitman-Gelles, 1989

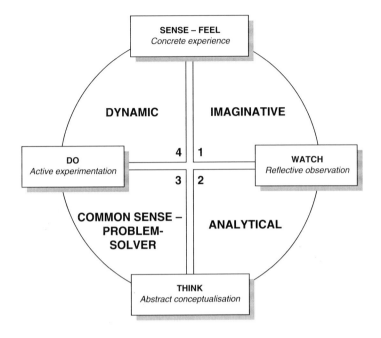

Figure 7.2   Some characteristics of different types of learner
Source: McCarthy and Pitman-Gelles, 1989

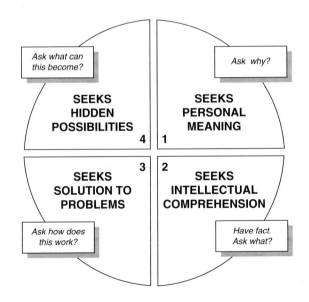

Figure 7.3 Four kinds of learners; from a lecture by Bonnie Pitman, University Art Museum, Berkeley, California

Style 4: Dynamic learners

- Seek hidden possibilities.
- Need to know what can be done with things.
- Learn by trial and error, self-discovery.
- Enrich reality.
- Perceive information concretely and process it actively.
- Adapt to change and relish it; like variety and excel in situations calling for flexibility. Tend to take risks, at ease with people but sometimes seen as pushy. Often reach accurate conclusions in the absence of logical justification.
- Function by acting and testing experience.

Strength:	Action, carrying out plans.
Goals:	To make things happen, to bring action to concepts.
Favourite question:	What can this become?
Careers:	Marketing, sales, action-orientated managerial jobs.

Style 1: Imaginative learners

- Seek meaning.
- Need to be involved personally.
- Learn by listening and sharing ideas.
- Absorb reality.
- Perceive information concretely and process reflectively.
- Are interested in people and culture. They are divergent thinkers who believe in their own experience, excel in viewing concrete situations from many perspectives, and model themselves on those they respect.
- Function through social interaction.

Strength:	Innovation and imagination. They are ideas people.
Goals:	Self-involvement in important issues, bringing unity to diversity.
Favourite questions:	Why or why not?
Careers:	Couselling, personnel, humanities, organisational development.

Style 3: Common sense learners

- Seek usability.
- Need to know how things work.
- Learn by testing theories in ways that seem sensible.
- Edit reality.
- Perceive information abstractly and process it actively.
- Use factual data to build designed concepts, need hands-on experiences, enjoy solving problems, resent being given answers, restrict judgement to concrete things, have limited tolerance for 'fuzzy' ideas. They need to know how things they are asked to do will help in 'real life'.
- Function through inferences drawn from sensory experience.

Strength:	Practical application of ideas.
Goals:	To bring their view of the present in line with future security.
Favourite question:	How does this work?
Careers:	Engineering, physical science, nursing, technology.

Style 2: Analytical learners

- Seek facts.
- Need to know what the experts think.
- Learn by thinking through ideas.
- Form reality.
- Perceive information abstractly and process it reflectively.
- Are less interested in people than concepts: they critique information and are data collectors. Thorough and industrious they will re-examine facts if situations perplex them.
- Enjoy traditional classrooms. Schools are designed for these learners.
- Function by adapting to experts.

Strength:	Creating concepts and models.
Goals:	Self-satisfaction and intellectual recognition.
Favourite question:	What?
Careers:	Basic sciences, maths, research, planning departments.

distinguishes people who prefer 'thinking' from those who are more inclined to a 'feeling', or more concrete, sensual experiences. The horizontal axis distinguishes those who prefer to 'do' from those who prefer to 'watch'. On this basis the authors of the scheme have created 4 learning types:

Type 1:   the imaginative learner
Type 2:   the analytical learner
Type 3:   the common sense, problem-solver learner
Type 4:   the dynamic learner

Figure 7.2 isolates some of the characteristics of the different learning types, and figure 7.3 is a summary of the general characteristics of each.

Of course any one individual is not just one type of learner (I assess my own strengths as primarily type 2, balanced by type 1 and 3, with type 4 as my weakest point!). But I find this classification a very useful scheme to think with.

If you read through the list of characteristics of each learning type, you will undoubtedly recognise people you know – if not yourself! (This understanding is indeed also a very useful management tool in its own right, and helps identify why you will almost certainly have communication challenges in a typical museum!)

So what does this tell us about museums and heritage parks?

First of all you should work out what kind of learner you are currently catering for. Then you can consider if you are indeed using the right kind of language or images to reach these people: and then you can ask yourself if you want to broaden the range of your visitors/learners.

In a museum it is a characteristic that the staff have all the fun; they learn by doing, by fixing things, by trying out things, by thinking and by analysing. Perhaps this is one reason why museum staff are usually so 'loyal' to their profession! However it has also been a characteristic of indoor museums until recently that their visitors were only allowed to experience type one or two learning – use your imagination, look, think, compare and classify.

In those museums (like the Otago Museum) which have science centres incorporated, the range of learning styles available to the visitor has increased dramatically. We are attracting a completely new clientele, the type 3 and 4 learners.

Similarly in heritage parks the chances are that your volunteers have all the fun of type 3 learning, of 'improving things', while the visitors may get a far less rich experience. You can also expect that your 'doers' will often be hopeless at communicating with, say, imaginative learners.

So each institution has a choice of strategy here. You can decide that you will cater only to certain kinds of learners, and perhaps broaden the range of topics or themes you consider; or you can choose to stick to one theme and explore it in ways that will attract all the different kinds of learners.

So if you decide that your theme is railway trains, you could run a 'Build-a-train' art competition for type 1 learners; publish endless catalogues of engine types for type 2 learners, each complete with a full history; and then let your visitors experiment with models of gears, steam boilers, different types of wheel cross-sections on rail curves, for your type 3 learners, and enrol your type 4 learners in your volunteer restoration teams! You can aim therefore to use all the techniques of a hands-on science centre, a park visitor centre, a typological museum and a volunteer workshop to enrich the experience of your visitors.

One thing you can expect if you broaden your range of learning styles is that you will attract more of your local community.

If your heritage park is to be supplemented by your own museum/information centre/experimental room, you will reach a much wider range of people than just those who want an instant re-enactment experience.

Does your Experience have Depth?

The second concept which I have found useful is that of stages of learning; or the idea that good learning will be achieved through a series of processes.

The example I use here is Joseph Cornell's 'New learning' sequence, from his book *Sharing the joy of nature: nature activities for all ages* (1989). In figure 7.4 I have set out his stages on the left, with my own notes on the right.

Figure 7.4 Sequences of learning
Source: Cornell, 1989

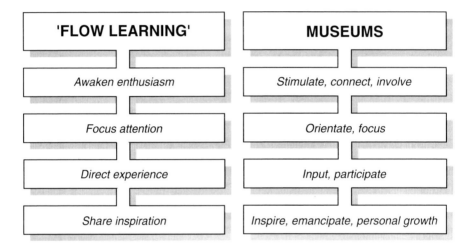

Thus stage 1 of a good learning experience is to awaken enthusiasm – to stimulate people and involve them. Typically this is something that heritage parks, with their live actors, reconstructed villages, hissing steam trains or paddling steamers, have no problem with – and which is much more of a challenge for 'indoor' museums.

Cornell's second stage is to focus attention. Indoor museums do this naturally because their objects have been extracted and isolated from their environment, and so attention is already focused. In heritage parks however the wide-eyed, wind-blown, 'interacted-with' visitor may well be unable to focus on anything at all.

Stage 3 involves the learner participating, having some input. Museums now do this to some extent with such devices as interactive displays or videos, hands-on models, etc., but the results are rarely open-ended. Heritage parks do it brilliantly for their volunteers; but can you offer your visitor some elements of this experience?

Stage 4 is sharing inspiration, so that the visitor is inspired to go out into the world with a new vision or passion or commitment. Some museum displays achieve this. For example very good environmental displays in a natural history museum can mould new 'greenies' and social history displays can build a deep sense of social justice or help a person to become aware of their own subtly hidden racism or ethnocentrism.

Do you have issues in your heritage parks which you really wish to impart to your visitors? Perhaps they already came with them, for example anti-mining or anti-technology views or views on the oppression of mine workers or the mindlessness of agricultural labour? Here is material for you to build on.

In your heritage park, is there anywhere to think and reflect upon what you have seen? Have you addressed the more difficult and sensitive issues of the era you are portraying, such as racial conflict, racism, subordination of women, massive environmental destruction and exploitative attitudes to resources . . . ? How can you do this in a place that relies on keeping visitors entertained, happy and coming back? How are you going to encourage your visitors to develop and pursue a real interest in the subject matter? How are you going to inspire and uplift them?

One answer to this is to have an indoor museum as part of your park. The chance to reflect and consider difficult issues is the strength and power of indoor museums, so if you can't beat them, join them – build your own!

You may like to combine this 'museum' with another element of parks that is commonly lacking, the 'exit experience'. I am a great believer in contact with visitors as they leave; to enquire how they found their visit; to help nurture, develop and direct any interest that may be aroused by the visit; and to encourage them to go on and visit another heritage park, museum, historic building or even their public library.

Visitors should leave on 'a high', so fire them up and bounce them out. Build your indoor museum for reflection and arrange your 'exit experience' as a spring board to further learning and discovery.

What I am saying about depth of experience is not unlike the message of the different learning types. Consider what you have already got, and then ask yourself how it might relate to the different types of learner, how you can make an even deeper impression on your visitor and how you can encourage them to go even further into the subject.

Heart and Soul: the Maori Experience

Many heritage parks are very monocultural, usually concentrating on the European material culture and social history of the last 150 years.

So the last thing I want to say about learning is to do with really 'getting through' to visitors, and it is based on my museum experience of the impact of Te Maori and biculturalism on what was a very monocultural museum tradition in New Zealand.

In the last decade Maori people really 'took on' New Zealand museums. Speaking as a European New Zealander, Maori challenged our ethnocentrism, our academic posture, our non-emotional style, our lack of spirituality. To justify the holding of Maori treasures, New Zealand museums had to change, and in many cases they did.

In figure 7.5 I have tried to summarise, from a European point of view, some of the differences between the Maori and the European views of museums. I apologise for the extent to which this is a caricature, or over-stereotyped, but I believe you will recognise the differences I am talking about.

Figure 7.5 Some differences between Maori and European views of museums

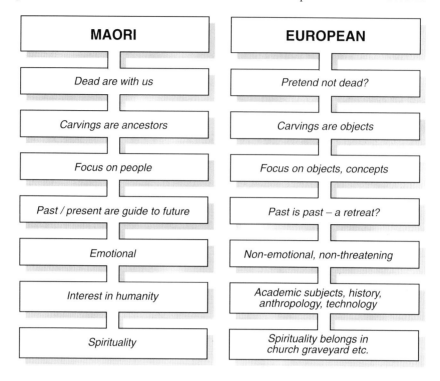

MAORI	EUROPEAN
Dead are with us	Pretend not dead?
Carvings are ancestors	Carvings are objects
Focus on people	Focus on objects, concepts
Past / present are guide to future	Past is past – a retreat?
Emotional	Non-emotional, non-threatening
Interest in humanity	Academic subjects, history, anthropology, technology
Spirituality	Spirituality belongs in church graveyard etc.

From the Maori point of view then, much of the European style museums or heritage parks is sterile; there is no mention of death, yet the exhibits are all about people; the institutions avoid emotion in favour of information; they operate either academically or in a Hollywood Wild West mode, with all its associated powerful editing of reality.

In the European heritage park the graveyard has no place; yet in the Maori view the two are inextricably linked.

So what is the lesson for heritage parks? Indeed this raises even more questions. As we receive visitors from more and more different cultures, what is their world view? What are their cultural assumptions? Are they the same as ours? Are they relating to our heritage parks as an extension of Hollywood? Do they expect more cowboys? Or do they see ancestors everywhere?

Secondly, would it be appropriate to acknowledge the dead specifically? Perhaps we should consider what they might say if they were alive today? Perhaps a situation of some reverence might be appropriate – a place attached to your heritage parks, where some reverence and contemplation could take place?

Soul

To conclude, I think we all have to stop periodically and think, 'what is the soul of this organisation?' Are we still true to that 'soul'? Because once we are sure of our 'soul', everything else will follow – collecting policy, marketing strategy, exhibit design, etc.

In travelling around New Zealand I have often felt the 'soul' of our heritage parks; the snowy mountains, barren stony soil, freezing winds and hand-built stone houses of the Otago Goldfields Park; the powerful 'Jewishness' of Olveston; the centuries of competition for Pukekura (Dunedin's Albatross Colony/Taiaroa Head settlement and fortifications, ancient pa), the greed and wetness of the West Coast goldrush as reflected in Shantytown, the craving for Englishness and security at Howick, the disharmony between the male settlers' obsession with technology and the nature of the Canterbury landscape at Ferrymead, the unbelievably short-term perspective of the kauri industry as shown at Otamatea. However, only you will really know your business, your soul, and if you are in touch with it, you will reach for your visitors at the most powerful level of all – from mind to heart and soul.

References

Cornell, J (1989). *Sharing the joy of nature: nature activities for all ages*, Nevada City, California, Dawn Publications.

McCarthy, B N D and Pitman-Gelles, B (1989). 'The 4MAT system: teaching to learning styles with right/left mode technique' in *The sourcebook 1989*, American Association of Museums.

Section Three   Audiences

Introduction

Exhibitions are for visitors, and analysing potential audience types and their needs should be an integral part of all exhibition planning. In Britain, the fact that this stage of the process is often neglected may be due in part to the scarcity of useful information. We have found it difficult to find published material on many of our principal audiences, and that which is available is patchy. Far more research time has been devoted to studying family learning than, for example, adult learning in a museum context. We also lack longitudinal studies on the impact of the museum experience on lifelong learning. Nevertheless, the selection of writings included here should provide a useful framework for analysis of audience learning needs.

This section starts with extracts from *By popular demand* (1994) by Stuart Davies. In this report, a recent study of who visits museums in Britain and what the future might bring, Davies draws attention to the unreliability of much of the available statistical material. Comparison with 'The future demand for museums 1990–2001' by V T C Middleton (1991) in Kavanagh, G (ed.), *The museums profession: internal and external relations* (Leicester University Press) demonstrates the different ways in which statistics can be used to forecast trends and what a difficult business predicting the future can be. If you are interested in consulting some of the more general statistical information produced by and about museums you should also see 'How can we find out?' by Eilean Hooper-Greenhill (1994) in *Museums and their visitors* (Routledge) pp. 49–52.

Visitor surveys undertaken by other institutions offer a starting point for those on exhibition teams. Some illuminating focus group work has been carried out by the Museum of London, the Museum of Science and Industry in Manchester, the National Museums of Scotland and Croydon Museum Service. For innovative ways of identifying potential audiences at one local museum consult 'Changing our minds: planning a responsive museum service' by Sally MacDonald (1995) in Hooper-Greenhill, E (ed.), *Museums, media, message*, pp. 165–174 (Routledge). Marilyn Hood (1986) in 'Getting started in audience research', *Museum News* 64(3), pp. 25–31 suggests more general approaches to this topic.

By looking at past and current trends in museum visiting and other social behaviour, project team members can identify actual and potential audiences in terms of age, education, social and economic background, attitudes, motivations, leisure needs and educational goals, across the whole museum sector. For those examining the social, cultural and psychological factors which affect visiting patterns, N Merriman's chapter 'Museum visiting as a cultural phenomenon' in Vergo, P (ed.) (1989) *The new museology* (Reaktion Books) provides a valuable analysis.

All of this may help those working on exhibition teams to put their own work in context and alert them to trends in visiting and the possibility of attracting new audiences. But it would be unwise to depend on surveys conducted at other institutions as the sole basis for decisions about the audience at your own institution. Much of the data that have been gathered are specific to particular museums. There is no agreed definition of important terms such as 'education' which means that the resulting data cannot easily be compared. Much of the data are quantitative not qualitative, which places a disproportionate emphasis on visitor numbers rather than visitor experience and gives little guidance to exhibition teams on how to translate these numbers into better displays. Data from other institutions can be interpreted in many different ways and local interests and preconceptions may have affected the conclusions, and by the time the data have been analysed and made available in published form, some may be out of date. There is, then, no substitute for conducting your own audience research for specific purposes in your own area or your own museum.

Davies suggests, for example, that children account for one third of museum visitors and come with friends or family. It would be worth exploring whether this holds true in your own museum or gallery and, if so, whether you should adapt or re-display the collections accordingly. Other general conclusions in his report could also be used as pointers for further research: are your visitors mainly local, as Davies suggests is often the case?

Identifying potential audiences and attempting to meet their needs in exhibitions is only the first stage in reaching audiences. Marketing, which in a museum context should mean using an understanding of the needs of an audience to inform appropriate and effective promotion of the product, is an essential part of the process. Short extracts from Sue Runyard are reproduced here to raise awareness of this element of targeting, reaching and winning over new audiences.

The next two articles (McManus and Macdonald) investigate audience behaviour once visitors are in the museum. McManus looks at the motives and personal agendas of those visiting a science museum and how visitors' social groupings and expectations affect the ways they communicate with the exhibits. She suggests exhibitions can be designed to encourage social interaction, which in turn will facilitate improved communication with exhibits. Macdonald's study is based on several years of research. She examines the reactions of audiences to a specific exhibition and looks at the preconceptions people bring with them and how they construct their own meanings. Her findings serve as a warning to all those who claim to know what visitors want and understand without conducting research into visitors' views of the exhibition subject. She also suggests that visitors tend to receive stronger messages from certain types of exhibit, notably three dimensional and interactive ones, than from others. This leads visitors to create their own meanings and may result in them ignoring those of the exhibition makers.

Both articles thus emphasise how those on exhibition teams should take into account audience expectations, preconceptions, and reactions to exhibit type, at every stage of the planning process.

Subsequent articles focus on specific audiences and raise issues of which planners should be aware. These audiences include adult learners (Matthew), adults and children in museums (Cohen), families (Wood), and children at different stages in their development (Thomas).

For many museums, school visits are important not only because of the number of visitors they account for but because they are a way of forging strong links with the local community. A number of museums are planning displays closely related to the requirements of the curriculum but we have been unable to find a suitable article about designing such displays.

Local and/or national curricula will be the starting point for anyone trying to target schools in their displays. Local schools and libraries will almost certainly have the information you require or point you in the right direction. If you want to know what children can do as a result of museum visits and how teachers can best prepare pupils, there have been a series of Her Majesty's Inspectors of Schools reports on the use of museums by schools and other educational institutions. These are listed in the GEM bibliography, and an article based on some of this work, 'The use of museum resources by young children in England' by Hazel Moffat (1992) was published in the *Journal of Museum Education* 17(1), pp. 4–6. The Schools Curriculum and Assessment Authority (1995) has also published some guidelines called *A guide to the National Curriculum for staff of museums, galleries, historic houses and sites* (SCAA).

8 The Museum Visitor: Statistical Information and Trends

Stuart Davies

Extracted from *By popular demand: a strategic analysis of the market potential for museums and art galleries in the UK*, Museums and Galleries Commission, 1994, pp. 33, 48–49, 61, 89.

The environment in which museums and art galleries exist, contains an almost infinite number of variables, each of which, when altered, will have a corresponding impact upon the museum sector. A combination of an ageing and slightly increasing population and increasing trends in early retirements, together with an overall increase in mobility would imply that the market potential for museums and galleries is increasing. Furthermore, higher standards of education would imply a further increase in potential visitors. However, such factors must be set against the increasing number of competing attractions, many of which have greater financial support available, with which they improve the quality of their attractions and employ more aggressive advertising campaigns to attract more visitors. Another important variable is policies, direct and indirect. Finally, the impact of economic factors must be mentioned. The effects of economic trends generally have a large impact on the leisure patterns of the population. Having recently emerged from the depths of a recession, the effects of high unemployment and fears of redundancy have been observed in the lack of demand for non-essential goods, which have included leisure activities. Furthermore, a combination of economic crises and the resulting pressure upon government to cut spending may result in the reduction of government support for tourist attractions such as museums and art galleries. All these factors should be considered when analysing the environment in which museums, art galleries and numerous other institutions are trying to survive . . .

The last ten years have, therefore, been a time of only modest growth in demand within the sector overall, but with quite widely differing experiences between sorts of museums and art galleries.

The Market: Key Points

- There are between 2,000 and 2,500 museums and art galleries in the UK, over 1,600 of which are registered by the Museums and Galleries Commission.

- The most commonly accepted estimate of the number of visits made to museums and art galleries each year (79 million in 1992) is an under-estimate. A more accurate estimate would be 110 million, based on data as collected from source and not amended to remove any biases in the collection method.

- Analysis of participation and frequency data suggests that 40 per cent of UK adults visit at least once a year ('regular' visitors), a further 40 per cent are occasional visitors and 20 per cent rarely go.

- There is an obvious and simple correlation between regular visitors and local visitors, a fact which ought to influence marketing strategies.

- There is a strong core of committed and loyal visitors at all museums and galleries.

- Visit and visitor figures are the only widely recognised measure for both performance and market size. This dual role for the same data is unhelpful because it is too easy to overstate the one and make the other over-optimistic.

- The common perception of steady growth in visits to museums and art galleries during the 1970s and 1980s is challenged.

- The 19 national museums and art galleries account for about one-third of all visits each year.

- Non-national museums and art galleries have been responsible for more than two-thirds of the growth since 1982.

- By analysing only the most reliable data, a previously accepted growth rate of 16 per cent since 1987 is modified to one of 10 per cent.

- The greatest percentage growth has occurred among medium and small museums and art galleries, most notably those with fewer than 30,000 visits per annum.

- It is the free admission museums and art galleries which have sustained such growth as there has been.

- Since 1987 visits to free museums increased by 34 per cent while those to charging museums decreased by 23 per cent.

- The national museums and art galleries have increased their visit numbers by 9 per cent since 1987, the local authority services by 17 per cent and the independent museums by 6 per cent.

- Few significant regional trends were observed, although Area Museum Council marketing campaigns have resulted in above average growth.

- A regional case study confirms the broad picture of very slow growth in demand, especially since 1989.

- The overall trend is one of slow growth which may even have reached a plateau by 1994 . . .

Market Segmentation: Key Points

- Supply is slowly exceeding demand. There are too many museums and art galleries chasing too few visitors.

- To get the most from resources, managers should be looking to identify segments of the market which are most appropriate for their museum or art gallery to target.

- Traditional market segmentation is not always appropriate for museums and art galleries.

- Five possible ways of segmenting the museums and galleries' market are suggested: demographics; lifestyle; geography; schools, and special interest.

- Museum and art gallery visiting is a phenomenon enjoyed across all age groups.

- Children appear to make up the single largest age group among visitors. Among adults, visiting is more popular with the middle-aged and those with families than with the young or the elderly.

- Marginally more women than men visit museums and art galleries.

- Museums and art galleries attract visitors from the whole class/occupational spectrum and are not an elitist preserve as sometimes supposed.

- The longer someone has spent in formal education, the more likely they are to visit.

- For many (perhaps most) museums and art galleries (especially those outside London), the local residential population (the 'community') will supply the core of annual visits, supplemented seasonally from other segments.

- Most people spend less than 30 minutes travelling to a museum or art gallery.

- Most visits made by children are with friends or family rather than in a school party.

- Special interests are an under-exploited segment . . .

What's New?

Like most other pieces of research, this study has built on existing knowledge and information. The museums and art galleries sector in the UK is slowly developing an understanding of the factors which help create success and those which account for poor performance. What has this study specifically added to this understanding?

The Uptake of Services (the Market Size) is Larger than has Been Thought

In the absence of any other reliable data the base market size is usually derived from the British Tourist Authority's *Sightseeing in the UK* series. For 1992 this suggested nearly 80 million visits per annum. This study has demonstrated that 110 million is actually a more accurate estimate.

Visiting is More of a Mass Phenomenon than is often Accepted

This research has shown that museum and art gallery visiting is experienced by large numbers of people across age, gender, occupational and educational divisions. Virtually everybody will be a visitor at least once in their lives, and about 40 per cent of all adults are regular visitors, going at least once a year.

Children Rather than Schools Should be a Focus for Strategy

Children account for up to one-third of visitors and perhaps 80 per cent of those are concentrated in the 10–13 year old age group. But less than a quarter of them visit as part of organised school trips and their motivation (just like their adult counterparts) is rarely 'educational'. This study's findings would imply a need for museums and art galleries to give at least equal weight to the 'experience' that they offer as to their 'educational' mission.

Geography Rather than Demographics Should Determine Strategy

Much talk about the 'ageing population' and the need to attract the over-50s may be unhelpful. The core audience will, at least for those other than the London nationals, be the local population and especially local children. This will, in turn, have implications for the type of services offered.

The Data Base for Marketing and Decision-making in the Sector is Woefully Inadequate

Many may have long suspected (or realised) this, but this study can confirm that a complete re-think about how the sector informs its action is now urgently needed.

Growth has Currently Reached a Plateau, but Enormous Potential Remains

Since about 1987 there has been relatively little growth in the market. This has considerable implications for the 'viability' not only for the numerous new museums proposed each year, but also those in existence and holding important collections. The sector is suffering from over-capacity, and needs to tap into the potential market of 130 million visits which this study has identified.

9 Targeting Specific Audiences

Sue Runyard

Extracted from *The museums marketing handbook*, HMSO, 1994, pp. 57–59, 68–70.

New Markets

Almost invariably, new markets are harder to win than extending existing markets. There are several reasons for this:

- you cannot apply knowledge gained through experience;
- starting from scratch is more challenging than building on what you already have;
- there is usually a good reason why that market has not been won already.

There are two reasons why you might believe that, despite the difficulties, you should venture into new markets. First, you might realise that it would be a financial advantage to attract a particular group, or more of a particular group, because you want to persuade them to become Friends or donors. Second, it would help to fulfil your mission statement, because they are a group which should be served by the museum. Sometimes it will be a combination of these two reasons. Whatever the motivation, it is important to be aware of the resource implications such a decision carries.

Let us take, as an example, one decision to target a particular group of disabled people, those with impaired vision. This is a group to whom many museums feel a particular responsibility, since so little has been done to make collections accessible, but where it has, the results have been dramatic and appreciated. Targeting blind and partially-sighted people is not simply a matter of extending mailing lists. The key to working this area is an appreciation of how long it takes for information to filter through the chain of communication to the point where action is taken. Publicity has to start far earlier; exhibitions need to run for longer, talking newspapers need to be researched and accessed; busy, preoccupied radio programmes need to be persuaded that this topic has sufficiently high priority – and to broadcast early rather than late; sighted helpers need to be targeted through normal channels of approach in time to arrange assisted group travel; and, because of general mobility problems, more time needs to be allowed for word to get around and action to be taken. All of this has cost implications.

Another common 'new' market are ethnic groups who rarely enter the museum. There are some interesting thoughts on this in *Could do better?* (1991) published by the West Midlands Area Museum Service. There is usually a reason why people of a particular racial group or different cultural background do not come to their local museum. It may be that museum-going is simply not part of their leisure habit, or that they feel the collections are irrelevant, or the atmosphere unwelcoming. There are big challenges to meet, because real change must be brought about. This is more than a promotional exercise. The resource implications are likely to be pressures on time, since much research and contact-making will be needed, with good internal communications allowing staff to explore issues which arise.

The same holds true whether you are trying to move your visitor profile up or down market. You need to discover preconceptions and resistance, and then work to put them right. This is a prime example of how marketing needs to intersect with every other aspect of museum activity, from public service to exhibition planning. New markets cannot be won without a co-ordinated approach . . .

Targeting

. . . What distinguishes marketing from a low level of general publicity-seeking is targeting. After considering who is and who is not using the venue, and considering objectives, decisions can be taken as to which types or groups of people should be the subject of special efforts on the marketing front. Many museums say that they are trying to serve the widest possible spectrum of people, so their marketing effort should be aimed at a broad general public. This is the least effective way to use resources, scattering them widely over a poorly defined area. A marketing strategy will allow for different groups to be targeted in different years, so that by having limited, or clearly identified objectives, real progress can be made, measured and built upon. It stands to reason that different types of people lead different lives and need to be reached in different ways, possibly with slightly different messages. Museums have many options here. Unlike performing arts centres, they are offering many different types of subject matter simultaneously. This is reflected in the broad social cross-section of people who use museums . . .

There are many different potential target groups. Here are some which could merit separate treatment and approaches:

- enthusiasts (for particular subject matter);

- clubs on group excursions;

- people undertaking further education;

- teachers and classes;

- family groups on leisure trips.

There are many more. Even within this short list, it is evident that different reading and social habits will require approaches to be made through different media, using different language. For example, enthusiasts will read specialist magazines, special interest features in general interest magazines, and possibly newsletters from societies. This doesn't mean that they don't read and listen to all the other general news and features output that everyone else is subjected to, but you don't have to pay for, or put effort into, reaching a hundred people in the hope of catching the attention of one who is already interested in your subject matter. Likewise, you wouldn't explain what you are offering in quite the same terms to an enthusiast with a bit of knowledge of the subject as you would to a family group looking for an entertaining day out. It is said that government ministers are the most difficult group to reach, since they read nothing but briefing papers and don't have time to watch TV or listen to the radio!

It should also be evident that you can't choose target groups at whim, without reference to what you are offering. Transport and military museums sometimes seek to bridge a gap in their female attendances, or seek to attract women because of their role in deciding on and organising family days out. The first step in doing so is to look at what satisfies and interests the particular group you are trying to extend. Museums like the Bovington Tank Museum and Fleet Air Arm Museum have both extended their female audiences by discovering that the social history aspects of their collections had more appeal to most women than the history of engineering. They have adapted their approach to the presentation of some of their exhibitions accordingly. This is not always possible. However, it does put the nature of a temporary exhibition programme in a new light. Museums which decide the content and style of their programmes according to the likes and enthusiasms of their curators may be out of step with the likes and enthusiasms of visitors already attending, and a long way from widening their market.

The factors or features which have the potential to interest people are called benefits. Brainstorming groups can help to establish the benefits offered. This may result in an over-lengthy list which needs to be selectively reduced, but it can offer some new angles on the subject. Here are some of the benefits offered by a modern jewellery exhibition:

- new – first time that some of the pieces have been shown;

- high standard of craftsmanship;

- decorative, ornamental pieces;

- many young craftspeople involved;

- unusual and unconventional pieces.

Such an exhibition begins to select its own audience, consisting of younger people; those with a special interest in decorative design and craft; people interested in fashion and dress. When this is put together with potential target groups within the catchment area, it suggests art and fashion schools, clubs and classes; craft venues; specialist magazines; teenage magazines and other media. It also suggests a young, avant-garde style, rather than a traditional approach.

This is a long way from standard mailing lists, one press release and a leaflet. It takes thought and imagination, but also a great deal of time and effort in order to communicate the appropriate benefits to the appropriate groups.

10 Visitors: Their Expectations and Social Behaviour

Paulette M McManus

Extracted from 'Making sense of exhibits' in *Museum languages: objects and texts*, Kavanagh, G (ed.), Leicester University Press, 1991, pp. 33–46.

What are Museum Visitors Like?

Visitors' Attitudes and Motivations

People choose to visit museums out of interest, for pleasure and because museums are places that can be visited with family and friends (Hood, 1983). Consequently, the social aspect of visiting is very influential on the communication situation in museums (McManus, 1988). Being able to have a relaxed time in social contact with family group members is very important to many visitors – often as important as the exhibits they will see.

Relaxation, pleasurable anticipation of a warm social quality to that relaxation, the opportunity to 'find out' and the expectation of pleasure associated with the reception of information, work together to colour the visitor's view of what will happen to them in the museum, even before they cross the threshold. Such feelings affect the manner in which visitors are 'open' to any communications presented to them so it is essential that those who prepare exhibitions are aware of them before they begin work. Fortunately, surveys of visitors entering museums are broadly similar in their reporting of visitor motivations and attitudes so it is possible to look at a particular survey as representative of a general trend in behaviour. During 1989, it was decided to conduct an entry survey of visitors' views of the Science Museum, London, to help in the preparation of a major new exhibition. One hundred visitors, chosen as a quota sample which mirrored the visitor age and sex distribution reported in the last major visit study in the museum (Heady, 1984), were interviewed as they began their visit. Two out of every five visitors interviewed were making a repeat visit.

Table 10.1   Motivation to visit the museum

Family visit with children	20%
Recreation	20%
Reputation of the museum	18%
Interest in science	17%
Revisiting the venue/an exhibit	17%
Museuming	8%

Source: Science Museum, 1989. Quota sample (*n* = 100)

Table 10.1 summarises the visitors' motivations in planning their visits. It can be seen that the responses centre around general interest in science and social relaxation. Around one-fifth of the audience at the Science Museum can be expected to be focusing on making an enjoyable family outing, while a further one-fifth is prompted to visit for recreational reasons. Slightly over one-third visit because of the reputation of the museum or because they have a general interest in science. As the Science Museum is in the South Kensington 'museum district', a small percentage of the visitors at any particular time can be expected to be in the building because they are 'museuming' and making many museum visits that day.

The team preparing the exhibition also wanted to focus on what the visitors' expectations were of them so that they could build their communications around these as much as possible. A visit to a museum is more than a visit to an exhibition, or exhibitions, so a general question was posed to the same quota sample asking what they hoped to get out of the time they spent in the museum. Table 10.2 reports the attitudes visitors brought with them to the museum with regard to the 'museum side' of the communication situation. It can be seen that more than a quarter of visitors hoped to gain information or understanding about unspecified scientific subjects, while a further one-fifth visited to satisfy and feed a general interest in the subjects presented in the building. That is, almost half of the visitors to the Science Museum can be expected to hold, as a first priority, hopes related to the educational mission of the museum. This group is bolstered by a further one-fifth of visitors who came wishing to see specific exhibits or exhibitions of which they are fond or have learnt about recently. In all, around 65 per cent of the sample reported that the main hopes for their visit were related to satisfactory communication from the displays presented in the museum. A further 22 per cent of visitors hoped to get fun and enjoyment from their visit – an aspiration not incompatible with good museum communications.

Generalising away from this particular survey, and noting that its findings are broadly in line with surveys conducted in other museums (for example, Alt, 1980), we can say that visitors are highly motivated to attend to exhibit communications within a social recreational context. Their interest is general and not focused in a studious, academic style.

Table 10.2   Expectations of visit

Finding out/learning	26%
Fun	22%
General interest	21%
Specific aspect of museum	18%
No structured plans	7%
No	6%

Source: Science Museum, 1989. Quota sample (*n* = 100)

Visitor Behaviour Patterns

It is possible to categorise visitors according to the patterns of behaviour they show when they interact with exhibits (Diamond, 1986; McManus, 1987). In a study I conducted in the Natural History Museum, London, the behaviours of reading, talking to companions, interacting with exhibits and spending time at exhibits were particularly considered. Styles of behaviour within these categories were closely related to specific types of social groupings amongst the visitors to the museum. I call the social groupings constituencies. I believe that exhibits must cater for the four distinct styles of making sense of exhibits shown by these constituencies, described below.

Groups containing children: The largest constituency was of groups containing children. Such groups were very likely to play at interactive exhibits, had long conversations and tended to have longer visits. It was not easy to observe reading behaviour unless there were adults in the group and then it was likely to be brief glances at text. The characteristic style used in engaging with exhibit communications displayed by the Groups Containing Children Constituency involves lots of talking and discussion and active participation and play, where this is possible.

Singletons: The next largest constituency was composed of people visiting alone. Males outnumbered females two to one in this social grouping. Singletons tended to pay brief visits to exhibits and read the labels in great detail. They were 50 per cent more likely to read labels thoroughly than any other constituency. When compared to females, male singletons were twice as likely not to play all interactive exhibits. The characteristic style used in engaging with exhibit communications employed by the Singletons Constituency involves a focus on the text of labels, rather than on artefacts or games in the display.

Couples: This, the next largest constituency, was characterised by a lack of conversation in comparison to other constituencies containing companions. Nearly 50 per cent of couples did not talk at all. On the whole, couples tended to stay at the exhibits for a longer time than members of all the other constituency groupings and were, in general, likely to read the labels comprehensively. The characteristic style used in engaging with exhibit communications displayed by the Couples Constituency involves much reading and browsing with a tendency to process communications independently before, perhaps, drawing together for discussion.

Adult social groups: This constituency appeared to pay the least attention of any constituency to exhibits as they read less than other adult constituencies and spent the least time at exhibits. The characteristic style used in engaging with exhibit communications displayed by the Adult Social Group Constituency involves rather rapid browsing. This may be because such groups are skilled processors or, alternatively, because the main focus in such groups is social interaction within the group, so leaving less attention time for displays.

The categories of behaviour displayed by the four constituency types are brought to the museum as a part of the social context of visits. They are natural behaviours, dependent on the companions with whom one comes to the museum. That is, a particular individual will be very likely to process communications in the museum differently, on differing occasions, depending on the type of constituency in which he or she visits. We see that there is no single type of visitor audience and exhibits have to cater for the variety of behaviours shown by visitors.

The Effects of Social Intimacy

The analysis of the data collected in the Natural History Museum also showed that groups of visitors which had good social relationships and moved around the museum in closed units were more likely to engage in behaviours which would allow them to process information from exhibits satisfactorily. Groups who communicate well with each other also communicate well with museum staff via exhibits. Museums cannot choose their visitors for the quality of their social interactions, but they can encourage intimate social behaviour by designing exhibits which lead groups to cluster about while they sort out what is happening within the exhibition.

Exhibits can be organised so that face-to-face communication or equal status interaction within the group are possible . . .

References

Alt, M B (1980). 'Four years of visitor surveys at the British Museum (Natural History) 1976–79', *Museums Journal* 80(1), pp. 10–19.

Diamond, J (1986). 'The behavior of family groups in science museums', *Curator* 29(2), pp. 139–154.

Heady, P (1984). 'Visiting museums', in *A report of a survey of visitors to the Victoria and Albert, Science and National Railway Museums for the Office of Arts and Libraries*, London, HMSO.

Hood, M G (1983). 'Staying away: why people choose not to visit museums', *Museum News* 61(4), pp. 50–57.

McManus, P M (1987). 'It's the company you keep . . . the social determination of learning-related behaviour in a science museum', *International Journal of Museum Management and Curatorship* 6(3), pp. 263–270.

McManus, P M (1988). 'Good companions . . . more on the social determination of learning-related behaviour in a science museum', *International Journal of Museum Management and Curatorship* 7(1), pp. 37–44.

11 The Influence of Visitors' Preconceptions on Their Experience of Exhibitions

Sharon Macdonald

This article 'Cultural imagining among museum visitors: a case study' appeared in *Museum Management and Curatorship* 11(4), 1992, pp. 401–409. The original contains notes about method and references to interview numbers which have been omitted here.

Introduction

A museum exhibition can, I suggest, be regarded as a 'technology of imagination'. It is an ordered site where the sensory and the cognitive are brought together; and where, through experience, visitors may extend and reinforce or re-shape their knowledges. This process, however, is not one in which visitors can be seen simply as passive, more or less resistant, recipients of the knowledge disseminated. Rather, they themselves come with their own visions and predispositions for particular imaginings. My aim in this paper is to illustrate something of this visitor activity through specific case study material and to discuss some of its consequences.

Research on the understandings of visitors in museums (particularly science museums) has tended to focus on questions of what visitors learn. Within these cognitive approaches, the work of Minda Borun (1982) on 'naïve conceptions' has been a significant advance. Her approach is to look at ways in which visitors may misunderstand the nature of the exhibitions because of the prior conceptions with which they come to the exhibition (e.g. 'naïve conceptions' about gravity). However, visitors inevitably come to any exhibition laden with cultural preconceptions which shape the nature of their visit and affect their response to it. This is a much bigger issue, then, than one of individual and specific 'naïve conceptions'. Indeed, the kinds of social and cultural conceptions which people may hold are often difficult to detect because far from being 'naïve' they are embedded in everyday life and make a good deal of sense within it. The kinds of cultural conceptions under consideration may also be of various orders, and about more than cognition alone. They may entail, for example, emotive attraction towards or avoidance of certain kinds of representations; tendencies to make particular classifications or order sense-data in specific ways; or the creation of personal stories, say, or the instigation of group activities in response to some kinds of exhibits. A good deal of the response to an exhibition may well be individually variable, but within this there will be certain recurring, though not necessarily universal, patterns. These patterns – cultural imaginings – are imaginative in that they involve creative interaction between visitors and the exhibition; and they are cultural in that these interactions are influenced by all kinds of expectations and ideas about the nature of museum visiting, science and so forth . . .

The Study: 'Food for Thought'

The detail of this paper is based on a study of visitors to *Food for Thought: the Sainsbury Gallery*, an exhibition which opened in the Science Museum, London, in 1989 (Macdonald and Silverstone, 1990). The study was principally qualitative, its central aim being to encourage visitors to talk about their experience of the exhibition rather than to enumerate responses to closed format questions. The methodology was devised around an intention of looking at the kinds of readings of the exhibition which visitors would make; and it entailed semi-structured interviews with families – the main target audience of the exhibition – in the groups in which they visited. Responses were all recorded and transcribed and the negotiations and occasional arguments recorded are an important part of the data (Macdonald, 1992).

As its name implies, *Food for Thought* is an exhibition about food. It is a large (810 m^2) permanent exhibition, expected to be in place for about 10 years. It cost approximately £1.2 million, excluding staff costs. It is a mixed media exhibition, containing a high proportion of interactive exhibits. The exhibition was specifically designed to be as accessible as possible to the lay-person, and it uses a number of specific strategies, such as simple, multilevel text, to be so. The following account does not by any means cover all dimensions of the exhibition, or of the visitor study. Instead, it takes three examples of ways in which visitors bring their own, patterned, input to bear on the exhibition.

Example 1: Readings of the Exhibition

The first example concerns the overall readings of what the exhibition is about. The overall theme devised by the exhibition makers was 'To help people understand the impact of science and technology on our food'. Perhaps surprisingly, given that the exhibition is in the Science Museum, few visitors mentioned science or technology in their answers to our questions about the theme of the exhibition. Instead, visitors predominantly verbalised the theme in two ways – both relevant to the makers' intentions – though not, perhaps, quite as they would have anticipated. These were: (1) 'history'; (2) 'healthy eating'.

Readings of the exhibition: some examples.

History
'It's got to do with food through the ages hasn't it?'
'History of foods in the shops and what it's like, or in the home.' . . .

Healthy eating
'I suppose it's trying to promote healthy eating.'
'Food and health – healthy living.'
'It seems to be geared towards healthy eating which is good.'

More interesting than the fact that they give these as the themes, however, is that they reconstruct the gallery in terms of them. In interviews, the first thing that visitors were asked to do was to talk about where they went and what they saw in the exhibition. The idea here was to try to get visitors to generate their own accounts of the visit. One thing that happens in many of these accounts is that visitors link together particular exhibits into patterns of 'history' and 'healthy eating'. What happens in the case of 'history' is that visitors link together some or all of the following exhibits: 1920s Sainsburys, larders and nippy and kitchens (occasionally, also the street seller and snacks section), marked by * on the exhibition plan. They talk about these one after another as though they form a continuity. For 'healthy eating', visitors join together some or all of: additives, the mirrors and scales and the exercise bikes and the nutritional puzzles and food pyramid, marked by + on the plan.

Figure 11.1   Schematic groundplan of *Food for Thought: The Sainsbury Gallery* at the Science Museum

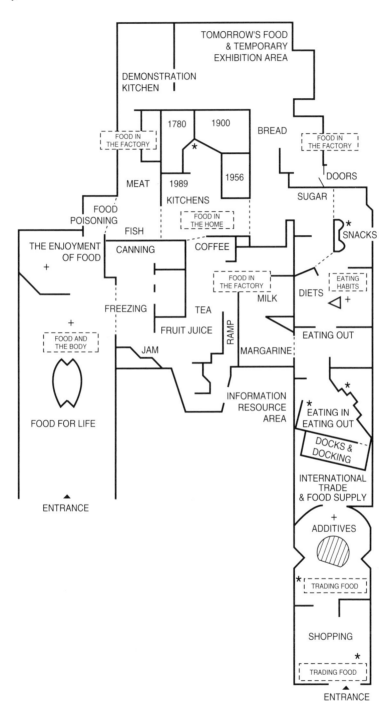

There are, I suggest, factors both external to the exhibition and unintended suggestions within it which play a part in promoting these particular readings. Within the exhibition it seems that a key to the linking of these sections by visitors may be the media used. The 'history' sections that visitors join together are all historical reconstructions and most also contain a model of a person or persons . . . The 'healthy eating' sections, on the other hand, all involve interactive exhibits, and it is these which visitors seem to pick up on in their accounts.

One external factor involved in these particular linkages and the identification of them as themes may well be experience from other types of exhibition. (Our study suggested that the majority of the visitors seemed to be general museumgoers rather than specific Science Museum aficionados.) The 'history' theme may be one that is particularly expected from heritage-type reconstructions, while the 'healthy eating' theme may have derived from health education-type exhibitions. More generally, of course, both historical narratives and messages about health are extremely prevalent within the general culture from which the visitors come, and perhaps these – rather than ideas about sciences and technology – are dominantly associated with the subject matter of the exhibition, namely food. Certain exhibits, because of their contextual location outside the exhibition may act as particularly dominant triggers for specific readings. Scales, exercise bikes and mirrors, for example, seem to spark off a personalised discussion of self, of body shape and of a concern with health.

Example 2: 'Good' Foods and 'Bad' Foods

The second example of visitors bringing their own messages to the exhibition concerns the subject-matter of the exhibition still more directly, and continues the 'healthy eating' theme. When visitors talk about healthy eating they very frequently claim that the exhibition is telling them which foods are 'good' and which foods are 'bad'.

'Good' foods and 'bad' foods: some examples

Do you think that there is a theme to the exhibition?

'Good foods and bad foods'

'I suppose in a way . . . showing you what's right to eat and what's not right to eat. Round here it had the Mars – what was in the Mars – and what was in the carrot and things like that.'

'Telling you more about food than just eating it. It tells you more about it. What's good for you and what's bad for you, ain't it?'

However, this was a point which the exhibition makers had not wanted to make and indeed at one point the text of the exhibition directly states: 'Most scientists agree that no one food in isolation is "good" or "bad".' Despite this, the neat discrimination between good and bad foods is prevalent among visitors. What is more, although the exhibition-makers had hoped to avoid being narrowly prescriptive about diet – favouring notions of balance and choice instead – visitors nearly always themselves phrase the exhibition's message in terms of 'being told' or shown what is right and wrong, what should or should not be eaten.

Again, there is a culturally dominant assumption involved here. Classifying foods into 'good' and 'bad' is one of the main ways in which food is thought about in the cultural contexts from which the majority of visitors come (Sahlins, 1976; Coward, 1989). For an exhibition to give a message counter to such a deeply rooted notion it would clearly have had to do so in a very much more direct way. Secondly, however, there are elements in the exhibition which can be read in terms of right and wrong, and good and bad. In particular, this applies to some of the interactive exhibits. When visitors talk about good and bad foods they never mention the text panels but instead talk about some of the interactive exhibits. In this particular case they talk especially about the scales and the exercise bikes and about the food pyramid, an exhibit which involves constructing a healthy diet by fitting different types of foods into different sections of a wire-mesh pyramid . . .

This raises a number of more general points for exhibition making. The first is that of from where in an exhibition visitors are going to get their 'messages'. This research suggests that – in this type of exhibition and this type of visit – messages come principally from the three-dimensional exhibits rather than from the text itself. There are relatively few instances in the interviews overall where visitors mention things which they read in the exhibition. It may be the case, of course, that this tendency to 'read' messages into, or off from, three-dimensional exhibits rather than the text is something which is particularly likely to be the case for the family group visitors which were the subject of this study. However, even if this is not a tendency which necessarily occurs among all types of visitors, it is nevertheless clearly significant and something which exhibition makers need to take into account. This example shows that written messages which contradict visitors' preconceptions may even be ignored, a possibility which suggests that careful investigation of preconceptions and careful co-ordination of countervailing messages is essential to successful exhibition making.

The second point here concerns the nature of the messages which can be conveyed by three-dimensional exhibits, or in this case, specifically by interactive exhibits. There are two cases to be made here which seem to pull in different directions. One is that any non-text exhibit is especially capable of being read in diverse ways. This means that exhibition creators need to be especially attentive to alternative possible readings. The second, however, concerns the use of puzzles more specifically. Puzzles invite visitors to 'get it right' and, inevitably, to possibly 'get it wrong'. The very fact of right and wrong answers to the puzzles seems to set up a more general expectation of right and wrong answers throughout the exhibition, and as such may be difficult to use alongside more subtle messages of balance and choice.

Example 3: Making Science Everyday

This example provides further material on which to reflect about the nature of interactive exhibits. It concerns the exhibition makers' intention of countering the distant and difficult image of science and technology and instead introducing ideas about them via the familiar and everyday. The aim was to break down that vision of science as a separate domain from ordinary everyday life. This was tackled on many levels in the exhibition design. Interactive exhibits were a key part of this in that they physically allowed visitors to participate rather than be debarred from the world of science; a strategy of introducing science and technology via familiar objects and experiences, e.g. shopping, piles of food, was used throughout the exhibition, and the exhibition avoided the use of unexplained technical jargon.

Visitors themselves frequently voiced approval of the fact that the exhibition is comprehensible and that there is a hands-on element. Whether the exhibition managed to alter preconceived views about science is the more important issue, however, and more difficult to determine. In the study, one of the questions asked was: 'Did it strike you as a scientific exhibition?' There were three main types of response to this:

Science is something else: A minority of respondents simply said that the exhibition did not strike them as 'scientific' and was not 'scientific' – sometimes saying that 'science' was about subjects like physics and chemistry as studied at school. These interviewees see the exhibition, realise that it does not accord with their preconceptions, and respond by dismissing it and retaining their previous definition unchanged.

Science is everyday: Another minority held a view that science was, of course, thoroughly concerned with the everyday and so, of course, the exhibition was scientific.

There are types and levels of science: The majority of respondents, however, seemed to be rather ambivalent and the question generated discussion. They often replied to the effect that the exhibition had not struck them particularly as a 'scientific' exhibition – and here they identified 'science' as distant and difficult, as anticipated by the exhibition makers. However, they also recognised that it must be scientific because of its location in the Science Museum. This power of the Museum to say what counts as science, to define and legitimate science, is very important here. What then happens for these visitors is that, faced by this challenge to their preconceptions, they try to resolve the mismatching visions. And they do so either by moving towards the boundary-less vision, or – more often – by partitioning science into levels or types. In some cases this has the effect of shifting 'real science' elsewhere.

Challenges to images of science: some examples.

Does this strike you as a scientific exhibition?

'No . . . Studying science at school – physics and chemistry and so on – it doesn't really come into it in my view.'

'I just didn't think that food was very . . . was *science*. I just didn't think food was science, but now I know.'

'Not really, no . . . It doesn't go into that great an analysis – it's . . .'

'No, not substantially.'

'Science is everyday and if that is the case then, yes, but . . .'

'Not in the sense of pure science as it were . . . There's levels of scientific thought . . .'

'Well, it has to be – it's in the Science Museum.'

Conclusions

Visitors bring to any exhibition particular preconceptions – particular tendencies towards certain imaginings. Clearly, the more that exhibition makers can manage to detect of these predispositions, the better they will be able to work with them. As we have seen from the example of the explicit and multipronged challenge to expected public images of science, exhibitions can at least shake preconceptions which visitors may hold.

Exhibition messages may be more likely to be made through three-dimensional media – at least in an exhibition of this type and with a family-group audience – than through the text panels . . . However, the media of an exhibition may give rise to readings which had not been anticipated by its makers. There have, of course, been doubts raised about the effectiveness of interactive exhibits to further public understanding of science. For example, Diane Saunier (1988), a French museums' consultant, has cautioned against assuming that presenting science *as* accessible is the same as actually making it accessible: 'the presentation of science and technology as spectacle leads to a belief in the accessibility of knowledge, yet knowledge remains concealed'. Understanding of scientific principles or of scientific processes is misleadingly conveyed – or not conveyed at all – by interactives, she claims.

However, although many of these arguments clearly deserve attention, we must be wary of seeing 'understanding' in too narrow a fashion. The understanding of scientific principles and processes may well be difficult to convey – and museums *might* not be particularly good at it in any media – but they may be very good at something rather less narrowly cognitive. That is, less at getting across scientific facts and details, than furthering understanding through more general images and messages about the nature of science, its possibilities, its relevance *and* its limitations.

The same arguments might be made about other kinds of museums and exhibitions, such as social history and ethnographic exhibitions. The kind of research into visitors' likely preconceptions which this paper calls for is particularly crucial where the subject matter of exhibitions touch on politically and socially sensitive topics: and these days that seems to encompass more and more exhibitions. Although this paper is based on research carried out subsequent to the opening of the exhibition, formative evaluative research could be based on the same principles and methodologies (see for example Miles et al., 1988). More generally, this kind of research should be adopted alongside more thoroughgoing development of broadly semiotic techniques for understanding the kinds of implicit 'messages' which may be inadvertently written into exhibitions. It has already become widely regarded as inadequate for exhibition makers to ignore their potential visitors altogether, but there is still a long way to go before they are taken fully into account in exhibition making . . .

References

Borun, M (1982). *Measuring the immeasurable*, Franklin Institute of Science, Philadelphia. (3rd edition).

Coward, R (1989). *The whole truth*, London, Faber and Faber.

Macdonald, S (1992). *'Food for thought': visitors to a Science Museum exhibition*, Unpublished report.

Macdonald, S and Silverstone, R (1990). *'Food for thought: the Sainsbury Gallery': some issues raised by the making of an exhibition in the Science Museum, London*, Brunel University, London, Centre for Research into Innovation, Culture and Technology.

Miles, R S et al. (1988). *The design of educational exhibits*, London, Unwin Hyman. (2nd edition).

Sahlins, M (1976). *Culture and practical reason*, Chicago, University of Chicago Press.

Saunier, D (1988). 'Museology and scientific culture', *Impact of Science on Society* 38(4), pp. 332–353.

12 Adult Learners

Maureen Matthew
This article 'Adult learners in the invitational environment of the museum' appeared in *Dawson & Hind* 14(1), 1987/88, pp. 4–6.

. . . We must remember that museums have extended the invitation to all to come to the museum. However, do we invite them to visit the museum, thereby improving our visitor statistics, or do we invite them to use the museum and do their learning there? The first question that we must ask ourselves is, how committed are we to turning visitors into users/learners? Are we willing to change our methods and approaches so that they more clearly reflect the ways adults learn?

What Do We Know about Adults as Learners?

We can make some projections about adult learning in museums from what we know about adult learning in general. First, when adults come to the museum, unlike children, they already have relatively stable perceptions about the world around them. What the museum says through its exhibits, pamphlets or educational programming must fit into an individual's past experience. Those parts of the museum's message that are in too much discord with the individual's previous experiences, and the beliefs and values that are grounded in those experiences, may be rejected or evaded altogether.

Some educators maintain that adults have to be un-taught before they can be re-taught the museum's message. But that undermines the adult's learning. Museum staff should be less concerned about transmitting a body of knowledge to visitors. When we set out to transmit a certain amount of knowledge, we are doing something to the person regardless of his needs and even his wishes. Museums practise a form of one-way communication with little reference to the existing knowledge, abilities and experiences of the adult visitors. We need to incorporate into our exhibits and programming, methods to encourage a two-way street of learning which allows visitors to give the museum information that they know about a topic, so that museums can use that information. Our adult visitors are a rich resource and many know things that we, the professionals, do not.

Secondly, a schoolchild's visit to a museum is part of his major concern, while the adult's visit is one concern among many in their lives. Museum personnel have to remember that just because adults don't happen to think it's important that they learn the information we think they should learn right now does not mean that they are not capable or motivated to learn. Adult learning is intensely personal and private. One of the frustrations of working with adult learners is that they rarely wave their hands wildly in the air when they want to show that they know something. As an educator, you have to believe, on faith, that adults are capable of learning all the time.

Thirdly, the teacher/student relationship changes drastically when working with adults. As an educator, you are working with people who are your peers –

your ability to control them to do anything is rare. Remember, visiting a museum is voluntary on the part of the visitor. They do not have to be there and if they feel that they are being forced into doing something they will leave and may never come back. Because of the conventions that adults have been socialised to, they will probably not make a fuss but they will still leave, either mentally or physically . . .

Finally, adult visitors arrive at the museum with very divergent interests. No museum can expect to meet all the interests of all their visitors. However, museums need to be more aware of the unexpected dimensions of adult learning. In preparing our exhibits and educational programming, we tend to become focused on *our goal* for the exhibit and exclude the discovery of learning that may be relevant and important to the adult visitor . . .

Museums conduct surveys on visitor demographics, on what museums are interested in the visitor learning, but can there not be an on-going visitor survey with the focus on the visitor's perspective on their own learning? Regardless of the original intent of the exhibit, what did the visitor learn that was important to him or her? Museums could then begin to get a handle on the divergent interests of their visitors and attempt to incorporate them into future exhibits and education programmes.

What Do Studies Tell Us about Adult Learners?

Most of the studies on adult learners have focused on adults enrolled in formal education institutions such as community colleges, universities and technical schools and generally do not provide useful information on learners in the informal environment of the museum . . .

A tremendous amount of independent learning is happening in each of our communities. While dealing with the adult audience can be a daunting task, the fact remains that adults are out there actively learning and, as research is discovering, learning very successfully. Museums can certainly tap into certain portions of an adult's learning, if we are aware of some other dimensions of their learning efforts . . .

Why Do Adults Decide to Learn Independently?

. . . The following four reasons are mentioned frequently when learners decide to plan their own learning (Penland, 1977):

- Adults desire to set their own learning pace – to do their learning when it fits into their schedule. It is important for museums to remember that adults have many activities in their lives that affect when they can learn. Museums need to look closely at how accessible they are to learners. When are learners available? Probably in the evenings and weekends. When are museum staff, the people with the information, available? Weekdays. This would seem to create a problem in matching learners with the resources or experts.

- Adults desire to use their own style of learning. Most adults already know what style of learning works best for them and which style does not and they adapt their learning activities to reflect their own style of learning. Museums need to offer a wider variety of formats for the learner to take advantage of. Those adults who are not attracted to a lecture series may be interested in a study circle approach where the curator assumes the role of facilitator rather than teacher. One reason that motivates people to become involved in learning is the social aspect of learning. In a study circle the friendship and community of effort towards a common learning goal satisfies that need. However, study circles are very frustrating experiences for the organiser because they rarely go in the direction that the organiser had planned and it is difficult to demonstrate that a body of information was learned.

- Adults want to keep the learning strategy flexible and easy to change. Again, adults are busy people, few can commit themselves to 12 weekly classes without missing a few. If the learning strategy cannot accommodate this, it will not serve the needs of the adult and he will go elsewhere.

- Adults desire to put their own structure on the learning project. Adult learning often takes a very wandering path, partly because the adult is exploring various options and becoming acquainted with the topic that he wants to learn and what parts of that topic are relevant and meet his needs. On the surface, learning structured in this way may appear disorganised and a waste of an individual's time. The learner, however, is able to explore dimensions of his or her learning that may prove beneficial but are not necessarily obvious at the start.

Common to these reasons is that the adult learner wants to *maintain control over his learning* – the pace of the learning, the structure, the learning style and obviously the contents. The fact that adults want to maintain control over their learning is understandable – it is probably the one area in their lives that they have control over. They want an active role in planning and conducting their learning . . .

Reference

Penland, P R (1977). *Self-planned learning in America*, Pittsburgh: Book Center, University of Pittsburgh.

13 Children and Adults

Stewart Cohen

Extracted from 'Fostering shared learning among children and adults: the children's museum' in *Young Children* 44(4), 1989, pp. 20–24.

The Museum as Joint Adventure

For effective integration of child and adult participation, a children's museum needs to determine what challenges it can present to children and adults alike.

Two questions need to be answered:

1 How may adults assist children's appreciation and participation in such settings? (See McNamee, 1987, on the role of adults in preparing children for the art museum.)
2 In what ways can children's museums inspire intergenerational learning? . . .

Contemporary museum philosophy, inspired in part by educators, as well as the success of the children's museum, lends support to the belief that learning is multidimensional: it is not limited to the acquisition of information, 'but also involves the development of attitudes, skills and values' (Hoyer-Hansen, 1984, p. 179). In addition, the modern children's museum has evolved as a 'research laboratory' whose exhibits and practices encourage children and adults to find out about themselves, their environment, their relationship to their environment, and their relationship to other members of the world (Schlossberg, 1975).

For children, the advantages of this philosophy are readily apparent. Children learn by doing (Dewey, 1902; Piaget, 1926/1967; Bredekamp, 1987; Elkind, 1987). The child is an active participant in her world; she manipulates and explores, and thereby discovers (Banaigs, 1984; Weiser, 1986; Williams and Kamii, 1986).

For the involved adult learner, museums may re-ignite a long forgotten dream, a postponed interest, or even a misplaced curiosity. Clearly, as former concerns are re-kindled, they may now be examined with different insight and renewed vigour.

Children expand existing knowledge (from an understanding of himself grows the child's understanding of his environment and, subsequently, an understanding of others). Adult learning focuses on attempts at re-orientation and re-integration (i.e. re-discovery). Here, much new learning consists of experimenting with previously acquired information in novel ways. Children's museums encourage adults to explore different forms of knowing, as well as different levels of knowing. Museum settings that emphasise child-adult inquiries favour concrete over abstract learnings, physical over verbal interactions, experiential over conceptual understandings, and sensory over theoretical encounters.

Exhibits in children's museums can help children and adults understand the complex ('What is Life?') and the perplexing ('Why are we different?') features of human existence . . .

Children's museums have increasingly addressed disabilities, using medical props such as wheelchairs, casts, and bandages, to encourage children through hands-on experiential role-playing to examine life under various handicapping conditions . . .

For minority families, ethnological exhibitions may provide a source of ethnic pride. Children's museums can help the child and other family members expand upon their sense of cultural pluralism and develop a better appreciation and understanding of many differences that make each person and culture unique (Corder and Quisenberry, 1987). Negative stereotypes and myths may be somewhat dispelled, making the children's museum a useful part of our informal anti-bias education efforts. By sitting on tatami floor mats at the Japanese House or sipping tea in the Chinese Garden, children and adults directly experience customs and cultural perspectives characteristic of other kinds of families.

It is very important not only that the teachers of young children take advantage of the rich educational opportunities available in children's museums, but that teachers also use this wonderful opportunity for parent participation in their children's school life, and for intergenerational learning. As has been demonstrated over and over, children learn best when their families are involved in their experience (Powell, 1989).

Judging Children's Museums

Museums vary in their mission and purpose. They often differ in terms of the diversity of specificity of clientele they seek to serve. Consequently, some forethought is advised when selecting a museum that will serve the needs of children and adults alike . . .

For the early pre-operational child (2 to 5 year olds), we seek museum exhibits that allow for frequent repetition of activities, require little instruction, do not demand word comprehension or reading skills, provide playful opportunities in the use of manipulative materials, and offer many props that encourage role-play and are age-appropriate.

Museum participations for children in early to middle childhood (ages 6 to 8) should also be developmentally appropriate (Bredekamp, 1987). As Banaigs, a museum educator, notes, 'School-aged children take an interest in those aspects of reality upon which they can exert some influence . . . Passivity is not the child's natural state, but one imposed by the educational system' (1984, p. 190). Consequently, for children of this age group, museums should feature hands-on activities, explorations allowing movement, and exhibits involving experimentation. They should avoid school-simulating programming (e.g. fatiguing mechanical seatwork, worksheet-dictated involvements, and topical lectures).

Considering the diversity of activities and exhibits that may compete for attention within the museum, Regnier (1987) developed guidelines to enhance the enjoyment and success of the museum adventure. For preschool and primary children and their families, successful exhibits usually include one or more of the following:

- Gross-motor activities (e.g. crystal climbing boxes and bridges).

- Multisensory exhibits (e.g. moving exhibits characterised by bright lights and sounds).

- Sand and water (e.g. large seascape settings featuring boats and ships).

- Collections that demonstrate classification (e.g. dinosaurs arranged in order of size; floral exhibits displayed by climate).

- Role-play (e.g. school, commercial, neighbourhood, and various historical settings).

- Dressing up in costumes and uniforms (e.g. explorer, archaeologist, or astronaut dress).

- Places to hide (e.g. animal homes, life in the forest, storybook gardens).

- Objects to assemble/disassemble (e.g. large-scale dinosaur or animal puzzles; matching jobs and tools).

- Age-appropriate activities (i.e. explorations children can reach, solve, or complete without adult intervention).

- Activities that provide choice and diversity (e.g. child-sized tools or equipment and opportunities to apply them to 'real' tasks).

Poorly conceived or unsuccessful museum exhibits are those that bore, confuse, or fatigue children and adults. Unsuccessful exhibits usually include one or more of the following components:

- School-simulating or imitative interactions – activities that ask children to listen in small groups or engage in focused discussions or specified interactions do not fare well in settings where the environment beckons exploration.

- Information/non-interactive components – non-participatory events that provide few opportunities for active engagement require revision. Such exhibits tend to fatigue children and emphasise child/adult learning differences. Moreover, they require adult-guided interactions, rather than underscore child-adult explorations.

- Intensive use of words or reading comprehension – activities with high word content, or that require reading ability, usually fatigue younger participants.

- Confusing or unclear purpose – spaces that do not inform participants about appropriate behaviour or expected outcomes create difficulties for both child and adult participants.

- Many abstract components – exhibits should reflect children's real life experiences.

- Subject matter or topics that require advanced comprehension – exhibits should not tax or discourage participant interactions and resources, but rather challenge them.

- Dependence on prior knowledge – developmentally advanced exhibits are usually inappropriate for young children.

- Demands for sustained attention span or high persistence level – extended, highly involved, or time-dependent interactions that conflict with a child's sense of here and now may discourage young children's participation.

Summary

Children's museums provide unique opportunities for engaging families in inter-generational explorations and discovery learning. There is a growing awareness of the need for addressing children's development within the context of the family. Such adventures, which represent a new thrust of museum educators, appear to recognise the value of fostering shared learnings among children and adults. Recent research findings indicate that child-initiated interactions in the children's museum account for the greatest proportion of family participation, suggesting both the viability and importance of child-oriented programming as a stimulus to intergenerational participation (Dockser and Gallagher, 1987).

The role of early childhood educators in recognising and encouraging shared learning opportunities has several aspects. We need to identify such opportunities in our communities for our client families. We need to encourage the development of participatory exhibits that serve young children and their families in museums that have them and in museums that as yet do not. We need to take our classes to the museum frequently. We need to bring museum educators into our classroom (Dunitz, 1985) to work with the children and with their parents and grandparents, who should be there too.

References

Banaigs, C (1984). 'Curators, teachers and pupils: partners in creating an awareness of modern art', *Museum* 36(4), pp. 190–194.

Bredekamp, S (1987). *Developmentally appropriate practice in early childhood programs serving children from birth through age 8* Washington, DC, National Association for the Education of Young Children.

Corder, L J and Quisenberry, N L (1987). 'Early education and Afro-America: history, assumptions and implications for the future', *Childhood Education* 63, pp. 154–158.

Dewey, J (1902). *The child and the curriculum*, Chicago, University of Chicago Press.

Dockser, L S and Gallagher, J M (1987). 'Parent-child interaction in a museum for preschool children', *Children's Environments Quarterly* 4(1), pp. 41–45.

Dunitz, R J (1985). 'Interactive museums', *Media & Methods* 21(8), pp. 9–11.

Elkind, D (1987). 'Viewpoint: superbaby syndrome can lead to elementary school burnout', *Young Children* 42(3), p. 14.

Hoyer-Hansen, T (1984). 'The museum as educator', *Museum* 36(4), pp. 176–183.

McNamee, A S (1987). 'Museum readiness: preparation for the art museum (ages 3–8)', *Childhood Education* 63, pp. 177–180.

Piaget, J (1967). *The child's conception of the world*, Totowa, New Jersey, Littlefield Adams. (Originally published 1926.)

Powell, D R (1989). *Families and early childhood programs*, Washington, DC, National Association for the Education of Young Children.

Regnier, V (1987). 'The children's museum: exhibit and location issues', *Children's Environments Quarterly* 4(1), pp. 55–59.

Schlossberg, E (1975). *The learning environment for the Brooklyn Children's Museum*, Brooklyn, The Brooklyn Institute of Arts and Sciences.

Weiser, M G (1986). 'Young children and the quality of life: Report of the XVIIIth world congress of OMEP', *Childhood Education* 63, pp. 74–77.

Williams, C K and Kamii, C (1986). 'How do children learn by handling objects?' *Young Children* 42(1), pp. 23–26.

14 Families

Richard Wood
This article 'Museum learning: a family focus' appeared in
Journal of Education in Museums 11, 1990, pp. 20–23.

> The attitude that museums are 'good places' to take children, and the fact that
> the largest postulated visiting group comprises families, [make] it . . . clear that a
> specific policy catering for this market should be further developed and actively
> promoted. (Prince and Schadla-Hall, 1985)

As we hack our way through crowded galleries on a drizzly afternoon during
half-term week, the evidence of our eyes may suggest that we are already satisfying the needs of families quite adequately. But are we? Trains are often packed,
too, but that is no indication of quality of service or customer satisfaction. To
evaluate our service we need to know something about our family clients, why
they visit museums, what and how they learn when they are with us and the
ways in which museums can facilitate or obstruct this learning process. This
article draws on research from museums in Britain and the USA to highlight
some of the specific needs and expectations of our family visitors.

Families are important

Museum visitor surveys note the statistical importance of families. At the
Natural History Museum, for example, nearly 50 per cent of visitors were found
to be in family groups, 70 per cent in groups of some sort (Alt, 1980). The
National Maritime Museum found 65 per cent in family groups and a further
18 per cent with friends, but only 5 per cent visiting alone (Smyth and Ayton,
1985). Falk's study (1985) of museum visitors in Florida found 68 per cent in
family groups, and a further 22 per cent in peer groups. Museum visiting is
obviously a social experience for most of our clients. However, not all types of
museums are equally attractive to families and even within particular museums
considerable variation in gallery use by families can be seen. At Norwich Castle
Museum, for example, even on the busiest days, family groups are conspicuously
absent from the art galleries. If museums are truly concerned with maintaining
or increasing attendances, then families offer potentially the most productive
target for promotions and publicity. The importance of families, however, is far
more long-term than our present statistics might suggest. In a real sense, the
whole future of museums rests on the impact they make on the families of
today. Families are arguably the greatest opinion formers, the greatest purveyors
of social, cultural and aesthetic values in our society. Evidence suggests that
adult recreational choices are far more closely linked to recreational experiences
begun as a child in a family than in school (Kelly, 1977). A poll conducted in
the USA showed that 60 per cent of regular museum-goers said that their
interest in museums had been shaped by a family member against only 3 per
cent who credited school visits (quoted in Wolins, 1982). Clearly if we hope to
earn the support of the adults of tomorrow we must respond to the needs of the
families of today.

Families are Different

Firstly, families are different from how they used to be. Yet until recently even children's museums (Zien, 1979) applied educational approaches and exhibition techniques based on assumptions about the relative roles of adults and children that had changed little for 50 years. Adults were cast in the role of chaperones and informants, leaving the children, familiar with television and Disneyland, even more bored than before. Families today are less dependent on each other and spend less time together, but expect a higher quality of experience than before (Yerk, 1984). There is no lack of choice. Further, the change from didactic to learner-centred discovery methods of education in schools may have permanently changed the expectations of informal, out-of-school learning too. Museum displays which cling to a didactic mode will not be appreciated and may not even be understood. Visitor surveys such as those at Hull and Greenwich, already quoted, have found dissatisfaction amongst family visitors with the methods and level of information provided. In short, museums that are more concerned with objects than with the effective communication of ideas about objects have little to offer families. As the Wright report commented 'A museum should not be regarded as a collection of objects . . . but as a service based on a collection' (DES, 1974). The nature of that service must keep pace with the changing nature and expectations of the clients.

Secondly, family groups differ from each other and from other visitors. They come for different reasons and with different expectations carrying different sets of social and cultural baggage. The seeming impossibility of communication with such diversity within a single museum or display sometimes results in a failure to communicate with anyone, except perhaps other curators. Can we, hand on heart, claim that all our displays are intelligible without some prior knowledge? If not, and we are relying on parents to supply or interpret that knowledge for their children are we encouraging and helping them to do so? Do our displays cultivate the curiosity of families by helping them to link the artefacts with their everyday knowledge, or 'find the *Me* in museum', as Waterfall and Grusin (1989) put it.

> The finding of the *Me* insures that the museum becomes a place to be comfortable exploring the mysteries of the world. The *Me* in the painting, or the beehive or the First Ladies' gowns make connections from the museum-goer to the museum world. A child who feels a connection with the world . . . regards the world with more care and interest. Children who value artefacts and creations of their culture grow into adults who create or preserve culture for the next generation.

All too often, the *Me* is nowhere to be seen. Art galleries, instead, tend to 'institutionalise the artist's marginality suggesting art is related only to other art. Our imagination is so stunted by art history that we hang pictures chronologically by isms' (Gilmour, 1979). Gilmour's criticism is not only applicable to art galleries. We all categorise in order to make sense of our experiences. Yet most museums use academic category systems ('archaeology', 'pleistocene', 'post-medieval') which are in stark contrast to the commonsense categories ('manners', 'meals', 'entertainment') of family life. If we wish to help families to understand and learn from our displays, we must find ways of bridging the gap between these two systems.

Visitor surveys invariably suggest that family visits are rarely planned more than a day ahead. Nearly all are casually made for purposes of leisure, pleasure or general rather than specialist interest (Alt, 1980). Though most people rate museums as 'educational' institutions, family visitors are predominantly 'tourist' in nature. Thus the learning which takes place is qualitatively different from that of either the unaccompanied adult or the child in a school group. Unlike the former it is social in context, and unlike the latter it is informal and voluntary in character.

'Social learning is the essence of the family museum experience', comments Wolins (1982). Other studies draw attention to different aspects of this process. Alberty (1982) speaks of the use of the museum visits as a 'cementing ceremony, thoroughly enjoyable and with implications that go well beyond the aesthetic and intellectual benefits intended by the museum', while Graburn (1984) describes the 'major *ritual* function of museum going . . . to serve as a social marker by punctuating personal and family life in a memorable and pleasurable way'. The importance of social factors is borne out by comparison of the behaviour of families with that of other visitors. McManus (1987), for example, found that families spent the most time at the displays they selected for attention, they engaged in the most conversation and were the most likely to use interactive displays. However, they were the least likely to read labels or graphics – even instructions were read only as a last resort if they failed to make manipulables work by trial and error.

This social quality of family learning contrasts with the individual-as-learner focus of formal education. Yet it is not a mere optional extra or bonus, it is the very means by which family learning takes place. Diamond (1986) observed 'teaching' behaviours such as showing, telling, naming, describing and questioning, practised by parents with their children. She concluded that learning resulted primarily from these interactions rather than from interaction between individuals and objects. She also found that easily intelligible labels or graphics considerably aided learning, despite these only being read at 9 per cent of exhibits visited.

Display design must facilitate, or at least not obstruct, these social learning encounters. Is this always so? Can families see and talk to each other while looking at our displays? Are all the objects visible from child height, or do the spotlights reflect on the glass if you are under five feet tall? Are comfortable spaces provided for families to sit together to discuss discoveries, or are displays only accessible for any length of time to those with Spartan endurance? A 1989 survey (Touche Ross, 1989) found that a remarkable 87 per cent of museum visitors rated provision of general seating areas as important or very important. Further, around 80 per cent stressed the importance of snack/coffee areas and museum shops. Clearly the social nature of the family visit makes these facilities essential. But does the cafeteria sell family-type food at affordable prices? Are high chairs and nappy-changing facilities available? And does the shop sell gifts and books for children as well as parents? When we look at the museum from our clients' perspective, these are not peripheral issues.

Museums are public places where particular codes of behaviour, probably unfamiliar to children, are expected. While some may use a museum visit deliberately to practise these behaviours, other parents may find their children's potential for non-compliance stressful. As Hensel (1982) found, museums can present challenges to parental roles, pit child against child, family against family and force parents into passive roles in the presence of authority. Equally, if displays take more account of museum priorities than visitor interests, if visitors are directed where they do not wish to go and if information panels read like comprehension tests, we have only ourselves to blame if families do not warm to our endeavours. How many museums even trouble to ask visitors what they think, or to collect comments and ideas in a suggestions book? If we want families to be open to museums, museums must be open to families. They will judge us, not just on our displays, but by everything we do.

Families make Choices

Family learning is free-choice and informal. Probably the principal reason for the continuing popularity of museums with so many families is that they provide a focus for informal learning together outside the home. But it is the quality of the whole experience that matters more than any specific set of learning goals. Rosenfeld (1982) found family visitors' expectations of zoos predominantly child-centred, and his observations of their behaviour showed children consistently controlling the pattern and pace of visits in 69 per cent of groups. Observations of family behaviour in different types of museums not only show children's interests paramount, but also illustrate their marked preference for interactive displays. Laetsch (1980) tells us that science centres are popular because they are multisensory

> unlike art museums where sight is the only sense observers enjoy. Active partici-
> pation – the ability to physically interact with objects and to manipulate variables
> – provides something for everyone in the family. Active participation increases the
> chance that social interaction during an outing will be successful.

Surveys show a similar concern for greater involvement with exhibits. Visitors to the National Maritime Museum (Smyth and Ayton, 1985) for example, expressed the wish 'to look through telescopes' or 'to have a feel of the material and be able to work models'. Nor is this just a wish to play (and even if it were, why should museums not gratify it?). The chance to press a button or make something happen confers a sense of well-being, of being in control. Museums can be great intimidators. Our clients deserve a few boosts to self-confidence. Koran (1986) related manipulation of objects to learning outcomes by observing responses to a display of shells first when closed, then open, then open with a microscope available. He found that one-third of visitors handled the shells when open, but two-thirds when the microscope was added. Visitors, notably children, spent more time at the open exhibit, and a higher percentage were attracted to it, regardless of whether or not they touched the exhibits.

Family learning in museums is informal. It has no predefined objectives or strategies or curriculum-determined outcomes. It is a free-choice, unstructured, casual activity. Falk (1984) likens museum visitors to shoppers in a department store. A small minority of adult visitors are 'serious' shoppers. They know what they want to see, they see it, they leave. Family visitors are 'window shoppers'. They browse around enjoying a pleasant social time, making a few purchases on impulse when something takes their fancy. The job of the museum, like the shop display, is to convert window shoppers to purchasers. Good displays and signs are essential, or how will they know where to go and what to see? Falk's observations (1985) of museum visitors in Florida showed a predictable pattern of behaviour by families. They first spend a few minutes in general orientation, then 30 to 45 minutes of attention to exhibits, and finally up to 30 minutes of 'cruising', stopping only occasionally and selectively. Beer (1987) found that only a third of museum displays were looked at for more than 30 seconds while almost half were skipped entirely. Those most likely to be attended to were large, or had manipulable or moving parts or audio-visual components. However, these 'attention-seeking' displays had a negative effect on adjacent displays, which were the least likely to be seen.

Other studies have shown a strong correlation between the position of displays within an overall museum layout and their likelihood of receiving attention from visitors. Surprisingly perhaps, Beer found that even people who visited with specific learning objectives in mind did not behave in a significantly different manner from those whose visits were merely casual or recreational. We must conclude that if we expect families even to notice our museum objects, let alone learn from them, we must first ensure that displays are appropriately sited, attention-seeking and, if possible, interactive . . .

References

Alberty, B (1982). 'A museum autobiography', *Roundtable Reports* 7(2), pp. 3, 10–11.

Alt, M B (1980). 'Four years of visitor surveys at the British Museum (Natural History) 1976–79', *Museums Journal* 80(1), pp. 10–19.

Beer, V (1987). 'Great expectations: do museums know what visitors are doing?', *Curator* 30(3), pp. 206–214.

DES (Department of Education and Science), (1974). Provincial museums and galleries, HMSO.

Diamond, J (1986). 'The behavior of family groups in science museums', *Curator* 29(2), pp. 139–154.

Falk, J H (1984). 'The use of time as a measure of visitor behavior and exhibit effectiveness' in Nichols, S J (ed.), *Museum Education Anthology*, pp. 183–189. Museum Education Roundtable.

Falk, J H (1985). 'Predicting visitor behavior', *Curator* 28(4), pp. 249–257.

Gilmour, P (1979). 'How can museums be more effective in society?' *Museums Journal* 79(3), pp. 120–1.

Graburn, N (1984). 'The museum and the visitor experience', in *Museum Education Anthology*, (ed.) Nichols, S J, pp. 177–181. Museum Education Roundtable.

Hensel, K (1982). 'A new look at our largest audience', *Proceedings of the AAZPA Annual Conference*.

Kelly, J R (1977). 'Leisure socialisation: replication and extension', *Journal of Leisure Research* 9(2).

Koran, J J, Koran, M L and Longino, S J (1986). 'The relationship of age, sex, attention and holding power with two types of science exhibits', *Curator* 29(3), pp. 227-35.

Laetsch, W, Diamond-Jeffry, J, Gottfried, L and Rosenfeld, S (1980). 'Children and family groups in science centres', *Science and Children* 17(6), pp. 14–17.

McManus, P (1987). 'It's the company you keep . . . the social determination of learning-related behaviour in a science museum', *International Journal of Museum Management and Curatorship* 6, pp. 263–70.

Prince, D and Schadla-Hall, R T (1985). 'The image of the museum: a case study of Kingston upon Hull', *Museums Journal* 85(2), pp. 39–45.

Rosenfeld, A (1982). 'A naturalistic study of visitors at an interactive mini-zoo', *Curator* 25(3), pp. 187–212.

Smyth, M and Ayton, B (1985). *Visiting the National Maritime Museum*, HMSO.

Touche Ross (1989). 'Touche Ross Management Consultants Survey', *Museums Journal*, 89(7), p. 8.

Waterfall, M and Grusin, S (1989) *Where's the ME in museum?*, Washington, DC, Vandamere Press.

Wolins, I (1982). 'Educating family audiences', *Roundtable Reports* 7(1), p. 2.

Yerk, R (1984). 'Families, what are we doing for our largest audience', *American Association of Zoological Parks and Aquariums annual conference proceedings*, pp. 380–386.

Zien, J (1979). 'Beyond the generation gap', *Museum News* 58(2), pp. 26–31.

15 Children

Gillian Thomas

Extracted from ' "Why are you playing at washing up again?":
some reasons and methods for developing exhibitions for
children' in *Towards the museum of the future*, Miles, R and
Zavala, L (eds), Routledge, 1994, pp. 120–130.

Multisensory Stimulation

Ask children to look at an object in your hands and they will automatically
stretch out to touch. Depending on age and experience with similar objects, a
child may also smell, suck, lick or bite the object. Training the eye is important,
but children find it easier to concentrate on an object that can be touched, held
or manipulated. The ideal object in a museum can thus be explored in a multisensory fashion and may also include physical movement. It is, however,
important to ensure that the action proposed has some relevance to the learning
experience. Crawling or climbing may well relieve the tension and will certainly
be popular with children, but if it is dissociated from the educational content, it
merely serves to excite. On the other hand, if the physical activity has relevance,
it enhances the experience. This is the case for the Inventorium's ant farm [in
Paris], where visitors can crawl underneath the ants' feeding area and discover
ants inside their nest, illuminated by red light. Here the action of crawling
reinforces the message that the ants are underground. The physical activity is a
means of encouraging observation. It enriches the experience and encourages a
'minds-on' experience . . .

Development Level

The majority of children under 12 are not yet at a developmental stage that
enables them to handle more than one variable at a time. Before the age of 6 or
7, even concrete experiences may not as yet be well established. At this age,
counter-intuitive effects may produce little surprise; odd events are an everyday
happening. Exhibitions thus need to emphasise the simple relationships between
the visitor's action and its effect. More complex phenomena, with multiple variables, need to be limited and presented in a different way, so that simply
acquiring the feel for the phenomenon, admiring its beauty, using it without an
attempt at an explanation, may be sufficient. This must, however, be a conscious
decision, rather than an overall justification for a high-play-level, low-
understandability exhibit.

While the developmental level of exhibits obviously needs to be simplified for
children, unsure adults also use a hands-on, concrete approach to solving
problems in the unfamiliar world of exhibitions. Designing an exhibition for
children can make it accessible for adults who would otherwise feel intimidated.

Role-Play

The use of role-play in an exhibition can help children to explore both a
situation and technical equipment. A happy equilibrium needs to be established

between the realism of the situation and the technical complexity of the materials. Too real a simulation will limit the imagination; too simple and unstructured an experience and the exhibit will be enjoyable, but not communicate effectively. 'Playing' both sets the scene and creates the context for learning. In what way this play differs in a young child from that of an adult engaged in role-play as a management training experience is difficult to define. The activity must be focused on the essential information to be communicated, and appropriate equipment integrated into the experience. The environment serves only to set the scene, the activity needs to be as realistic as possible.

Visitor Interaction

Few children visit alone; coming to an exhibition is a social event. How children react with other members of their group, or with other unknown visitors, varies with their development and is dissimilar to adult behaviour. At a young age, children are still developing awareness of the others as individuals; characteristic play is alongside rather than with others. At the Inventorium, the *Building Site* in the young children's section offers a structure sufficiently large for children to create their own corner for building and allows each child to develop an individual activity. At the same time, the size and weight of the high-density foam bricks and the crane to lift them to the upper floor of the structure encourage co-operation between the children. The exclusion of adults from the zone also encourages the child to develop a sense of autonomy, in an unfamiliar environment, with unknown people.

Once children are of school age, the importance of the peer group can become overwhelming. Children will often not attempt to investigate an activity until a group has been established. The first action is to occupy the exhibit, attract other members of the group to it, and only then does effective investigation occur. Exhibits that require the participation of several members of the group are necessary. Children will also adapt situations to conform to their current enthusiasms and interests. In this way, a coloured lights exhibit can be readily converted into a journey into space; exhibits on mechanics can be converted into a car race. However well the scene is set, the subversive spirit will appear. To some extent this also happens with adults; exhibits are used to further social contacts, to display knowledge or importance in a group. These would not be included in the exhibit developer's aims for the exhibition, and are less apparently subversive than creating a space setting in the coloured lights exhibit. Children are perhaps simply more honest.

With the approach of adolescence, two conflicting types of behaviour emerge. Young people are still predominantly in groups, and tend first to make a whirlwind visit of the entire exhibition, apparently paying very little attention to individual exhibits, often using them simply to display to their peers. However, the interest in individual exploration is growing, and this initial tour is effectively used to preselect items that are subsequently visited either alone or in smaller groups for more careful investigation.

The *Television Studio* at the Inventorium was an exhibit which appealed to a very wide age range and offered a considerable variety in the types of activity offered. At a simple level, children can appear in front of a camera and present the news, the weather or any other programme of their invention. They can also be the camera man, use the zoom or focus, or, outside the studio, use the mixing table to manipulate the camera images. Without recording, groups of children will use the studio and need little supervision. As the number of controls are limited and all the equipment is protected, visitors find out how to use the equipment with little instruction, and frequently tell one another how to make it work. The emphasis is on demystifying television and on acquiring technical mastery of the equipment. The quality of the programme produced is low, but the pleasure and sense of achievement is high. With an enabler, more emphasis on the production can occur. At the Inventorium, a whole range of types of use of the TV studio was developed, from the simple unassisted use of the material, through short 20-minute sessions with informal groups, to a series of sessions incorporating video material filmed by the group with hand-held material elsewhere in the science centre. This type of exhibit offers a wide range of types of use, and can both be adapted by the public for their particular interests and social needs and, at the same time, have structured activities proposed which encourage the public to pursue their nascent interests a little further.

The Development Process at the Inventorium and Eureka!

For the main exhibition areas at the City for Science and Industry [La Villette, Paris], as in the majority of museums, little attempt was made in the period up to opening to target the younger visitor, either for the content or for social needs. Only the Inventorium was considered as having a specific function for the younger visitor. As a direct consequence of this specific aim, the team developing the Inventorium contained a wider variety of specialisations and the educational programme was defined in terms of the process of learning rather than of subject fields. None of the exhibitions was based on collections, but outside the Inventorium the exhibition policy was defined by broad definitions of essential areas of knowledge, rather than by reference to the public.

The educational aims and objectives of the Inventorium defined discovery learning as the approach to be encouraged, and content was chosen which was close to children's knowledge about themselves and their experience of the everyday world. Twelve themes spanning biology, physics and technology were included, with an emphasis on learning in a context. Largely inspired by the discovery rooms of American natural history museums, and considerably influenced by institutions such as the Boston Children's Museum and the Exploratorium, the development team of the Inventorium aimed to exploit existing good practice but was aware of cultural differences between the American and French publics.

Criteria for the selection of exhibits were not whether the content was essential scientific knowledge, but whether the phenomena or information were of intrinsic interest to children, and whether an appropriate hands-on activity could be developed. Giving intellectual coherence to the exhibitions and making the themes intelligible for adults were reasons behind the decision to group exhibits in themes, rather than leaving individual stand-alone exhibits to be explored as in many science centres. None the less, careful attention was paid to ensuring that the content of each exhibit was clear and could be explained and justified scientifically. High-play value alone was insufficient to guarantee inclusion. Nor were any exhibits constructed on a putative 'Stun the Visitor' factor. An equilibrium was sought between the intrinsic pleasurableness of a hands-on activity and an intellectually stimulating, minds-on challenge.

For all members of the development team, a perusal of available American research made it evident that considerable educational and cultural differences existed between the USA and France. There was little information available as to how these would affect visitor behaviour. Observable differences in the education system and in family attitudes could be ascertained. These include, for example a carefully structured national education programme for the whole country in France, a lack of interest in experiential learning in the school context, more formal classes, little project or individual work in schools. Greater emphasis is placed on writing, observation and deduction in France. Attitudes as to the type of activities undertaken by families are also different . . .

Visits and Discussions

An initial feel for an exhibition area or theme can in some cases be established by visits with children. This technique is also used by toy manufacturers such as Fisher Price to establish initial interest for proposed toys where a relevant visit can be proposed, for example in developing a model fire station or garage. This technique is particularly appropriate at Eureka! in the *Living and Working Together* theme, which relies on role-play and learning in a context to interest children in the hidden aspects of the everyday world and, in particular, in design and technology. A set established around a town square will present a house, a shop, a factory, a bank, a garage, and a recycle centre for exploration. To gauge the interests of particular areas, visits and discussions were carried out with different school groups. Some unexpected interests have been revealed, such as enquiries as to relative pay levels of different staff members in the shop, or questions as to whether the manager had ever been sued. Simple discussions of this sort often reveal unexpected knowledge, and also areas of knowledge shortfalls. Some 8-year-olds have been unable to offer any concept of what a factory might be or do; the word has no meaning for them. In general, the range from lack of knowledge to detailed information is wider than would have been anticipated without such visits and discussions . . .

Write and Draw

One of the difficulties in ascertaining children's knowledge is that techniques applicable to adults are generally unsatisfactory when applied to young children, either because their reading and writing skills are insufficiently developed or because the techniques such as questionnaires and interviews have no relation to their habitual learning styles or social activities. Peer-group pressure is also very strong, and the school context often makes children unwilling to express their ideas. It is essential to develop techniques that will encourage all children to express their ideas individually, by a method that is familiar and reassuring.

Write-and-draw techniques encourage children in the security of their class or in a quiet museum space to respond either to questions or situations. Both writing and drawing may need assistance from a friendly adult, to help label an unclear picture, or to help spell words. It is the child who decides on the content and asks for assistance only when necessary. The activity can be presented as a game, a secret, so that each child gives an individual response. Children with a limited mastery of English can take part fully, provided an adult who understands what the child wishes to say is available. Initial ideas as to the questions or scenarios to be presented often develop after a few small trials. These can vary from simple word definitions, to continuing a story which sets a scene.

This technique was used extensively at the Inventorium, in particular for areas where there seemed to be little existing information about children's ideas. In some cases, preliminary research by this method caused a shift of emphasis of the content. In the *Techniques for Communicating* theme, a variety of different technical appliances was available for children to explore, with games designed to encourage investigation of the advantages and disadvantages of each . . .

Conclusion

Developing exhibitions adapted to a public of children and the adults accompanying them remains a skill rather than a science. Techniques for identifying children's ideas offer largely anecdotal evidence, relevant to a particular time and place, but guaranteeing no certainty if they were to be applied in another context. Nevertheless, a body of skills is being acquired, a methodology of development . . .

Section Four   Disability

Introduction

Through invoking their legal rights people with disabilities in the United States have been very successful in acquiring equal provision. Section 504 of the Rehabilitation Act of 1973 prohibited discrimination against people under any programme or activity receiving federal funding. Although people were slow to appreciate the significance of Section 504 it came to be seen as the core of the disability rights movement. In 1990 the Americans with Disabilities Act required that all public, commercial and government buildings and services should be made 'readily accessible' to people whatever their disability. In the last 15 years or so American museum literature has been full of articles addressing disability issues.

In Britain progress has been slower. People with disabilities have lobbied, so far with minimal success, for the same sort of rights, and many groups have become much more radical. Although not directly related to museums Simon Brisenden's article has been included because of the importance of its very clear statement about how some disabled people see themselves and what they identify as their distinctive and separate culture.

Both Rebecca McGinnis and Anne Pearson (whose book *Arts for everyone* was an important milestone in the British literature on access) offer practical suggestions for ways forward. The Museums and Galleries Disability Association (MAGDA) runs sessions on disability issues and the Museums and Galleries Commission have an Access co-ordinator who can advise. The MGC's *Guidelines on disability for museums and galleries in the United Kingdom* (1992) and their *Disability resource directory for museums* (1994) should also be consulted, but for an alternative model the Canadian guidelines on disability published by the Ontario Ministry of Culture and Communications (1985) could be studied. (See *Ontario museum notes – practical information on operating a community museum 12: The community museum and the disabled visitor*, The Ontario Ministry of Culture and Communications, Toronto.) Models of good practice throughout Europe are described in *Museums without barriers* (1991) (Fondation de France and ICOM/Routledge), and Eilean Hooper-Greenhill (1991) introduces some of the issues in *Museum and gallery education* (Leicester University Press).

Equal access for all is about intellectual access to collections as well as physical and sensory access to museum displays. Whilst this section focuses mainly on physical access the volume touches on other types of access through its emphasis on the analysis of audience needs. In Section Eight, 'Evaluation', there is an extract from an article by George Hein ('Assessing the hands-on learning process') about a research project which confirmed what many campaigners had been suggesting for a long time: that in adapting displays to serve the needs of people with learning difficulties museums can improve the gallery experience for the whole spectrum of their visitors.

16 Disability Culture

Simon Brisenden
This article appeared in *Adults Learning* 2(1), 1990, pp. 13–14.

What is Disability Culture?

This is a concept which has been made possible by the disability movement. It consists of two things – firstly, the skills which we have developed in order to live well with our particular conditions, and to communicate with fellow humans. Wheelchair skills, sign language, longcane skills, our humour, our 'secret' knowledge that we share only with each other, all this is part of our culture. Secondly, it is the development of our artists, poets, dancers, actors, singers, comedians, writers, filmmakers, photographers and musicians who are using our talents to express the experience of disability from our own perspective.

> Ultimately disability culture should be recognised as one of the many strands running through contemporary multi-cultural society. A lot of disabled people believe there is great value in making links between ourselves and other oppressed groups and artistic expression should facilitate this in all sorts of ways. In time we will have our own body of artistic work about, or informed by, the experience of being disabled in the same way as there is already much work created from the point of view of women, people from ethnic cultures, and from lesbians and gay men. (Sean Vasey)

Some disabled people avoid the issue of disability culture simply because it touches areas of their lives that they would rather not think about. If you have carved out a life against all the odds as an alien in a non-disabled world, you do not want to think too hard about the price you have had to pay.

You may not want to think, for instance, about the world of disabled people, for you now belong to a different world. The idea of a culture of people with disabilities, a set of common experiences and aspirations belonging to us all, seems to undermine everything you have achieved. It seems to threaten the basis upon which you live. If you have struggled and fought to become assimilated, to merge with the majority, you do not want this achievement to be knocked, you do not want to be reminded of what you have left behind.

The overwhelming urge to become part of 'normality' leads one to devalue the world of disabled people and to avoid contact with that world. It leads one to avoid like the plague any association with other people with disabilities and their organisations.

The concept of disability culture is deeply threatening to this point of view because it values the lives and experiences of disabled people as important in themselves. More than this, it says that the world of disabled people should be valued on a par with the world of 'disability'.

The idea of disability culture begins with the recognition that we are valuable people in ourselves, and that we need not avoid each other or hide behind a cloak of false integration. We no longer need to build our lives on a denial and devaluing of our background and the experiences of pain and triumph, sadness and joy, which form the reality of our upbringing. Disability culture is being built upon a ruthless honesty about the people we are and the role we play in society.

Out of the recognition of our value comes the ability to organise ourselves, to put on events, to mobilise our forces, to produce works of art, to run workshops and newsletters and generally to get together and share the common language of our experiences. Only people who value themselves and listen carefully to their own voices have a culture of their own rather than a secondhand culture gifted to them as the price of a silent acquiescence to unthinking 'normality'.

So what is disability culture? It is, in general terms, that which is common to our lives and which informs our thoughts and activities. It is our aspirations and our dreams as well as our struggles and our nightmares. It is the things we cannot forget as well as the things we want to remember. It is the schools we went to, the day centres we inhabit, but it is also the art we produce and the organisation we have built. It is so many things but it is no one particular thing.

Many of us have found the idea of disability culture extremely valuable because it has given us the opportunity to share experiences, to come out of the shell of private confusion and into the public world of politics and performance art. Speaking as a poet it has given me the one thing I wanted above all else – an audience I could identify with. This is true for other artists too, who have been given strength and encouragement by the realisation that the subjects they struggle with are not isolated incidents but have a deeper cultural significance.

Culture and Empowerment

We now live in a multicultural society and we must proudly take our place alongside the other cultures and lifestyles that are demanding a space to communicate and be themselves. We must learn to relish our differences and not disguise them. We must take control of our lives and our organisations so that we can create a form of politics that is born out of our uniqueness, and which is not led by professionals or other non-disabled people.

The culture of disability comes out of our ghettos as a form of defiance just as it comes out of the ghettos of women, black people and ethnic minority people, gay men and lesbians. A ghetto is not only a place of physical degradation, a slum, but can also be a spiritual dungeon, a psychological prison in which the mind is chained and tortured. So it is not just a question of closing down the special schools and the day centres but of opening up our minds to the value of our existence. We can only work against these mental ghettos by getting together and sharing the common themes of our lives. It can be a thrilling and liberating experience.

The culture of disability is the web that binds us together on the basis of what is common but leaves us room to move and grow. It is built upon appreciating and valuing many things, including things that may have been patronised or ignored in the past. For instance, an important element of our culture is our history. We should not wait for the academics to decide this is important, but we must begin charting it ourselves by listening to and recording the reminiscences of older people with disabilities. Their stories are our lost history, a central element of the culture we belong to.

But a disability culture is not only rooted in the proper appreciation of the past, it must also celebrate the present and the future. This sense of celebration and freedom has been strongly in evidence at some of the artistic events that have taken place up and down the country, where audiences and artists have merged together and participated in a collective event arising out of the desire to express themselves. Disability culture is about expressing ourselves in whatever way comes naturally, and about realising that these expressions are valuable.

It is not a question of shutting ourselves off from society, as some people seem to think. On the contrary, we must take our place in society fortified and empowered by the knowledge that we do not need to discard our cultural identity as the price of integration.

17 The Disabling Society

Rebecca McGinnis

This article appeared in *Museums Journal* 94(6), 1994, pp. 27–29, 33.

We are all aware of the need for improved access to museums for people with disabilities, but most of us regard it as a vague and abstract issue which barely affects our work. When access is addressed, it is often in the limited terms of a ramp, a toilet for wheelchair-users or perhaps a touch-tour for visually-impaired people. So how well do we actually understand the issue of access for people with disabilities and its relevance to all areas of museum work?

In recent years, disability has come to be understood as a condition imposed by an able-bodied society rather than the inevitable consequence of impairment. Barriers of attitude can be as impassable as physical and sensory barriers and there is no single disabled audience. There are blind and partially-sighted people, deaf and hearing-impaired people, people with mobility difficulties, people with learning difficulties and people with hidden disabilities such as back pain and epilepsy. Together, people with disabilities make up a larger audience than is generally recognised. There are about 6 million people in the UK with a disability; that is, one in ten. In fact, 6 million is a conservative estimate based on a narrow medical definition. One in four may be a more realistic figure.

Very often we find misconceptions about the relative size of groups of people with particular disabilities. Only about 2 per cent of these 6 million people use wheelchairs. Therefore 98 per cent are ignored when disability is equated to the use of a wheelchair. Although there are one million who could be registered blind and partially-sighted people in the UK, and an additional 750,000 people with severe visual impairments, only about 1 per cent of museums offer information in braille and only about 2 per cent provide information in large print.

Numbers of People with Disabilities

- 6 million in the UK have a disability, or one in ten people, according to the narrow medical definition.

- Some organisations estimate numbers as high as 15 million, or one in four people.

- 2.4 million people with disabilities are of working age.

- Only 31 per cent of these are in work.

- About 2 per cent of people with disabilities use wheelchairs.

- One million people could be registered blind or partially sighted.

- Another 750,000 people have severe visual impairment.

- Less than 3 per cent (about 20,000 people) of registerably blind and partially-sighted people can read braille.

• About 65 per cent of registerably visually-impaired people can read large print.

Consulting Disabled Audiences

Each group of disabled people must be located and targeted carefully. And this should be done by museums before they develop their programmes and facilities. Groups of disabled people should be consulted from the planning stage right through to the evaluation of the finished product. A good example of the importance of consultation concerns a large museum in the USA which planned a series of sign language-interpreted events on Friday evenings. No one turned up for these evenings. When evaluating what went wrong, the organiser found that Friday was the one evening each week when several television programmes were sign language-interpreted. One brief chat with a well-informed member of the deaf community would have prevented this disaster.

Many museums in the UK are now forging links with local societies of and for disabled people. However, this is still done haphazardly, usually on a one-off basis and relying on the initiative of one person rather than any museum policy. The Museums and Galleries Commission (MGC) Guidelines on Disability clearly state that 'regular consultation with disabled people and disability organisations [should be undertaken] in order to assist in designing, improving and developing the provision of services and the recruitment and employment of disabled people'. The guidelines also say that such consultation should be an integral part of a museum's disability policy.

Consultation develops in different ways according to the culture of an institution. Local authority museums may find it more natural to draw on links with local agencies and societies, whereas national museums, which cannot rely on a pre-existing network, may have to work harder to find sources of potential user groups. In the US, the consultative process has become an official procedure and is virtually standard practice. Committees called advisory boards, consisting of members of the target audience, are established and maintained.

Once programmes and provisions have been put into place, the audience must be informed about what the museum has to offer them. Museums do not have a good reputation for their accessibility, or for programmes for disabled people, so getting a positive message across can be a daunting task. People's mobility difficulties or their need for information in alternative formats may, in turn, slow the dissemination of information. For example, people with mobility difficulties may not get out as much as others and may therefore miss much of a museum's advertising. Blind and partially-sighted people may not have access to information about a museum unless it is available in large print, braille, or on tape or computer disk.

Museums must make it clear what they have to offer and what assistance can be given. Some of the most valuable contacts for marketing facilities and services are the press officers of organisations representing disabled people – they can advise on appropriate specialist disability publications that reach other organisations and societies, and on other methods of communication with the target group. The talking newspaper network, for instance, is an invaluable method of spreading information to visually-impaired people.

Many of the suggestions listed below would benefit all visitors, not just people with disabilities. Everyone appreciates clear print on labels, good lighting and good signs for directions. And certain facilities will also help children, people for whom English is not a first language, those with children in pushchairs, older people and those with minor or temporary disabilities, such as cataracts or broken legs.

What Can Museums Offer People with Disabilities?

General Services for Disabled

- access brochure
- advertising
- staff trained in disability awareness
- staff assistance

Services for Visually-Impaired People

- taped guides
- pre-visit information
- touch-tours
- handling gloves (only if absolutely necessary)
- handling sessions
- tactile plans
- tactile drawings of objects
- workshops
- braille information
- large print information
- objects for touch by all
- legible labels
- braille labels
- large print handouts of labels/text panels
- shop items
- tactile postcards
- good lighting
- clear signs
- guide dog access into the museum
- water for guide dogs

Services for Deaf and Hearing-Impaired People

- sign language-interpreted tours
- print transcript of taped tours and information
- staff trained in British Sign Language and deaf/blind alphabet

- fire alarms with flashing lights
- sympathetic hearing scheme
- hearing dog access into museums
- water for hearing dogs

Services for People with Mobility Difficulties

- ramps of a regulation slope near all steps
- public lifts (not goods lifts)
- accessible lavatories
- signs, labels and displays, as well as doorhandles, information counters and public telephones, at an appropriate height for people using wheelchairs (these facilities will also benefit children)
- doorways wide enough for wheelchairs
- wheelchairs for use in the museum
- stools for use on guided tours
- adequate seating in all galleries and public areas offering back-rests and different heights and degrees of hardness
- set-down point at the entrance to the museum
- maps showing seating
- ramped routes marked clearly on a map
- numbers of steps indicated in the brochure
- sessions where objects (possibly from handling collections) are brought to one place

Services for People with Learning Difficulties

- clear labels and signs
- large print
- specially tailored taped tours

Getting on Good Terms

Appropriate language is vital when talking with, or about, people with disabilities. Terminology surrounding disability has become increasingly problematic and politically charged in recent years. Knowing which of the many descriptions for various types of disability to use without giving offence can confound the best-informed person. Phrases can be cumbersome and awkward. Words move in and out of favour quickly and there is also a wide diversity of personal preferences but you can avoid resorting to stereotypes. Usually there is a comfortable middle ground. Indeed, understanding how to communicate, how to behave and how to assist disabled visitors are the first hurdles museums must face.

A vital first step is to address the person – the individual and not the disability. Avoid saying things like 'there are two wheelchairs on the first floor'.

To say 'there are two people using wheelchairs on the first floor' conveys a more positive message. Disability awareness training or disability equality training for all members of staff, particularly those who provide a first point of contact with the museum, is an essential first step towards accessibility.

The term 'access' itself should be clarified. Access means not only physical access, but conceptual, intellectual and multisensory access as well. A lift will not help a person with a learning difficulty or a partially sighted person to understand a museum's collection; but clearer layout and larger print on labels and signs will. Another important aspect of access is the employment of people with disabilities in museums. This side of the equation is almost always forgotten. In all, consultation between museum departments on issues relating to access must be developed and maintained. A committee consisting of curators, conservators, designers, educationalists, exhibition organisers, fundraisers, health and safety officers, personnel officers, press and public relations officers, printers and warders, would be an invaluable forum for these issues. Such a committee should draw on the expertise of disabled people, perhaps inviting representatives of different groups to the meetings.

Legislation and Equal Opportunities

There is no anti-discrimination legislation for people with disabilities in the UK. Until this changes, enforcing access and preventing active and passive discrimination in employment and visitor services will be impossible. Many museums have equal opportunities policies, but these usually vague policies tend to rely on the goodwill of personnel departments. These policies are rarely tested, since few people with disabilities are employed by museums. They are not enforceable by law and there are no clear mechanisms of recourse for dissatisfied employees.

Anti-discrimination legislation does exist in the USA. There the Americans with Disabilities Act of 1990 (ADA) has been a tremendous catalyst to the development of physical and psychological access to museums in the USA. In addition to anti-discrimination legislation, the ADA requires that public, commercial and government premises and services be made 'readily accessible'. This means that, for instance, access through the kitchen is unacceptable. Measures include everything from major structural alterations, such as widening doorways, to minor additions such as legible signs, good lighting and braille labels on lift controls. Of course, these regulations are relatively easy to follow in the USA, where most buildings are often quite new and there is lots of space. But historic houses enjoy no exceptions – they have to provide for people with sensory impairments and many have come to realise that loop systems, legible signs, information in large print, braille and on tape, good lighting and the like need not be defacing or expensive to implement. Though there are alternative minimum requirements for historic structures, one accessible route through the publicly used sections of the premises is still required.

In the light of this legislation, museums have had to address access and equal opportunities seriously and coherently. Many museums have access advisers and ADA committees designed to exchange ideas and air problems in every aspect of the museum's activities. In New York City, seven large museums have recently formed the Museums Access Consortium. It is hoped that this sort of structured communication between museums will spread to other cities and regions throughout the country.

Although the UK has no such formal links between museums where access is concerned, area museums services could and sometimes do perform similar functions. The Museums and Galleries Disability Association is another channel for exchanges of information and discussion.

The MGC *Guidelines on disability* give excellent recommendations for developing access and equal opportunities within museums, but the guidelines are problematic. As they are not requirements, they are often seen as extras rather than as an integral part of museum activities. They do not give any ideas about incorporating the recommendations into pre-existing structures and regulations. For example, equal access will contravene the fire regulations which recommend that only a limited number of wheelchair-users may be above ground-floor level in a building that does not have adequate lift access or a fire-safe lift. No solutions to such problems have been found.

The guidelines provide no practical help with creating a disability policy and action plan, nor with setting mechanisms for consultation with groups of disabled people, developing evaluation procedures, or implementing equal opportunities policies and positive action on employment of disabled people. All of these, none the less, are recommended in the guidelines. The MGC has recently published its *Disability resource directory for museums* 1994, which, for the first time, provides a thorough central point of reference to information pertaining directly to museums and disability. This document is a valuable tool for creating an accessible experience for all museum visitors. It is also a vital step in the process of informing everyone in museums of the needs and rights of disabled people.

As the Universal Declaration of Human Rights (article 27) states: 'Everyone has the right freely to participate in the cultural life of the community, to enjoy the arts and to share in scientific advancement and its benefits.' Only when these rights are recognised, understood and reinforced by legislation, can people with disabilities be empowered to take full advantage of all that museums can offer.

18 Physical Access

Anne Pearson

Extracted from *Arts for everyone: guidance on provision for disabled people*, Carnegie UK Trust & CEH, 1985, pp. 29–30.

Seating

More fixed seating in galleries is necessary, loose chairs being a security risk. Resting rails are also helpful.

> A feature conspicuously absent in many galleries is comfortable seating. Here a wheelchair bound visitor can be at an advantage. Sheer physical exhaustion is commonplace with the fittest and most devoted gallery goer. No wonder the average time spent looking at each painting is estimated in seconds rather than minutes in gallery surveys on the subject. Perhaps Matisse's dictum that a painting should be like 'a comfortable chair' should be taken more literally in art galleries themselves to encourage people to enjoy their treasures. (Keen et al., 1984)

If possible there should be some seating in the open air, perhaps in a garden or courtyard, where visitors can sit in the sun for occasional relief from the sometimes monotonous levels of temperature and lighting control required for protection of the exhibits in gallery areas. Robust sculpture suitable for touching could be sited here.

Levels and Obstacles

Changes in level are usually the greatest single danger to visually-impaired visitors as well as to elderly people and those who wear bifocal spectacles. Visitor gallery routes should be 'smoothed out' as far as possible by gallery designers. Varying floor levels in galleries, though interesting to look at, do deter many people, not only visually-impaired people. The beginning and end of a change in floor level should be marked with strips of contrasting tape.

Overhanging barriers on showcases are easy to walk into and designers should be aware that low rails, bars, jutting plinths, spreading rubber plants and contrasting light levels can be dangerous for those with impaired vision.

Floor Textures

Floor texture can add to the total experience of a museum visit for everyone, and if considered carefully can provide information for visually-impaired people by indicating the route to follow, or the location of a particular exhibit. For example, at the Museum of London floor surfaces are appropriate to the period of the display. There are squeaking floorboards in the Poyle Park Room and brick floors in the Tudor Gallery.

Lighting

Dramatic changes of light should be avoided in galleries because it can be disturbing for visually-impaired people to enter without warning into a dark space. It is not obligatory to have strong lighting everywhere, but steps and corners should be spotlit for safety, and wall panels, photographs and labels should also be well lit. Soft lighting may be required for protection of objects such as textiles and also to create mood. However, careful, soft lighting need not be incompatible with good vision. A greater emphasis on visual contrast in the display of objects in glass cases would help visually-impaired people.

Labelling

. . . Wall-mounted labels should have a matt surface. Avoid lighting a case from outside – the visitor will be trying to look at the object in his or her own shadow. If the lighting in the cases cannot be heightened, place the text outside the case and light the labels.

When labels may be difficult to read, a helpful solution is to have a number of chained magnifying glasses available for visually-impaired visitors.

Braille and Large Print Labels

In new galleries braille and large print labels should be considered. They should be simple, with a title and a brief description, and should be positioned outside the case so that they can be easily touched. They should also be placed in a similar position relative to each case or exhibit and should be fixed horizontally for ease of reading.

The Tactile Sense

The sense of touch is an important element which is neglected in the design of many museum displays. Most galleries could be enhanced by the addition of some tactile features. Developing this, however, requires careful thought and experimentation. Security and conservation factors have to be taken into consideration, and the provision of touch facilities will always require special controlled conditions. Tactile services in museums should nevertheless develop because touch is much appreciated by sighted visitors and is the only way some blind people can experience museum objects.

It should not be assumed that all blind people are touch-orientated. Those who are blind from birth will have learnt to use touch as an alternative to visual perception; those blind through illness or accident tend to rely more on memory. One cannot rely on blind or partially-sighted people being any more gentle with the objects they touch than are any other visitors.

There are various ways of presenting objects for touching; each museum must choose the way most suited to the nature of its collections, the number of its staff and the volume of visitors.

If at all possible, touch exhibitions, both permanent and temporary, should not be confined to visually-impaired visitors. When a touch exhibition is opened in a public gallery it always excites the interest of sighted visitors who may then resent being excluded. Most visually-impaired people much prefer to visit an exhibition with sighted friends and relatives and without having to make special arrangements beforehand. At recent touch exhibitions (Coles, 1984) many blind visitors have stressed that much of the pleasure of the visit derived from hearing the comments of sighted people around them about the objects on display. These provide an illuminating addition to the information being received through the fingertips. Furthermore, given the remarkably small number of visually-impaired people able or inclined to visit touch exhibitions, the gallery is likely to be empty for most of the opening hours if it is confined to the visually-impaired public. Given the labour intensiveness of preparing touch exhibitions, this is wasteful of time and resources. Conservation considerations are usually the main reason why touch exhibitions are confined to visually-impaired people, but as preservation techniques improve it may be possible to expose more categories of museum objects for tactile exploration. The future of touch exhibitions lies mainly in the hands of conservators and curators.

Relief Maps of Galleries

These can be very helpful for visually-impaired visitors especially those who are unaccompanied . . .

Textured Paths

When a gallery has a few exhibits with audio or tactile elements, thought should be given to connecting them with textured paths, floor ridges or handrails. All these methods present problems and more work needs to be done on perfecting such linking pathways in galleries . . .

References

Coles P (1984). *Please touch report: an evaluation of the British Museum's exhibition of animal sculpture*, Committee of Inquiry into the Arts and Disabled People.

Keen, C et al. (1984). 'Visitors' services and people with disability', *Museums Journal* 84(1), pp. 33–38.

Section Five   Exhibition Planning

Introduction

We still have a long way to go in developing planning models for exhibitions that recognise the importance of identifying and addressing the learning needs of visitors. Current research into the learning processes suggests that people learn in a variety of ways, and that recognition of these differences through the design of exhibitions enables more people to feel more comfortable. In the past, learning theories were often regarded as being of relevance only to education services. Today, as museums and galleries search for ways to deepen the experiences of current visitors and to develop new audiences, the insights that learning theories offer are beginning to be fruitfully deployed in exhibition planning.

Most discussions of exhibition planning and development concentrate on the process as a whole, with particular emphasis on project management and the management of objects. Two useful introductions to this are Belcher (1991) *Exhibitions in museums* (Leicester University Press), and Dean (1994) *Museum exhibition: theory and practice* (Routledge).

However, to develop exhibition planning models that respond to the learning needs of visitors, we need to adopt planning strategies that are informed by the learning theories presented in the second section of this book. We also need to take account of the experience of institutions where the displays have been developed in response to visitor learning needs.

We should acknowledge the important work which was carried out at the Natural History Museum during the 1970s and 1980s which is introduced by Roger Miles and his colleagues (1988) in *The design of educational exhibits* (Unwin Hyman). The papers in this seminal book address learning in exhibitions, and introduce detailed exhibition production procedures that pay attention to visitor needs. However, learning in the book is understood in a rather didactic way as the transfer of facts, and is limited to issues concerned with cognition.

Contemporary learning theories (see especially the extracts in this book by Hein, Gardner and Cassels) suggest that learning is a much broader process than the mere acquisition of facts, that it is dependent on the skills and knowledge that learners bring with them into the learning situation, and that learning takes place in social and cultural settings. We need therefore, more sensitive, flexible and complex exhibition planning models that require adaptability, humility, openness and responsiveness on the part of the exhibition team.

Policies need to go much further than merely listing which exhibition happens when. What are the philosophies within which choices are made? How do they relate to the museum's intentions as a whole? What are the basic 'givens' that all exhibitions should include? Policies, Hooper-Greenhill suggests, need to go beyond resource allocation to show how exhibitions are planned in relation to the museum's overall philosophies and objectives.

People from a range of disciplines, with different skills and expertise, including representatives of the intended audience for the exhibition, can contribute useful perspectives to a holistic planning process. Grasso and Morrison show how a varied team can work together in a non-hierarchical way, and Worts demonstrates how the specialist knowledge of the psychologist contributed to innovative approaches to visitor interaction at the Art Gallery of Ontario, Canada.

Worts shows how the meanings that visitors read from, or impose on, paintings are unique to their life experiences and personal psychological needs. When this happens, then a museum or gallery visit can become a very powerful personalised experience. It is neither appropriate nor possible for curators to control the meanings that people construe from their experiences. It is sensible, therefore, to design exhibitions that enable people to choose their own physical and conceptual pathways. Falk suggests that unstructured exhibition environments enable visitors to satisfy their own agendas more quickly and effectively than structured environments that require people to process the exhibition experience as dictated by the curator or designer. Having achieved their own objectives, some people are then willing to spend time on the museum's agenda.

Increasingly, exhibition producers and designers are developing interpretation strategies that encourage active participation. There is a danger that the focus on activity for its own sake takes precedence over genuine exploratory learning. Phillips introduces gallery-based ways of experiencing processes to do with picture-making and pattern-making. Serrell and Raphling describe some golden rules for producing computer-interactives that will be both used and enjoyed.

How do exhibition planners and designers think about the ways exhibitions might be used? Probably not very well. Bicknell and Mann provide the beginnings of an outline of how visitors respond to and use exhibitions at the Science Museum in London. Although there is a great deal more work to be done in this area, the findings so far have general application. An anonymous extract discusses ways in which people as physical bodies use spaces, which is important in thinking about the size and feel of exhibition spaces and display furniture. Bitgood's work on orientation and circulation within exhibitions offers general principles on the cues and information people need to find their way around an unfamiliar area.

19 The Exhibition Policy

Eilean Hooper-Greenhill
Extracted from 'Managing museums for visitors', in *Museums and their visitors*, Routledge, 1994, pp. 176–179.

The exhibition policy describes the underlying principles on which exhibitions will be based, and also sets out the intentions of a rolling exhibitions programme . . . It informs the exhibition action plan, which describes the actual exhibitions that are planned over a certain period . . . and may cover permanent and temporary exhibitions, and where relevant, travelling exhibitions and mobile museums.

The exhibition policy needs to address the following areas: target audience, resources, types of provision, roles and functions of temporary exhibitions and permanent displays within the museum, and in the community, research and evaluation. At one level these are practical questions, but at another they are deeply philosophical and relate to the very core of the identity of the museum.

In many museums, exhibitions occur for a variety of pragmatic reasons, rather than for a planned and carefully thought out purpose. Some museums do little except buy in temporary exhibitions from elsewhere. In some museums, the relationship between temporary exhibitions and permanent displays is tenuous, to say the least. The relationship between the two, the objectives of the one and the other and the resources allocated to each, should be part of the programmed and managed development of the museum.

The exhibition policy from the Museum of Contemporary Art, Sydney, Australia, provides an interesting example. The policy is prefaced by the following philosophical statement:

> The MCA exhibition programme constitutes its most immediate, varied and energetic interface with the community. All other MCA activities will be drawn together and pivot around the function of exhibiting works of art for direct engagement with a public audience.
>
> It is through the exhibition programme that both 'the latest ideas and theories' and 'the most recent contemporary art of the world' (as conceptualised by the founding benefactor, J W Power) will be brought into prominent focus within the life of the MCA. It is through the exhibition programme that works of art will be experienced not only as discrete objects, but also as vehicles of more comprehensive and complex meanings, within the wider context of the production, interpretation and experience of culture within the community. (Museum of Contemporary Art, 1992, p. 11.)

This statement provides a challenging context for the mounting of exhibitions. It goes beyond the functional organisation of objects in spaces, and acknowledges the social and cultural issues that arise when objects are placed within museums or galleries.

The policy goes on to discuss the scope and balance of temporary exhibitions (the responsibilities for the permanent collections are fully acknowledged in the General Policy), ethics, related events and support activities, audiences, sponsorship and funding and implementation of the policy.

Exhibition policies in Britain must acknowledge the guidelines on customer care (1993), disability (1992) and the use of non-sexist language produced by the Museums and Galleries Commission and the Museums Association. Approaches to display bearing in mind the needs of audiences should be considered. Phased renewal of permanent displays should be set out, with costings and target dates. Potential themes for displays and exhibitions, issues in relation to local circumstances, current gaps and omissions should be identified.

The exhibition action plan specifies what developments are taking place within which time-frame and at what cost. This is generally planned over a three- or five-year period, with staff time, resources, use of space, employment of outside contractors or designers and educational use carefully considered.

In Britain, at the present time, exhibition *plans* are frequently to be found within forward plans, where actions to be taken are described. It is much rarer to find an exhibition *policy* that takes a philosophical stance in relation to the functions of exhibitions, and makes statements about the issues that should underpin any exhibition, such as a commitment to disabled access, avoidance of sexist, racist or other bias, approaches to the writing of accessible text. It might seem that these can be taken as given, but where things are taken for granted this often means they have not been fully considered and therefore they will not be fully implemented.

In considering the role of the audience advocate, the staff member responsible for promoting the needs of visitors, in developing, reviewing and revising exhibitions, D D Hilke proposes that all exhibitions should be:

- accessible to the widest possible audience (including those with visual, physical, auditory, and learning disabilities);

- informative and relevant to the widest possible audience (e.g. beginners and scholars; browsers and studiers; first-time visitors and returning visitors; foreigners, non-native speakers and native speakers; visitors from diverse ethnic and other social backgrounds; children, teenagers and adults, etc.);

- effective in communicating their messages;

- structured to complement the natural learning strategies that visitors use;

- supportive of a variety of learning styles;

- supportive of the visitors' agendas as well as the museum's agendas;

- supportive of individual and group experiences;

- empowering, stimulating and fun;

- comfortable, uncrowded, and not overly structured or sequential. (Hilke, n.d.)

These are excellent guidelines, and museums and galleries should be working towards ensuring that all exhibitions and displays conform to them. To achieve these objectives it is necessary first to have general information about, for example, the nature of the museum's audience, the needs of people with a range of impairments, and an understanding of the range of learning strategies and intelligences people bring with them to any exhibition; second to have information on specific matters relating to each exhibition, such as attitudes and possible misconceptions in relation to particular topics, likely reactions to specific exhibition vehicles and particular factors that will influence the use of the exhibition by any particular audience segment.

An exhibition policy should be written to include these audience-related matters, rather than simply as a matter of resource allocation.

References

Hilke, D D (n.d.). What is an audience advocate? (unpublished).

Museum and Galleries Commission (1992). *Guidelines on disability for museums and galleries in the United Kingdom*, London, Museums and Galleries Commission.

Museum and Galleries Commission (1993). *Quality of service in museums and galleries: customer care in museums – guidelines on implementation*, London, Museum and Galleries Commission.

Museum of Contemporary Art (1992). *Collection/Exhibition/Education Policy*, Sydney, Museum of Contemporary Art Ltd.

20 An Exhibition Team at Work

Hank Grasso and Howard Morrison

This article 'Collaboration: toward a more holistic design process' appeared in *History News* 47(3), 1992, pp. 12–15.

Visitors to *American Encounters*, a Columbian Quincentenary exhibition [which opened] June 24, 1992, at the Smithsonian Institution's National Museum of American History, [saw] some of the ways American Indians and Hispanics have interacted with each other and with Anglo-Americans in New Mexico for nearly 500 years. Visitors to the exhibition . . . also [saw] the result of a unique, collaborative exhibit development and design process.

Nearly three years ago, the museum assembled a team of four curators, a scriptwriter, an education specialist, a designer, a New Mexico-based researcher, and a project manager; one of the curators served as project director. Such teams usually function as autonomous collectives in which individuals responsible for a particular domain meet merely to co-ordinate the execution of their separate tasks; but the *American Encounters* team functioned as a collaborative body.

Collaboration does not preclude individual responsibility and accountability; team members were assigned specific duties and areas of concern. But, at each crucial decision-making point, they *shared* roles and responsibilities. Everyone participated in the decision-making that determined the content and design of each part of the exhibition. Collaboration is more difficult when some team members are contractors rather than staff employees; contracts link payments to specific tasks and must be written to accommodate some blurring of the lines of responsibility.

Many exhibits might benefit from this kind of holistic approach. When the entire team participates in all aspects of the development and design process, individual differences in perspective and interpretation as well as in personality and agenda become assets rather than liabilities. There are fewer surprises, fewer last-minute (and therefore costly) demands for changes by competing interests. There are also more opportunities for sharing potential solutions with colleagues outside the team, test audiences, and a wide variety of consultants – in this case, tribal and community representatives, artisans, photographers, collectors, and scholars.

The challenge, as anyone who has ever tried to do anything by committee knows, was to establish a collaborative rhythm within a group of diverse individuals. What follows are brief descriptions of the series of group problem-solving exercises that allowed the *American Encounters* team to arrive at collaboration in the development and design of the exhibit.

Exercise 1: Identifying Interpretive Goals

What is the most important message the exhibit should convey to the audience? What is the essential aspect of that message that the audience must understand for the exhibit to have meaning? The first step in answering these fundamental questions was to allow each member of the team to express what he or she believed to be the purpose of the exhibit. The free exchange of ideas was crucial; for there to be collaboration, everyone on the team must have a say, must have a stake in the exhibit.

The *American Encounters* team retreated to West Virginia for three days of brainstorming with a professional meeting facilitator. The result was not consensus but a collection of wide-ranging, commonly acknowledged interpretive goals; to show cultural continuity, cultural change, cultural diversity, and cultural unity.

These and other goal statements provided the basis for in-depth audience studies using visitor surveys and interviews as well as focus groups. In addition, a broad-brush statement of purpose was presented in an illustrated brochure produced on a colour photocopier. The brochure was distributed to community and scholarly consultants as well as to potential financial backers.

Exercise 2: Orientating Concepts and Experiences

What core ideas should the exhibit present? What kinds of visitor experiences should it provide? Even though members of the *American Encounters* team had differing ideas on the exhibit's abstract goals, they were able to work collaboratively when answering these and other concrete questions.

For this exercise, everyone on the team literally had to put their suggestions on the table by means of a paper swatch floor plan. Each specific content idea or exhibit experience was written on a small, medium, or large square of paper and taped to a single oversized sheet of paper. Suggestions were assembled in relation to each other. Some needed to come before others; some after. Some were transitional; others were unrelated.

This exercise produced a seemingly helter-skelter wish list, but, in the process, core ideas and experiences began to emerge.

Exercise 3: Examining Possible Sequences of Visitor Experiences

By translating the swatches of paper into large and small circles, it was possible to lay out the interrelationships of concepts and experiences in a bubble diagram. The result was a schematic representation of the sequence and relative importance of ideas and experiences.

Exercise 4: Developing a Preliminary Floor Plan

Spaces in the exhibit were allocated by superimposing the bubble diagram on a plan that showed the size and configuration of the actual space available. How must the space be entered? How may it be exited? How many different ways can visitors move through the space? Team members, with pencils in hand, joined in marking up floor plans to develop various possible layouts for the preliminary floor plan.

The transfer of elements from bubble diagram to floor plan provided a reality check on the sequence and scale of proposed concepts and experiences. Ideas that were vastly too large for the space available were dropped or shifted to video or other media that can compress many images into a compact experience. Ideas over which the group disagreed often found a place in the exhibit simply by configuring a wall in a certain way or by changing the amount of space allotted to a certain element. Persistent disagreements were dealt with outside the group forum. A mediator shuttled between differing parties carrying proposals back and forth to work out agreements.

This exercise was the most difficult one in the series because the team had to define real visitor experience in terms of actual sections of the exhibition.

Exercise 5: Choosing Objects and Images

What objects and images are available to tell the stories identified on the preliminary floor plan? The team began to assemble snapshots of objects and graphics (paintings, illustrations, and archival photographs) in a series of plastic sleeves housed according to exhibit section in loose-leaf binders. Objects and images were shuffled, added, deleted, or returned to various exhibit sections with ease. In this way, team members defined sets of two- and three- dimensional items for each section of the exhibit. These interpretive sets in turn helped the team refine specific stories that would be told in each part of the exhibit. For example, pottery suggested itself as a metaphor for continuity and change among Pueblo Indians; weaving did the same for Hispanics.

Exercise 6: Visualising Exhibit Content

How will the objects, images, and stories selected for the exhibit actually work when they are brought together? The next step in the development and design process was to render the exhibit in a series of storyboards. Colour copies of graphic images and of photographs or drawings of objects were mounted to section-specific illustration boards along with a brief statement of teaching goals.

These storyboards provided an affordable way for team members to visualise the exhibit. The boards helped them to fine tune preliminary organisational decisions. Storyboards also provided colleagues, museum management, outside consultants, and ordinary visitors an opportunity to respond to plans for the exhibit. The boards produced for *American Encounters* were used for presentations and meetings. They were then installed in the museum's exhibit preview area where visitors were invited to write their comments on forms provided. A more formal audience survey was not conducted but would have been useful.

Exercise 7: Visualising the Exhibit Space

The next step was to build a three-dimensional foam core model of the exhibit. The model enabled team members to see in scale how spaces and elements within the exhibit related to each other when viewed during a walk-through. The model was a working tool not a presentation piece. Foam core walls went up and came down, exhibit cases were moved, and vantage points were shifted. To reinforce large interpretive messages, spatial patterns within the exhibit were derived from cultural forms: the Pueblo Indian section of the floor plan is circular, suggesting the cyclic patterns common in their culture, while the Hispanic community section is rectangular, like a village plaza.

After repeated trials and discussions, the model became the basis for detailed construction drawings. These drawings, which were prepared in consultation with an architect, included exhibit-specific information on wall placement and case openings as well as public space-specific information on acoustic attenuation and electrical, lighting, audio-visual, heating, ventilation and air-conditioning systems, and emergency systems.

Exercise 8: Selecting Forms, Colours and Textures

Team members re-grouped to decide on specific personalities for each section of the exhibit, using the model to test various solutions. They looked to objects in each section that suggested certain patterns and hues. They drew upon cultural or environmental elements related to exhibit content that could be abstracted in forms and textures. The team also decided to incorporate actual contextual elements from each community in New Mexico (being careful to avoid those elements that were clichéd or stereotypical): adobe and carved wooden architectural components, stone label substrate, coyote fencing, and signs.

Material palettes with samples of fabrics, paints, floor and wall coverings, and label substrate were developed for each section of the exhibit. Only materials that met durability requirements for public spaces, fire codes, and conservation mandates were considered.

Exercise 9: Developing a Graphic Image Vocabulary

The goal was to devise a palette of type styles and symbol sets that could be employed to convey ideas. Because the abstract qualities of typefaces and symbols are hard to articulate, the designer prepared several sample solutions for the group to consider. He selected a wide range of typefaces; he created symbol sets using various combinations of elements derived from cultural icons to identify things such as exhibit sections and labelling hierarchy.

The group discussed these and chose those that seemed better or more appropriate. The group selected a single typeface for the entire exhibit but used distinctive symbol sets for each section. For example, the section of the exhibit that looks at twentieth-century tourism in New Mexico uses a chili pepper symbol and graphic organisational bars that fuse dollar signs with patterns derived from weaving. A graphic designer could be engaged to assist with this exercise.

Exercise 10: Establishing Human Factor or Ergonomic Parameters

A full-scale mock-up of a typical exhibit component made using foam core, colour photocopies of objects and photographs, and photocopies of sample labels and graphics was used to address various design solutions as well as federally mandated accessibility requirements. The team experimented with the arrangement of objects and the size and placement of labels. They tested vertical heights, viewing distances, and angles of reading surfaces – exercises typical of industrial ways to code maps, time lines, and other information-dense graphics.

Once the team settled on a range of standards, the mock-up was moved to a public area. A visitor study was conducted using a mock-up of entrance panels and two exhibit cases, one from the Pueblo Indian section and one from the Hispanic section. Visitor observations and interviews conducted by an audience research firm suggested changes that were incorporated into the design control drawings.

Exercise 11: Finding an Exhibit Voice

The preparation of the label script for *American Encounters* began with three curators writing labels for specific content areas (the group as a whole had already established a four-level labelling hierarchy: main labels were written first, then section, group, and object labels). To make three different voices one, the team's writer re-worked each label, preparing a draft script for the entire exhibit.

The team re-grouped at this point to review the draft. Reading aloud, they went through the script line by line, day after day, considering everything from conceptual intent to word choice. *Every* team member participated; everyone made contributions to all sections of the exhibit, resulting in the final script. The document was reviewed by colleagues, the museum's director, its management committee, consulting scholars, and community members in New Mexico. Once revisions based on their comments were incorporated into the script, it was sent to copy editors.

Exercise 12: Considering Case-specific Solutions

Having begun this series of exercises with the broadest possible focus, the team made a series of decisions about increasingly specific design questions. As team members resolved each question, they moved on to the next one; they wasted no time re-tracing their steps. Now it was time for the last step.

The team used white models – renderings of each exhibit case with scale likenesses of objects, supports, pedestals, and graphic and label panels – to consider final designs for each exhibit case. The models enabled the team to decide not only on the placement of elements within the exhibit case but on other design questions as well. For example, should object supports in a given exhibit case be abstract or realistic?

In the course of their discussions, the team (joined by a collections manager) worked closely with conservators to ensure that the overall design of each exhibit case as well as specific object supports and brackets met conservation guidelines.

The final designs for each case were rendered as case elevations or production drawings and turned over to exhibit fabricators.

These problem-solving exercises allowed the *American Encounters* team to arrive at collaboration. Why? The exercises provided the structure that made it possible for team members to set aside job-title divisions; at crucial decision-making points they were able to share roles and responsibilities in a non-competitive environment. The exercises gave team members a common language and made it necessary for them to use it; when they spoke to each other of alternative solutions, they were spared the confusion that results from speaking in curatorese or designerese or educatorese. Finally, the exercises were solution specific; team members had to focus on the narrowly defined problem at hand, ensuring that their discussions were creatively motivated. The cumulative result was a kind of Gestalt that influenced the development and design of the exhibit at every step . . .

21 Assessing the Impact of Exhibit Arrangement on Visitor Behaviour and Learning

John H Falk
This article appeared in *Curator* 36(2), 1993, pp. 133–146.

The museum is a physical setting that visitors usually freely choose to enter. The physical context for all museum visits (Falk and Dierking, 1992) includes the architecture and 'feel' of the building as well as the objects and exhibits on display. A significant percentage of museum research has considered how visitors respond to the physical context at both the macrolevel of visitor pathways, orientation, and museum fatigue and the microlevel of exhibit-label font size and content. As museums continually strive to communicate better with their publics, a relevant physical context concern is how best to sequence information to facilitate understanding. Most exhibit designers begin with the implicit assumption that the order in which a visitor encounters information will affect his or her understanding. This assumption has never been directly tested. Previous studies provide some insights into the significance of exhibit sequencing and arrangement.

Considerable research exists showing that on the macroscale of the whole museum, sequence matters. Specifically, the research on museum fatigue (e.g. Robinson, 1928; Melton, 1935; Falk, 1991) and the research on the effects of setting novelty upon visitors (Balling and Falk, 1981) document the importance of time and space. As they begin to feel museum fatigue, visitors spend increasingly less time looking at objects and reading labels. Visitors respond qualitatively differently to exhibits, depending upon their level of familiarity and comfort with the setting; familiarity and comfort levels can change dramatically during the course of a visit (see Falk, 1983). Also relevant to this analysis was the demonstration of Cohen et al. (1977) that the 'popularity' of exhibitions often was a major factor in the order in which visitors viewed exhibitions rather than location within the museum.

At the other end of the continuum, research has shown that visitor responses to exhibits may be affected by the character and content of individual objects and labels (Bitgood et al., 1986; Bitgood, 1993). A variety of investigations have revealed that visitors respond in different ways to such microscale influences as object size and background shape and colour; visitors have even been shown to select among different objects within an individual display case (Munley, 1983; Thompson, 1993). Thus the nature of specific objects, rather than the nature of intended messages, may be the primary influence on visitor behaviour.

In the middle of this continuum is the issue of the sequencing of exhibition elements – whole modules of an exhibition. A considerable body of research documents that visitors to museums rarely follow the exact sequence of exhibit elements intended by the developers (e.g. Porter, 1938; Nielson, 1946; Melton, 1972; Cone and Kendall, 1978; Falk et al., 1985; Taylor, 1986; Falk, 1991). Visitors will fulfil their own agendas, for example, turning right (Melton, 1935; Porter, 1938) or leaving from the first available exit (Melton, 1972), rather than doing what the developers intended.

A reasonable question to ask then is: does the arrangement of exhibit elements within an exhibition space really matter? Would visitor learning and behaviour vary significantly if the same exhibition elements were sequenced in a different order? The research summarised above would suggest that exhibit sequence matters, but the question has never been directly addressed nor satisfactorily answered.

Logic suggests that the order of exhibits should influence visitor response, just as logic suggests that organising the chapters of a book in two different ways should influence a reader's experience. Exhibitions, however, are not books; and the visitor experience in a museum cannot be directly compared to the experience of reading a book. As the research cited here attests, museum exhibit 'reading' is a much more random, non-linear experience than reading a book. Exhibit designers tend to sequence information in museum contexts so that visitors will encounter them in one of two primary ways: (1) strongly linear, logically structured arrangements of hierarchically arranged elements; or (2) non-linear, unstructured arrangements of self-contained elements.

As part of the formative evaluation process of the redesign of the National Museum of Natural History's (NMNH) coral reef/sea-life exhibition, I had an opportunity to assess the impact of these two modes of exhibit sequencing . . .

Background

The problem: The exhibition design process was a collaborative team effort that included scientists, exhibition design and development professionals and education and evaluation professionals. The team determined that an initial prototype exhibition would be developed with the goal of facilitating public understanding of marine ecosystem functioning and conservation. Without significant disagreement, a list of key concepts and design approaches was developed to fulfil this goal. All members of the team agreed that the exhibition should accommodate the needs of both short-time/limited-interest visitors (assumed to represent the majority of visitors to this exhibit space immediately adjacent to the Rotunda) and visitors wishing to invest longer amounts of time in the topic and exhibit. What the team could not agree upon was how to structure the space to best communicate ecosystem concepts to these two kinds of visitors.

Two competing theories of how to structure the space emerged. These became known to the team as the 'Structured' approach and the 'Unstructured' approach. These two modes represented two conceptually and functionally different approaches to presenting information to the public. The structured mode was designed to channel the public into two distinct tracks, a short tour and a long tour. The short tour was intended to provide a brief overview of the concepts while facilitating a quick flow-through of visitors who desire simply to move into the next gallery. The long tour was designed to engage the visitor in a more comprehensive experience with the sequence of information carefully controlled to maximise comprehension of the concepts presented. Long-tour visitors were to begin with a video introduction to the subject, followed by exposure to a series of living and non-living displays that built upon concepts introduced in the video. Ideally, only visitors willing to commit the time to watching this video would be permitted into the long-tour section of the exhibit – the area containing the large ecosystem tanks and the majority of the other exhibit elements. This behaviour could be enforced, using a 'pulsing' procedure

Figure 21.1 Floor plans for the structured and unstructured versions of 'What is an Ecosystem?' exhibit. Numbers refer to specific modular exhibit elements

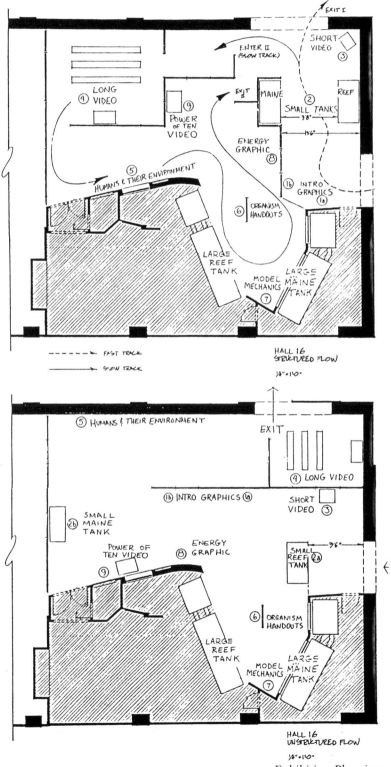

that only permitted visitors to enter the long-tour area at the beginning of each video cycle.

The unstructured mode was intended to permit visitors to move freely anywhere in the exhibition space. The assumption was that visitors would self-select which exhibit elements to view and at what level of intensity. It was left to the visitor, rather than the museum, to determine the exact sequence of viewing.

Since the team could not agree as to which of these modes would work best, it was agreed to test both modes and let the evaluation research process inform the course of the future exhibition layout. To facilitate a test of these two competing models, the team agreed to design all text, graphics, interactives, video units, and even two smaller ecosystem microcosms as modular, movable units. These elements then could be formatively tested within both the structured and unstructured modes; the only difference between the two exhibition modes would be the placement of these elements. To reiterate, visitors would encounter the same information, the same videos, the same tanks of organisms, but the arrangement of these exhibit elements, and presumably the order in which they were experienced by the visitor, would be very different in the two modes.

What was tested: Two basic issues were explored as part of this evaluation study: the effectiveness of each exhibit element and of note here, the impact of the arrangement and sequencing of exhibition elements upon visitors. Which arrangement would better facilitate the attainment of the project's overall goals and specific educational objectives? . . .

Discussion

What was the effect of the two floor plans on visitor use of the space, interaction with the specific exhibit elements, and general attitudes towards the exhibit? Overall, the differences do not appear to be dramatic. Although visitors in both the structured and unstructured floor plans accomplished most of the cognitive goals set out for the exhibit, the public found the unstructured floor plan more spatially inviting and were better able to comprehend the exhibit's intended purpose. In addition, the living exhibits and the text and video material in the unstructured mode were more extensively utilised by visitors – despite their content being identical in the two trials. In sum, the unstructured mode would have to be considered more successful than the structured mode.

A very interesting result of this study was that the difference between the two modes was not readily apparent from the 'quantity' measures of visitor utilisation such as time of use and cognitive gain. The distribution and mean time of use of the two modes was identical, as was cognitive learning on most questions. It was the quality measures that revealed differences. Visitors appeared to spend more time at the exhibit's elements, they seemed to find the experience more pleasant, and they evidenced a greater comprehension of what the exhibit was intending to communicate.

It could be argued that the 'success' of the unstructured mode seemed to be its ability to more successfully permit visitors to self-select aspects of the exhibit on which to focus. It was not that visitors spent more time in the exhibit, it was that the time they spent seemed to be somehow 'better' for them. For example, visitors exhibited, and reported, less confusion in their use of the unstructured mode.

The logic of the structured mode was that visitors first needed to have the information contained in the videos and textual material in order to fully appreciate and understand the living displays. The layout of the unstructured mode permitted visitors to move quickly to those parts of the exhibit they found most compelling. Although not reported, for most visitors, the unstructured-mode exhibit elements first visited were the living systems. Contrary to the assumptions underlying the structured mode, comprehension did not seem to be impaired by a lack of orienting material. In fact, the unstructured-mode visitors were significantly more willing than structured-mode visitors to read textual information and watch videos.

Several possible explanations could be given for this. One is that the living materials provided a motivation for reading the text or watching the videos. Or put in another way, the living material stimulated curiosity that was satisfied, at least in part, by the textual and video material provided. Even though the textual and video material was scripted to provide visitors sufficient introduction to the topic of ecology so that they could appreciate the living systems, the public preferred to use the sources provided in the opposite order.

An alternative explanation would be the 'visitor agenda' explanation suggested initially by Falk and Balling (1977) and most recently by Falk and Dierking (1992). This argument suggests that visitors entered the exhibit with an agenda (e.g. to see the whale or coral reef) that took precedence over the museum's agenda (e.g. to teach the public about ecosystems). However, once the visitors' initial agenda – curiosity about the living material – was satisfied, visitors were willing to accommodate the museum's agenda – read content information about ecosystems. Either of the explanations offered – increased visitor motivation and/or curiosity or facilitating satisfaction of visitor agendas – could explain why unstructured-mode visitors evidenced a better comprehension of what the exhibit was all about. One thing is clear, at least from an attitudinal perspective: the freedom of choice afforded by the unstructured mode appeared to better meet the needs of most visitors.

In conclusion, although the research reported here documents that the unstructured arrangement proved moderately superior to the structured arrangement, the generalisation worth taking away is that the physical context of an exhibition does influence visitor behaviour and learning. This experiment reinforces the long-held, but rarely-tested belief among exhibit developers that the visitor experience is synergistic, including elements of exhibit spatial arrangement, content and design, as well as factors less manageable by exhibit developers, such as a visitor's prior knowledge and experience and the social arrangement of museum visits. In the test described in this study, it was not the structured linear arrangement that was most comprehensible and inviting to visitors but rather the unstructured free-choice arrangement. Equally important, permitting visitors to access information in a random manner was as effective at conveying an abstract concept such as ecosystems as was imposing a more linear, hierarchical arrangement of information access. The results of this study suggest that exhibitions should be designed so that: (1) there is an array of individual elements, each of which is conceptually coherent; (2) they are arranged to make sense to the visitors, whether they are viewed in a hierarchical, linear manner or not; and (3) they not only facilitate viewing but invite visitors to choose freely their own modes of viewing – whether that be for a long or short time, in a linear or nonlinear fashion. I suggest that further research be conducted to validate these conclusions.

Finally, an important by-product of this study is that it reinforces for the field the importance of approximating, as closely as possible, the final exhibition configuration when formatively evaluating exhibits. Although testing mock-ups in 'testing rooms' is superior to not testing exhibits at all, results of those sessions need to be tempered by the knowledge that the final products, when placed in a different physical context, may engender different visitor responses. As this research documents, the physical context in which exhibits are displayed can, and generally does, directly influence visitor behaviour and learning.

References

Balling, J D and Falk, J H (1981). 'A perspective on field trips: environmental effects on learning', *Curator* 23(4), pp. 229–240.

Bitgood, S (1993). 'The anatomy of an exhibit', *Visitor Behavior* 7(4), pp. 4–15.

Bitgood, S, Patterson, D and Benefield, A (1986). *Understanding your visitors: ten factors that influence visitor behavior*, Technical Report 86–60, Jacksonville, Alabama, Psychology Institute.

Cohen, M S, Winkel, G H, Olsen, R and Wheeler, F (1977). 'Orientation in a museum: an experimental study', *Curator* 20(2), pp. 85–97.

Cone, C A and Kendall, K (1978). 'Space, time and family interactions: visitor behavior at the Science Museum of Minnesota', *Curator* 21(3), pp. 245–258.

Falk, J H (1983). 'A cross-cultural investigation of the novel field trip phenomenon: National Museum of Natural History, New Delhi, India', *Curator* 26(4), pp. 315–325.

Falk, J H (1991). 'Analysis of the behavior of family visitors in natural history museums: The National Museum of Natural History', *Curator* 34(1), pp. 44–50.

Falk, J H and Balling, J D (1977). *An investigation of the effect of field trips on science learning*, Final Report Grant Number SED77–18913. Washington, DC, National Science Foundation.

Falk, J H and Dierking, L D (1992). *The museum experience*, Washington, DC, Whalesback Books.

Falk, J H, Koran, J J, Dierking, L D, and Dreblow, L (1985). 'Predicting visitor behavior', *Curator* 28(4), pp. 249–257.

Melton, A (1935). *Problems of installation in museums of art*, AAM Monograph, New Series No. 14, Washington, DC, American Association of Museums.

Melton, A (1972). 'Visitor behavior in museums: some early research in environmental design', *Human Factors* 14(5), pp. 393–403.

Munley, M E (1983). *Visitors' views of the 18th century*, unpublished evaluation report, Washington, DC, National Museum of American History.

Nielson, L C (1946). 'A technique for studying the behavior of museum visitors', *Journal of Educational Psychology* 37, pp. 103–110.

Porter, M C (1938). *Behavior of the average visitor in the Peabody Museum of Natural History*, Yale University Publications of the American Association of Museums, New Series No. 16, Washington, DC, American Association of Museums.

Robinson, E S (1928). *The behavior of the museum visitor*, AAM Monograph, New Series No. 5, Washington, DC, American Association of Museums.

Taylor, S (1986). Understanding processes of informal education: a naturalistic study of visitors to a public aquarium, doctoral dissertation, University of California, Berkeley, California.

Thompson, D (1993). Considering the museum visitor: an interactive approach to environmental design, doctoral dissertation, University of Wisconsin-Milwaukee.

22 Visitors Make Their Own Meaning

Douglas Worts
Extracted from 'Extending the frame: forging a new
partnership with the public' in *Art in Museums*, Pearce, S (ed.),
Athlone Press, 1995, pp. 165–166, 168–181, 188–191.

Museums have long been considered special places where the authoritative
insights of trained experts are shared with members of the public. It is true that
we as an institution have something unique to offer the public – the collections
we amass and our intellectual insights into the creativity of artists. However, to
paraphrase Picasso (and many other artists for that matter), in producing an art
work, the artist carries the creative process *half* way – it is the responsibility of
the viewer to complete the process. This visitor-centred half of the creative
process is based on the personalising of symbolic objects. This process is not
prescriptive, so institutions cannot control how the personalising occurs.
Museums can, however, be supportive of visitors as they personalise their
experiences with the art works.

What does the visitor side of creativity look like? This creativity is idiosyncratic – sometimes tentative, sometimes dogmatic; at times it is intensely
moving, other times shocking, while at other times it is insightful. To this writer,
visitor-based creativity provides a powerful complement to the intellectual
insights of the museum experts. Accordingly, I submit that one of the core
partnerships that needs to be fully developed in museums (and particularly art
museums) is an honest and respectful relationship between the public and the
institutions – a partnership in which the many meanings of art can be explored
and honoured.

About the Canadian Historical Galleries

Much of the initiative for the progressive approach to the new Art Gallery of
Ontario evolved from work done by the team responsible for the Canadian
Historical Galleries. In 1988, this team of educators, curators and designers was
the first such group in the Gallery to form a partnership that was dedicated to
improving exhibition techniques, based on visitor experiences of the exhibits. As
part of this undertaking, the team developed, for the first time, audience
research projects dedicated to exploring the complexities and variations of
visitor experiences in exhibits. Based on research results, many interpretive
strategies, such as the use of computers, audio and interactive labels, were fully
integrated into the displays with the aim of supporting the visitors in focusing
on, enjoying and making sense of the displays. The results were very positive
and have been summarised in several publications (Worts, 1990a, 1990b and
1991a, 1991b, 1991c).

. . . One of the leading areas for the team to explore was how personal meanings related to viewing an art work – ones that do not necessarily fit into the
critical framework for understanding objects – functioned in an art gallery setting.

With funds received from the Government of Canada, the Canadian Historical Collection team hired three consultants to assist in exploring three areas of psychology that were felt to be important to understanding how people make meaning with art works in museums. These areas were environmental psychology, cognitive science and depth psychology. The team met regularly with the consultants for a period of about a year, working through a set of exhibit-related issues and strategies that was to become critical to how the new Canadian Historical Wing would be developed . . .

All of the new galleries in this wing reflect our visitor-oriented philosophy that there are many meanings associated with a work of art. This approach is manifested in several ways. One is the use of binders in which questions are asked concerning, for example, the importance of an artist or his/her art work, and for which responses are provided from many different and often conflicting perspectives. By offering a range of plausible reactions to an issue, it is hoped that visitors will feel more comfortable that there is no 'right' answer. This tactic is supplemented with a request for visitors to reflect on what the art work(s) mean to them. 'Share your reaction' cards are dispensed in about two dozen locations throughout the Canadian Historical Wing for written and drawn responses to the exhibits. Additionally, audio programmes, computers, visible storage, wall signs and text panels have been added to the displays to encourage more focused exploration of the art works.

'Share your Reaction' Cards

One of the most interesting outcomes of the re-installed galleries relates to the use of the 'Share your reaction' cards. Over a period of about nine months, approximately 12,000 cards were used – and at least 5,000 of these were left in the drop-off bins in the galleries. The cards have proved to be quite remarkable for their diversity of form and content. We are finding that comments are not superficial judgements, such as 'loved it' or 'hated it', which often characterise comments books. Instead, the bulk of comments are personal and reflective. Many provide insight into how visitors are interacting with particular objects or groups of art works. Often there is great sensitivity and intensity in the responses. A large number of visitors who use the cards choose to draw imagery of one kind or another. Some people copy pictures on display. Others adapt images on display to their own creative ends. Still others will create wholly new images, presumably inspired by their time in the gallery, or which reflect what is on their mind at the moment. Often, people seem to want to see themselves reflected, either literally or symbolically, in their imagery – and in their writing for that matter. This has been an important psychological phenomenon for Gallery staff to become aware of – people want to see themselves reflected in their visits to museums. This has the potential to affect dramatically the way in which art displays are conceived and installed.

The following visitor responses, (numbered 1–4) [considerably reduced from the number in the original article], present some of the public's written and drawn responses to their experiences in galleries, as reflected in the 'Share Your Reactions' cards. In the interests of space, written responses are quoted in full, while drawn responses are reproduced. This idiosyncratic material provides a glimpse into a powerful area of creative meaning-making that is part of the potential of every visitor . . .

Figure 22.1   Reaction card: Adaptation of landscape by Arthur Lismer

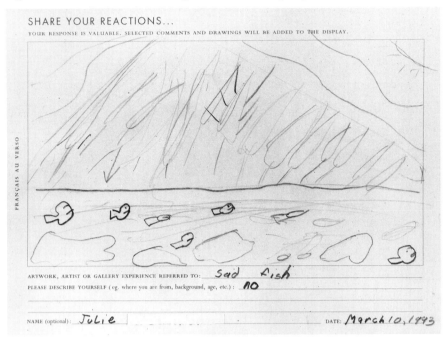

Response 1 – (Figure 22.1) An adaptation of a landscape by Arthur Lismer, 'Sand Lake, Algoma', in which the visitor has turned the original waves into 'sad fish'. This seems to be an example of an instance in which the mood and identity of the visitor projected into their reaction to the art. I feel it is important that the institution understand that this kind of experience exists and that it must be acknowledged and respected. Trying to 'teach' visitors about the historical dimensions of the Group of Seven would be largely pointless for visitors having this type of experience.

Response 2 – (Figure 22.2) A visitor's reflection on a painting that depicts the town in which her grandmother was born. The experience has filled a gap in an important personal relationship.

Response 3 – A visitor wrote:

> I would like to know why in this entire Art Gallery, people of colour are not represented. I would like to see more art about the Indian culture and also on the Black race. I am really disappointed that in a city where we are so multicultural, only European cultures are seen in the art gallery. I would not bring my child here, because we are not represented. We are not recognised for any of our talents. – I am a black woman, who is a Canadian (born).

This critical attack on the institution results from this visitor not seeing herself or her race reflected in the exhibitions. She forcefully raises an issue that the institution needs to address if it really wants to be an art gallery for the people of Ontario. She makes it clear that there is a problem, and that the solution must be negotiated between the public and the institution.

Figure 22.2   Reaction card: a written response

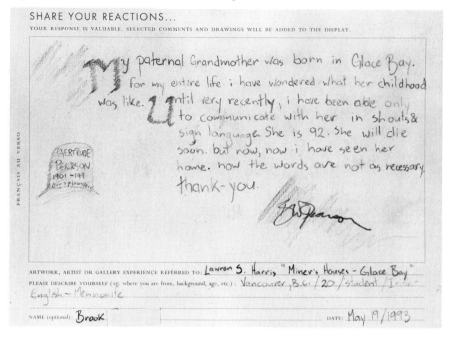

SHARE YOUR REACTIONS...

YOUR RESPONSE IS VALUABLE. SELECTED COMMENTS AND DRAWINGS WILL BE ADDED TO THE DISPLAY.

My paternal Grandmother was born in Glace Bay. For my entire life i have wondered what her childhood was like. Until very recently, i have been able only to communicate with her in shouts & sign language. She is 92. She will die soon. but now, now i have seen her home. now the words are not as necessary. thank-you.

GERTRUDE PEARSON 1901 –199

ARTWORK, ARTIST OR GALLERY EXPERIENCE REFERRED TO: Lawren S. Harris "Miner's Houses - Glace Bay"
PLEASE DESCRIBE YOURSELF (eg. where you are from, background, age, etc.): Vancouver, B.C. / 20 / student / I
English – Mennonite

NAME (optional): Brook   DATE: May 19/1993

Response 4 – A visitor wrote:

> The 'new' galleries are a tremendous improvement over the old. Coming here is now an engaging and intimate experience. One feels able to concentrate more clearly on works of art or particular periods without feeling overwhelmed or alienated. Coming here is now a joyous experience, whereas before it felt like a duty! Thank you. – I am an illustrator and painter, living in Toronto.

For those who worked on developing these exhibits, this reaction is very satisfying.

The range of responses is quite remarkable – and they display a kind of personal insight into the art experience that the Gallery itself could not articulate. For me, these images and comments need to be seen by the Gallery, so it can learn more about the felt power of the objects in our collections, but these reactions also deserve to be integrated into the interpretive strategy of the exhibits themselves and experienced empathically by other visitors. One possible outcome of such an integration is that other visitors may find greater comfort in entering the realm of personal meaning-making in a more conscious way.

'Explore a Painting in Depth'

The *Exploring a painting in depth* viewing facility consists of a seating unit, with sound-proofing material on three sides, and the painting ['The Beaver Dam' by J E H MacDonald], located directly in front of the seats and surrounded by three walls. Through this design, visual and auditory distractions coming from nearby exhibit areas are minimised. By using the headsets and CD technology provided, visitors can choose to listen to three audio programmes while they focus their attention on the painting. One programme carries the curator's engaging insights into the art work. A second provides several dramatised comments about the artist, by friends and family of MacDonald. The third, which is the most innovative technique currently in use at the Gallery, is a reflective imaging exercise that leads visitors into a reverie with the painting – encouraging their imaginations to create highly personal links with the painting. In it, the 12 minute recording encourages the viewer to relax and enter into a semi-dream-state with the picture. The first task is to establish a strong mental image of the painting. Then the viewer is invited to enter imaginatively into the space of the picture and to experience the sights, sounds, smells and potential of being in the setting. The wide range of response cards filled out in this facility has proven to be a very rich resource that provides many insights into the viewing process, the painting and the visitors.

Responses 5–7 illustrate a range of creative, visitor experiences relating to this picture . . .

Response 5 – A visitor wrote:

> I enjoyed the sensual journey into the painting. Sight, smell, cool/cold autumn day was evoked. Clear air and water. Loneliness – the empty canoe vaguely depressing. The suggestion(s) of human form in the rocks and sticks of the dam add another dimension of questioning the artist's interpretation of the scene. Thank you for making me enter the world of the Canadian north! – I am 56 years old, WMF, from USA, some art training.

This response demonstrates how some visitors use their imaginations to enter the world of the painting and create personal meanings for themselves. Many users of this facility experience the smells, sounds and textures of nature, as well as other powerful associations with the image.

Figure 22.3 Reaction card: projection of self into a picture by a child

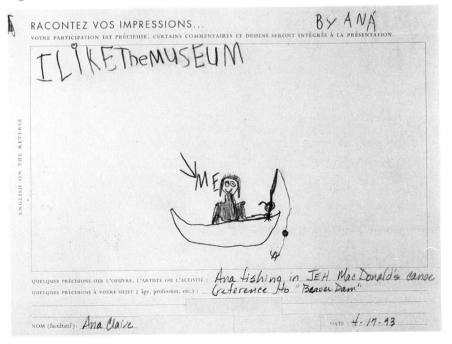

Response 6 – A visitor wrote:

> I hate to be negative, because on the whole the new gallery is wonderful. But programme no.1, female voice, 'The Beaver Dam' exploration is very silly. I was hoping to hear about art – and maybe the other selections cover this – but this heely-feely approach to art is just a bit much! Less new age, more content, please.

Not everyone likes the imaginative approach to viewing art works – or at least not the approach taken here. This visitor is expressing a desire for 'content', as presented by the experts in the institution. By referring to the tape as 'heely-feely' the visitor is clearly dismissive of the subjective approach in this programme. A certain portion of our audience has difficulty with, and perhaps even feels threatened by, a non-analytical approach. However, a significant portion of the audience feels very good about making personal connections with art works.

Response 7 – (Figure 22.3) A common theme in animating the imagination of visitors is the projection of the self into the response. In this case, a child has entered the picture, hopped into the canoe and gone fishing. She also declared 'I like the museum'. She has concretised the experience in a way that hopefully will remain memorable.

Figure 22.4 Conceptual model of museum experience

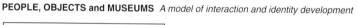

PEOPLE, OBJECTS and MUSEUMS *A model of interaction and identity development*

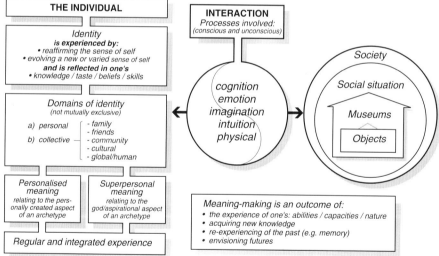

   ... I would like to offer up a conceptual model of the visitor experience (figure 22.4). The emphasis in this model is on the individual and the many processes and products of experience that happen during interactions with objects, people and places. Here, five processes of interaction mediate between the individual and the world in which that person lives (and all of these processes have both conscious and unconscious aspects). Cognition, emotion, imagination, intuition and physical interactions all contribute to the experience of an individual's sense of identity – either by affirming an existing sense of self, or by providing an impetus for an evolving sense of self. This identity is generally reflected in one's knowledge, beliefs, taste and skills.

Identity is a very complex notion, particularly because it involves both conscious and unconscious aspects. However, for my purposes here, the concept has been broken down into two general categories, which are not mutually exclusive – that of one's personal identity, or the sense of distinctiveness; and that of one's sense of belonging to a collective identity, such as a family, community or culture. Experiences of cultural objects can set in motion symbolic and literal experiences that can re-enforce, undermine or develop one's sense of identity.

This model implies that museums have traditionally honoured certain types of meaning-making processes with museum objects, but have largely ignored others, which are equally important. One hypothesis here is that museums have created an imbalance in how the public experiences symbolic objects and that this imbalance needs to be corrected. Specifically, most museums seem to focus their attention on rare and unusual objects in order to spotlight the extraordinary, superpersonal aspects of human experience. It is assumed that an inspired painting by Van Gogh, for example, is a source of an archetypal experience of nature or humanity. Yet the success of a Van Gogh painting depends on the particular way in which a viewer experiences it – and there is a great range of powerful responses to such art works. The painting must be experienced as something both outside the individual, but also within that person. I have come to think that museums generally encourage visitors to defer any personal, idiosyncratic meaning-making processes to the meanings that conform to the expert consensus (which is itself something of a myth). By encouraging people to experience objects with all of their perceptual capabilities (cognition, emotion, imagination, intuition and physical interaction) the museum can become a much richer forum for the showcasing of living cultures.

Conclusion

All of the 'Share your reaction' cards demonstrate to me how much creative energy exists within the public – it is a powerful energy that has many faces – unpredictable, moving, insightful. Even when visitor reactions seem elusive and idiosyncratic it is possible to relate to them empathetically, and I believe it enriches everyone's experiences when we do so. As a cultural institution, museums do have a great deal to offer – insights based on research – and we need to share our insights as effectively as possible. But, museums have limitations. They cannot experience artworks creatively, but rather must rely on the public for this function.

For me, museums in future years will include a new form of partnership with the public – where the many ways of meaning-making are encouraged, supported and respected. I imagine that museums will become places that more effectively present information which interacts with visitor imagination and emotional responses – and which in turn blend with social dynamics. The result will be museums that function more as places of a living culture. If the museum is truly the place of the muses, then museum professionals must realise that the physical and intellectual aspects of our current operations must function more symbolically as triggers that support visitors in activating the muses within all of us. It is this inner space that, in my view, is the real museum.

References

American Association of Museums (1992). *Excellence and equity: education and the public dimension of museums*, Washington, DC, American Association of Museums.

Worts, D (1990a). 'Computer as catalyst: experiences at the Art Gallery of Ontario', *ILVS Review*, 1(2), pp. 91–108.

Worts, D (1990b). 'Enhancing exhibitions: experimenting with visitor-centred experiences at the Art Gallery of Ontario', *Visitor Studies: Theory, Research and Practice, Volume 3*, Jacksonville, Alabama, Center for Social Design, pp. 203–213.

Worts, D (1991a). 'Visitor-centred experiences', in A Benefield, S Bitgood and H Shettel, (eds), *Visitor Studies: Theory, Research and Practice, Volume 4*, Jacksonville, Alabama, Center for Social Design, pp. 156–161.

Worts, D (1991b). 'In search of meaning: "Reflective practice" and museums', *Museum Quarterly: Journal of the Ontario Museum Association*, Fall, pp. 9–20.

Worts, D (1991c). 'The Art Gallery of Ontario's search of the muse', *ILVS Review* 2(1), pp. 109–111.

23 Recipe for an Interactive Art Gallery

David Phillips

Extracted from an article in *International Journal of Museum Management and Curatorship* 7(3), 1988, pp. 243–252.

Art galleries tend to present the history and contemporary progress of art and design through their collections in much the same way that traditional museums of science present scientific and natural history: through arrays of judiciously chosen specimens grouped by type. However, whereas science museums are nowadays often complemented by science centres, such as *Launch Pad* in London's Science Museum, where visitors can explore not history through collections, but principles of science through demonstrations which they may try out for themselves, art museums have few equivalent displays permitting informal exploration of visual experience.

. . . Nowadays, our galleries encourage those visitors who leave their easels at home, but bring with them skills in visual literacy which they apply to a kind of art appreciation which can seem more exciting socially than visually. It is a formula on which great collections in major cities seem to thrive, but which often leaves more modest collections in smaller towns rather under-patronised. Perhaps some of these might think of trying to set themselves up as places where, whether on a casual visit or an organised one, we are invited not exclusively to look at works of art, but to explore our own visual experience actively as well, in the way that science centres offer us the chance to experiment actively . . .

The most obvious way to start is to provide artists' materials for visitors to try their skills. To accompany the *Paint and Painting* exhibition at the Tate Gallery in 1982, the sponsors, Windsor and Newton, funded two tents full of materials and equipment in the grounds, which were used by some 700 to a 1,000 visitors a day, even though children under fourteen were not admitted to the tents in order to give priority to serious adult artists (Jupe, 1982) . . .

In the late 1970s the Education Department of the Art Gallery of Ontario used equipment for projecting on a huge scale children's abstract scribbles executed in translucent paints on clear plastic. The effect is spell-binding, and can be successfully imitated just with felt-tipped pens, 35 mm transparency holders and an ordinary projector . . .

Drawing and painting are not the only ways of exploring artistic effects. Leicestershire Museums devised, to accompany their exhibition in 1986 of French painting of the seventeenth century, *Masterpieces of Reality*, a pair of boxes full of objects of the kind found in the pictures in the exhibition, wired up so that visitors could try out different lighting effects. The devices proved so popular that they have often since been on display. With a somewhat similar set-up, it would be possible for visitors to explore some of the display options which we usually reserve for designers and curators. There are few occupations more enjoyable than seeing how the qualities of a glass, or a sculpture, or for that matter a whole room, can be brought out with different arrangements of lighting and background. We might be reluctant to allow visitors to handle objects so as to try out such manipulations, but it would be quite feasible to display some specimens surrounded by glass or perspex, in displays wired up to allow of variable illumination controlled by the visitor.

All the activities mentioned so far relate to specifically artistic experience. However, there is also a case to be made for including in galleries demonstrations of the kind more usually found in science centres, which allow visitors to explore aspects of vision which are not necessarily thought of as artistic. The main purpose of this article is to describe some of them, which relate to picture- and pattern-making or to perception, and then to suggest why some current directions in scientific research make them of interest for gallery curators. There are a surprising number of devices to choose from, mostly with a distinguished ancestry in scientific research from the nineteenth century or even earlier . . .

The picture-making devices are the most familiar. Of all the available demonstrations, camera obscuras have much the longest pedigree. They were fully described in the sixteenth century and used extensively by artists from the seventeenth century onwards. Many versions of them can readily be constructed, to show how an image can be projected on a screen, either in a blacked-out room, looking out onto a brightly lit scene, or within a box, which the viewer can move around like a camera. Either version will work just with a pin-hole if the scene is very brightly lit. We installed one on a deep window-seat in Nottingham Castle in 1974, with pin-holes of various sizes which the visitor could select, and it worked adequately on sunny days for many years. A much better image is given by even the cheapest lens. It is not always easy to find a lens giving a focused image sufficiently far away to make a large device, but we found that even the kind of large crude plastic magnifier, several inches wide, sold as an aid to embroidery, worked quite well. A number of professionally constructed camera obscuras with good lenses have been a popular feature of the National Museum of Photography, Film and Television in Bradford since it opened, looking out onto the animated city centre . . .

Instructions for using hinged mirrors to help discover designs suitable for formal garden layouts appear in the early eighteenth century (Bradley, 1731), and the principle was formally investigated first by Sir David Brewster, who coined the name kaleidoscope and published his discoveries about the idea in 1816. Brewster's instruments, like the earlier versions, used just two mirrors to give rosette patterns. Demonstration versions can easily be made to sit on pattern boards on table-tops. If three mirrors are used, joined at 60° angles along their long edges, whatever shapes appear in the plane formed by the short edges of the mirrors at one end of the triangular tube will appear to a viewer at the other end to fill the plane with hexagonal patterns. Small versions, a few inches [a few centimetres] long, are commercially available equipped with lenses so that as the viewer peers through them, as through a telescope, a reduced view of whatever is in front of the tube is fragmented into these patterns, which transform magically as the instrument is moved around. Larger versions can readily be made with ordinary glass mirrors. We have used versions up to 5 ft [1.5 m] in length, with mirrors up to fifteen inches [38 cm] wide, and a translucent screen over one end onto which colour-slides, film or shadows, can be projected . . .

Visual perception began to attract the attention of such major physicists as Helmholz, Mach and Maxwell in the nineteenth century, and a whole gallery of figures demonstrating effects and illusions has accumulated since. There are hundreds to choose from and they offer a very simple yet popular form of display. A splendid and easily imitated set, showing effects a little reminiscent of much op art of the 1960s, was published by James Fraser in 1908 . . . The curves of his 'spirals' have to be traced with a point for us to be convinced that they are really nests of concentric circles, though even then they obstinately appear to the eye as spiral patterns (Fraser, 1908). The demonstrations of figure and ground effects by gestalt psychologists of the 1930s (Beardslee and Westheimer, 1958) have parallels in the work of many painters, and had a direct influence. More recently the texture perception demonstrations of Bela Julesz seem to indicate the pattern elements on which the mind relies most for its initial analysis of what the eye sees. The figures devised for all these areas of research and many others are fascinating when presented as passive displays, but some can be used interactively too. The Bristol Exploratory includes a large magnetic picture board with movable picture elements with which visitors can try out effects of size constancy against a background of strong perspective distance cues . . .

None of the demonstrations mentioned so far need be very complicated from a technical point of view, and down-market versions of all of them could quite easily be built [at a fairly low cost]. There are positive advantages to their simplicity. For the organisers they are easy to maintain as well as cheap, whilst for visitors, blasé about the prodigious performance of technological consumer goods, there is still a sense of wonder to be aroused by the discovery that simple looking devices can produce remarkable effects . . .

Another most interesting area which is not easy to explore without expensive equipment is the way in which abstract patterning is involved in making recognisable pictures of things. This is not something which is at all well understood yet, which makes it all the more fascinating as an area for intuitive exploration. Perhaps the main difference between the picture we see in our mind's eye and drawn pictures or photos is that only the image in the mind's eye is devoid of any apparent patterning which is not inherent in the shapes of the objects we see. By contrast, even a photograph, if we examine it closely enough, shows patterning characteristic of the imaging process, optical patterning from blurring and the graininess of the emulsion. Most forms of painting represent things in terms of a language of far more obvious patterning, characteristic of the medium, or of the artist. The heavy impasto of a painting by Van Gogh is an obvious example, but even a lithograph imposes both stylistic shapes and textures characteristic of the process on whatever it represents. One of the impressions given by current research in perception is that the apparent absence of pattern from the image in the mind's eye disguises a considerable amount of pattern analysis in the brain during the process of turning the images on our retinas into the grand and perfect colour transparency we seem to see spread before us. Perhaps the aesthetic qualities of the patterning inescapable in so many pictures somehow depend upon these hidden perceptual processes. The patterns in pictures are certainly fun to explore. We tried doing so in Warrington by presenting visitors with reproductions of freely painted pictures (a Renoir and a Van Gogh), concealed by a succession of hinged masks so as to reveal at first only patches so small that only the patterning of the paint could be seen, then larger areas in which objects could begin to be recognised, and only finally whole sections of the paintings. These proved amusing, but more could be done with expensive equipment.

For instance, one of the fundamental areas of picture research over the last 30 years has concerned the abstract property of images known technically as spatial frequency, which we can very roughly think of as the distribution of shading across a picture surface. Suppose you are looking at a picture of a fluted column illuminated by soft light from one side. There will be an overall gradation of dark and light which follows the overall roundness of the column, and much sharper gradations where the fine structure of the fluting catches the light. Properties of optical systems make it possible to filter pictures so as to emphasise gradations of shading at different scales and orientations. We could filter an image of our column so as to suppress the sharp gradations from dark to light representing the fluting, in order to emphasise the gentle gradation suggesting its overall roundness. Alternatively we might play down the roundness in order to see the flutes more clearly. In fact, in any scene at all, changes in three-dimensional shape at different scales are often associated with gradations of dark to light at different scales in an image of the scene, and this kind of filtering is often applied for shape analysis in technological imaging. The same kind of analysis can be applied to any two-dimensional pattern of light and dark, whether or not it contains information about three-dimensional shape. Sometimes the dominant contrast components of this kind in a scene are very obvious, as they would likely be in a picture of a fluted pillar, but they are there embedded in the distribution of light and dark in any scene. This is therefore a way of exploring abstract qualities in any picture at all, however devoid of pattern it might appear. Even at the most superficial level the transformations of images which it allows are intriguing. They could be provided for visitors to a gallery to explore either with optical apparatus, or with computer processing (Taylor, 1978).

This kind of research may be in the process of transforming the business of making pictures. The field known as pattern recognition is slowly unravelling two different problems, teaching machines to recognise what they 'see', and trying to understand how we recognise what we see (Pinker, 1985). Perhaps discoveries made on the way will eventually offer ways of putting on a systematic footing effects, like those of symmetry and spatial frequency mentioned above, which artists have played with intuitively. That might sound frightening, but after all it is only what the development of perspective procedures between 1400 and 1650 did for all those effects of convergence for which previously there had been only rules of thumb. The result did impose a new discipline on artists, but one which released imaginative possibilities. Perhaps the analysis of two-dimensional surface pattern in pictures, and of its role in recognition, which is currently being pursued on many fronts will offer a comparable release of unguessed-at imaginative possibilities. Art in the past never remained in innocence of either technical advances in picture-making or new theories of perception, and there is no reason to expect it now.

Even if it is accepted that there are interesting connections between art and developments in contemporary scientific research, it remains to be seen whether visitors to a gallery would make the connections, given amusing demonstrations to play with on the one hand and collections on the other. Of course, the interactive display could be organised on sequential, didactic lines, so as to explain matters point by point, perhaps with illustrative works of art included in the display. But this approach would have drawbacks. For visitors seeking simply to look at the illustrative works the display would be a distracting setting. Nor would the display be likely to work didactically for casual visitors. It is even harder to follow any kind of sequence in a crowded interactive display than it is in a crowded passive display. Perhaps, anyway, it is a mistake to expect interactive displays to function didactically, so as to teach testable facts. What they do well is to provide a vivid experience, to stimulate subsequent learning . . .

Not enough experiments have been made for the success of a scheme of this kind to be guaranteed. Just the opposite, the interactive component of the displays could quite fairly be criticised on the grounds that the immediate stimulus it would offer might mask the subtler qualities of works of art, and make it less rather than more likely for visitors to be able to muster the quiet attention which such works need. I would argue that any distraction which interactive visual displays introduce into galleries is trivial beside the problem which conventional displays of static art now face in any case, because we are all so attuned to the instantly appealing stimulus of moving television and computer images, accompanied by sound, not to mention the aggressive effects of the commercial displays and advertisements around us. We live in a sensational culture, and a gallery full of pictures and sculptures is no longer the spectacle it was for turn-of-the-century audiences visiting recently established municipal galleries. Nowadays we need to be led into the quiet and unfamiliar languages of the art of the past. Perhaps just playing around with low-level visual experience, using both traditional materials and new technological methods, offers one route.

Some gallery directors might be happy to accept novel displays if they just succeeded in providing a vivid visual experience, not necessarily an artistic one, for a wide range of visitors. The experience could still be educational, in an increasingly visual age. Pictures have played a growing role in everyday communication over the last few centuries, and are likely to continue to do so given the possibilities of electronic imaging. This could be strategic territory in which some art galleries might stake a claim. The communication is too important and the possibilities are too delightful to be left to the brilliant engineers who have made it all feasible. It is an opportunity which galleries who find most of their audience puzzled by collections which seem remote from modern life might think about.

References

Beardslee, D C and Westheimer, M (1958). *Readings in perception,* New York.

Bradley, R (1731). *New improvements of planting and gardening,* London. (6th edition).

Fraser, J (1908). 'A new visual illusion of direction', *British Journal of Psychology* 2.

Jupe, R (1982). 'Paint and painting: a model sponsorship', *International Journal of Museum Management and Curatorship,* 1(4), pp. 365–70.

Pinker, S (ed.) (1985). *Visual cognition,* Boston, MIT Press.

Taylor, C A (1978). *Images,* Wykeham Publications.

24 Computers on the Exhibit Floor

Beverly Serrell and Britt Raphling
This article appeared in *Curator* 35(3), 1992, pp. 181–189.

Delivery-based Rationales

Often, what is presented in computer interactives is born of the content expert's desire to provide detail to interested or motivated visitors. Is this really appropriate? The term 'more-interested visitor' is a code phrase used by content experts to describe people like themselves – in other words, their peers. In fact, visitors with high levels of expertise make up an extremely small portion of the actual audience: usually fewer than five in 100 have any relevant background or training. Rather, the vast majority are lay-people with varying degrees of enthusiasm for the exhibit subject. A computer program, label, or exhibit written for only 5 per cent of its visitors has little validity in a public museum, which is accountable to a broader audience.

The notion of 'more-information' programs and the assumption that visitors really want all those data is problematic. Computer information storage is so efficient that visitors are often faced with hundreds – even thousands – of options to explore in a single database-type program, which is almost always too much to expect of visitors' casual interest and precious time. This 'information-dump' model is severely under-utilised and, therefore, a bad investment. For example, in a programme called *Desert Explorations*, which contained 325 images of desert-dwelling animals that visitors could select and learn about, on the average, visitors chose only five of these images (Diamond, 1989). In *Otters and Oil*, a much smaller information-dump program with 24 available screens, the median number selected was six (Serrell and Raphling, 1992b).

Sometimes the information-dump program is disguised by putting it into a game format. Even this will be under-utilised, because the game activity overwhelms the learning. People will be more interested in guessing and scoring points than learning facts. An illustration of this is a Jeopardy-style computer game, where visitors were observed excitedly trying to guess the correct answers to improve their scores and ignoring the supplementary-information paragraphs that were part of each answer screen.

Receiver-based Rationales

So developers should drop the information-dump model that relies on the notion of a fantasy visitor who has the time and interest to get lost in a sea of facts. Instead, exhibits need to contain computer interactives that work for real visitors. A better alternative is a computer interactive whose objective is to help users *construct meaning* through a tightly focused set of activities. It requires and inspires active involvement so that learning can be a result of manipulation of both technology *and* content. Educational psychologist Chandler Screven has said, 'Higher order learning is an active process of gathering information for making decisions'. He suggests that programs encourage visitors to seek out information and then apply it to solve a problem (Screven, 1990). In other words, exhibit developers should think not only about what *information* to impart, but about what visitors will *do* with it.

The following are three good examples of programs that help users to construct meaning. The first is called *Continental Puzzle*, and it is part of the *Earth Over Time* videodisc, a geology interactive produced for the Interactive Videodisc Science Consortium (Flagg, 1990). The puzzle allows visitors to take what they know and can infer and to come up with new information by manipulating the computer images. Continents are scattered around on the screen, and the visitor can drag them together until they form the ancient supercontinent Pangaea. A 'hint' screen may be accessed, but the activity involves making inferences from the available information and experimenting with shapes of the land masses in order to fit them together properly. The end result is literally a whole from the sum of its parts – a concrete experience which allows visitors to actively manipulate information to arrive at a new understanding.

Another example is a program about the future evolution of humans, called *Homo Nextus*, developed by the New England Technology Group. In it, visitors review and select the social and environmental factors they think will influence evolutionary changes in people and then see the results of those changes.

The third example, also from *Earth Over Time*, is *Save the Beach*. In this segment, viewers can hear different opinions about how to prevent beach erosion from people living in a shoreline community. After taking in these viewpoints, visitors can vote on a strategy and see how their choice would have affected the beach and its community.

Each of these three examples was based on clear, concise objectives; and each required and inspired personal involvement of the visitor. Personal involvement arises from a situation where visitors are able to see the consequences of their choices and actions. With a program similar to those described above, visitors can manipulate and use information interactively to create new and concrete understanding of a problem, question, or concept.

Ten Design Principles

Good examples and an understanding of some of the theory is an important place to start, but they won't build an interactive program. To design something that audiences will use, exhibit developers need to know specifics about how visitors behave around computers on the exhibit floor. The principles that follow are based on observations of visitor behaviour made by us and others and are offered as a reality check for making decisions about concepts, communication goals, learning objectives, software, and hardware.

1 *Expect not more than 30 per cent of the exhibit audience to be attracted to the computer.* This is a fairly reliable figure. In the Field Museum's *Nature Walk* exhibit, the *Deer Game* attracted a little over 20 per cent of both a child audience and an adult audience (Serrell & Associates, 1992); *LIFEmap* at the California Academy of Sciences attracted 21 per cent (Inverness Research Associates, 1991). A computer interactive that was one of 12 exhibit elements in the *Lasers at 25* exhibit in the Maryland Science Center attracted 29 per cent of the audience (Hilke, 1988). Computers in the *Otters and Oil Don't Mix* exhibit at the Shedd Aquarium were two of six exhibit

elements and attracted a total of 19 per cent of the audience (Serrell and Raphling, 1992a).

These data are not surprising. A computer interactive is an individual station, commanding limited square footage. At most, only a few people can use it at a time. Also, computers have less intrinsic interest than do the real objects and animals in an exhibit. In fact, computer interactives often have no more attracting power than other low-tech interactives.

That 30 per cent figure can be improved by offering more stations in a single exhibit. At the Art Gallery of Ontario, visitors were offered three computer stations to support eight paintings in a small exhibit; in that gallery, 96 per cent of the visitors looked at at least one computer (Worts, 1990). However, if that finding were broken down by individual terminals, it would probably turn out that each was attracting closer to 30 per cent. Thirty percent is *good*, given the free-form nature of a museum visit, and should be a goal.

2 *Less is more. Provide two minutes of information – total.* A computer interactive should not occupy a disproportionate amount of visitors' time and attention relative to other exhibit elements. Since people usually average around 30 seconds at an exhibit element (Miles,1991), even a five-minute program is too long. There are a number of good reasons to limit the total program:

- Keep it short for financial reasons. A short program will cost less. For the best return on the museum's investment, visitors should be using at least half of the program; and, given the amount of time people tend to spend at exhibit elements, a two-minute program has a better chance to be used more fully.
- Keep it short for personal reasons. The team's programming and design effort will have gone to waste if no one bothers to look at most of the product.
- Keep it short for logistical reasons. Shorter time will increase turnover so that more visitors can use it.
- And lastly, keep it short for the visitors' mental health and well-being. They will feel satisfied that they 'got it', their competence and confidence will have been promoted, they will not have been overwhelmed, and they might even have learned something.

3 *Each screen should require a reading time of not more than 12 seconds.* In fact, 10 seconds is a useful amount of time to spend with a screen of information. This is not as short as it seems. Try looking at a watch for 10 seconds, and you can imagine that quite a bit of information could be absorbed from a computer screen during that amount of time.

4 *Make sure instructions are intuitive, and keep technology response time short.* Visitors should be able to learn how to use the interactive in 10 seconds or less, because time spent learning is time taken away from total use. This also keeps visitor *frustration* levels down. There are advantages and disadvantages to both trackballs and touch screens, but regardless of what hardware is chosen, remember that it should be kept simple. Most important, don't *assume* visitors will be able to learn the mechanism. Test it on them first, because what is intuitive to programmers may not be to visitors.

Response time of the hardware should be 1 second or less, or else visitors will abuse the machine. In a recent AAM paper, Jim Oker, of the New

England Technology Group, offered this caution: 'A poor interface will be perceived as a broken program. It will invite your visitors to bang on your touchscreens, to try to wrench your joysticks out of the countertop. And it will not achieve your goals' (Oker, 1992). Barbara Flagg, of Multimedia Research, also refers to 'enthusiastic users pounding trackballs to the bottom of a kiosk' (Flagg, 1991).

5 *Build in free-choice and control for visitors.* This is an extremely important principle to remember, because ignoring it can have disastrous consequences. Think of the visitors' movement through the computer program as analogous to their movement through the entire exhibit or museum. Most visitors browse in museum exhibits, stopping at what catches their eye or piques their interest. Sometimes they follow a sequence and move on to the next case, sometimes they quit and walk across the room. They know that they have the choice to move through an exhibit however they want.

   The same must be true for the computer environment. In a study of the *LIFEmap* interactive, which *did* require movement through a specific information sequence, the evaluator found that visitors got bored or turned off when they couldn't get out of the loop, often giving up in the middle (Inverness Research Associates, 1991). This is not to say that screens of information can't *relate* to one another, but expect and plan for visitors to browse, sample, quit, or start over if they want.

6 *There should be access to the beginning at all times.* This is another aspect of the free-choice issue: the learner should always have control over what is being learned. Visitors should be able to investigate material how *they* want to, not how *we* want them to. An overview or index screen can be extremely helpful both as an advance organiser or reference for visitors to help them direct their experience. It *will* be used. For example, in the *Otters and Oil* program, visitors referred to the index three times more often than to any other screen.

7 *Use the same principles of language as you would for any good interpretive museum label.* Among these are the following: screens should not contain more than 50 words: sentences should be short, clear, concise, and free of technical terms or jargon. Remember that legibility issues are especially important for the high-contrast computer screen. Use legible fonts, with no 'shadows', italics, or harsh contrast between text and ground.

8 *Visitors are seeking the experience of technology, not content.* Visitors are not really dying for more information. Their basic motivation is 'What can this thing do?' or 'What can I do with this thing?' Only if the program is really engaging will it be able to teach them something *as* they manipulate the technology.

9 *Remember the 10–12 year-old boys!* They will be a major portion of the audience regardless of content, so make sure there is something for them to do. For example, *Otters and Oil* was a program designed for 'interested' adults; but through summative evaluation, we learned that the majority of its audience were young children (Serrell and Raphling, 1992a).

   Even if most children's motivation comes from their desire to play video games, that's okay, and what's more, it can't be helped. What exhibit developers *can* do is recognise that children will be attracted to the machine itself and give them something to do when they get there. Boys and girls 10–12 years in age are verbal, have good attention spans, are beginning to engage in abstract thinking, and are stimulated by it. In fact, 10-year-olds can be a benchmark. If they can understand and be intrigued by the program, most visitors will.

10 *Make the program fun – and make sure to include sex, humour, or grossness.* This is not so difficult to do. In *Otters and Oil*, sex and humour were combined subtly in a screen about breeding, which included a spoof on a 'personals' ad. An animation sequence in the *Global Warming* software produced by the AMNH features graphic sound effects as a cow emits methane gas (from both ends of the digestive system)!

Working Within the Visitor Relationship

Imposing limits on computer interactive design can help to achieve a better fit with the visitor's experience. By working within the *visitor relationship* rather than with whatever is technically or financially possible, development teams can come up with creative, thoughtful solutions that should achieve the goals set for both the exhibit and the audience. Designing and spending money *for the visitor* means that the product will be more intellectually and financially responsible.

As we must always remind ourselves, the museum environment is variable; any learning that takes place is informal; and any use of exhibit elements is casual and often cursory. Visitors can be impressed by technology, but they are also intimidated or frustrated easily; they might desire more information, but will seldom spend the time and energy during their visit to get it; and while they might enjoy the fun of playing computer games, they can easily overlook any didactic message. Making objectives and rationales *receiver-based* – that is, basing planning objectives on what is known about how visitors behave and learn in museums will help to create an engaging, fun, informative computer interactive experience that visitors *can* and *will* use.

References

Diamond, J (1989). ' "Desert explorations": a videodisc exhibit designed for flexibility', *Curator* 32(3), p. 170.

Flagg, B (1990). *Implementation formative evaluation of 'Earth Over Time'* Res. Rep. No. 90–004, Bellport, NY, Multimedia Research, pp. 24–26.

Flagg, B (1991). 'What research says . . . 16: visitors in front of the small screen', *ASTC Newsletter*, Nov/Dec, p. 9.

Hilke, D D (1988). 'The impact of interactive computer software on visitors' experiences: a case study', *ILVS Review* 1(1), p. 41.

Inverness Research Associates, (1991). *An initial study of the LIFEmap exhibit*, unpublished study, New York, NY, American Museum of Natural History, p. 2.

Miles, R (1991). 'The impact of research on the approach to the visiting public at the Natural History Museum, London' *International Journal of Science Education*, 13(5), p. 546.

Oker, J (1992). 'Reliability of interactive computer exhibits', *The Sourcebook 1992*, Washington, DC, American Association of Museums, p. 167.

Screven, C (1990). 'Computers in exhibit setting' in S Bitgood, A Benefield and D Patterson (eds), *Visitor Studies Theory, Research & Practice*, Volume 3, Jacksonville, Alabama, The Center for Social Design.

Serrell & Associates, (1992). *Nature Walk evaluation*, unpublished report, Chicago, IL, p. 11.

Serrell, B and Raphling, B (1992a). *Summative evaluation of the underwater viewing gallery at Shedd Aquarium's Oceanarium*, unpublished report, Chicago, IL, p. 10.

Serrell, B and Raphling, B (1992b). *Tool or Toy: an interactive computer program evaluation*, unpublished report, Chicago, IL, p. 9.

Worts, D (1990). 'The computer as catalyst: experiences at the Art Gallery of Ontario.' *ILVS Review* 1(2), p. 100.

25 A Picture of Visitors for Exhibition Developers

Sandra Bicknell and Peter Mann

This article appeared in *Visitor Studies Conference 5*, Science Museum, London, 1993, pp. 88–98.

Introduction

This paper is intended to provide the beginnings of a blueprint to help exhibition developers, in whatever role they may hold to understand how visitors use exhibitions and exhibits. The picture which is painted is still a little fuzzy but some of the detail is clear.

The Original Idea

The Science Museum in London, UK, is committed to the enhancement of public understanding of science and to improving the accessibility of the museum to its visitors. One of the ways we believe we can help achieve these aims is through the development of an idea one of us had when acting as project manager of a major re-display. For this task, it was felt desirable for the project team to have an agreed-upon 'model of visitor behaviour', even if the model was wrong. There were two reasons for doing this. First, to encourage consistency within the team by providing a shared view which would help avoid endless documents about undefined assumptions regarding our potential visitors. Second, should we wish to actually test such a model, it would provide a mutual starting point.

The model aimed to incorporate four main points:

- How visitors approach galleries as a whole. For example, do they want to envisage the gallery as a whole, or do they prefer a maze?

- How visitors approach the exhibits within a gallery. Do they read everything in sequence, or do they browse at random, only stopping to look at something that catches their eye?

- The quantity of information visitors require. Do visitors read anything at all, or will they read 400 words if it interests them?

- How the project team should view the visitors. Should they be seen as passive recipients of the information which is provided, or as active participants in the process of acquiring the information?

A literature search resulted in the construction of a model which suggested the following:

- Visitors do indeed appreciate a comprehensible structure to the exhibition as a whole, even if they don't follow it. They like to be able to orientate themselves within the exhibition.

- Few, if any, visitors will have the time, concentration, determination, or interest to look at everything in the exhibition, let alone read everything.

- Visitors browse through an exhibition looking for cues to make them stop.

- Most people spend only a short time at most of the exhibits they come across, and pass by having seen little to tempt them to stop. This is not a pejorative statement, nor is it assuming visitors are not taking anything in or not enjoying the experience.

- Perhaps most importantly, most people spend a much longer period looking at a small number of exhibits – the ones they actually stop at. It is at this point that the museum has the chance to put its ideas across to the visitor.

These suggestions had consequences for exhibition layout:

- There should be an understandable logic to the arrangement of the exhibits, so that visitors can know where they are and can identify where they want to go next.

- Where there are groups of exhibits, the physical and conceptual boundaries of each group should be clear, as should the relationship between the groups.

- Within a group the links between exhibits should be clear. Each exhibit should have a considered physical and textual structure so that each exhibit can be 'read' in the same way without having to learn a technique for each exhibit.

- Each exhibit and each group should have a bold title to be read from approximately 5 metres. The title should allow people to sum up the exhibit as they pass by, and decide whether they want to stop and spend their time there. Alternatively, the title should be intriguing or interrogating if its intention is specifically to draw people to it. These are the cues which are provided to allow them to decide whether they want to stop.

- Each exhibit and each group should have a piece of introductory text which briefly says why the exhibit or group is there and what the main theme is.

- Each object label should have the same structure so that they can all be 'read' in the same way. These labels should be comprised of a title to be read from approximately 3 metres, an introductory paragraph to say why the object has been included, and the remainder of the text to include other necessary information.

The model also had consequences for evaluation of the particular exhibition which was being created. Literature on the use of formative evaluation to improve attracting power and holding power seemed to be of little practical use and was felt to have the potential to be simplistic and misleading. Such indices did not address what would happen when such an exhibit is placed in a gallery of exhibits developed in a similar way. Would they simply be in competition with each other? Consequently it was decided to focus only on the attracting power and holding power of certain key exhibits where the intention was to attract and hold all visitors. This focus would be directed primarily toward the siting of key exhibits, and on formative evaluation to improve their attracting and holding viewers relative to all the others in the exhibition.

In the main it was believed that the project team should concentrate on the use of formative evaluation to improve the comprehensibility of an exhibit so that:

- as visitors passed by they could decide, on the basis of the cues they were given, whether or not they wished to stop or not;

- once they decided to stop, the concepts, information, and relationships between the objects presented should be capable of being understood by the target audience;

- once they stopped they would be provided with the amount and level of information appropriate to the target audience;
- the target audience for a particular exhibit would include those visitors who stop to look at that exhibit. This is not meant to imply that such visitors are a subgroup of visitors. On the contrary the model assumes that all visitors will stop at one exhibit or another. Rather it means that the text for a particular exhibit could be targeted at those who stop at it and are in, for example, the top 10 per cent of time-spenders at that exhibit. This is perhaps a rather unusual idea and will be developed later.

Our criterion of success was taken from the work of Steven Griggs who recommends that 'an exhibit communicates its message if a visitor, on seeing the display, can comprehend the information without any misunderstanding or misconception about its conceptions and intention' (Griggs, 1984, p. 416). It is then up to the visitor to decide whether he or she wants to learn or to forget the information with which they have been presented.

Unfortunately, since the project was not continued, the model was not developed further. However, a new project has provided an opportunity to resurrect the original model of visitor behaviour. This resurrection has involved updating the model to accommodate the evidence of internal evaluation work, more general visitor research, and the growing body of visitor studies literature.

Developing the Idea

The original model provided something practical and tangible that can be adapted for other project teams within the Science Museum. The four main areas addressed by the model were:

- how visitors will approach the gallery as a whole;
- how visitors approach the exhibits within the gallery;
- the quantity of information they require;
- the type of behavioural response (how visitors should be viewed) . . .

Exhibits Within the Gallery

In the original model it was felt appropriate to use John Falk's analogy of museum visitors being like people who are out window shopping – when something catches their eye they stop and look, and may eventually take away a purchase, i.e. take away ideas and information. Thus most people will spend a significant amount of time at a small number of exhibits at which they have decided to stop. It is this circumstance which makes possible the exchange of ideas and information by looking, listening, reading and discussing with party members (Falk, 1982). The work of Paulette McManus points out that 'a visitor reads up to 20 words in 5 seconds as he or she walks towards an exhibit, without an observer being aware that reading is taking place' (McManus, 1987, p. 265). Visitors appear not to be reading but in fact they are scanning objects and text, looking for cues to help them to decide if they wish to stop and invest their time.

One of the ways to portray where visitors stop and invest their time is to translate the results from behavioural mapping into contour maps [contour maps show by graded shaded areas the percentage of visitors which stop in any one area]. The inference here is that few, if any, of the visitors look at everything in an exhibition. To misquote Abraham Lincoln:

> you can encourage some of the people to read/look all of the time, you can encourage all of the people to read/look some of the time, but you can't encourage all of the people to read/look all of the time.

Steven Bitgood has said: 'It is my opinion that at least 50 per cent of the visitors should read a label' (Bitgood, 1987, p. 3). However, this can be unrealistic within the Science Museum. For example, the Land Transport Gallery has 126 cases, 122 free-standing objects and 1,158 object labels. Even if the labels were only 50 words long, visitors would have to spend some four hours just reading the words (assuming a reading time of 250 words per minute). There are 20 further, equivalent gallery spaces in the Science Museum – some three and a half days' worth of continuous reading . . .

[Research] serves to confirm the suggestion of the original model that few, if any, visitors will have the time, concentration, determination, or interest to look in depth at much of an exhibition. In general, visitors browse through an exhibition looking for cues to encourage them to stop and invest their limited time. Most people spend only a short time at most of the exhibits they come across.

Quantity of Information

Initially no published data were found to support the belief that visitors could be spending a considerable time looking at objects and reading labels they are interested in, since no researchers seemed to have observed or questioned visitors to ascertain the times they spent at those exhibits to which they devoted most of their time. It was therefore a hypothesis waiting to be tested.

This paper proposes an exponential model for visitors' investment of time in a label. The model encompasses the sort of label in widespread use in the Science Museum: title, summary paragraph and a paragraph of secondary information. In other words there are three levels of information. It is suggested that each label has three populations of visitors which correspond to these levels: title-readers, title-and-summary-readers and whole-label-readers. There are of course other populations, perhaps the largest of all being non-readers. There are also those who perversely read only the beginning and the end! . . .

Each label should be seen as a unique event, and the individuals that constitute its population of readers will vary from label to label. In other words, it cannot be assumed that the whole-label-readers will be the same people for each label.

This introduces a paradox; the model described here suggests the possibility of providing a substantial text for the small percentage who have accepted the cues to stop and invest their time in that exhibit, yet this substantial text may be the very cue that causes the majority of visitors not to invest any of their time in that exhibit. This is not an invitation to write a small book and call it a label. The evidence for numerous visitor studies is quite clear: increasing the number of words decreases the number of readers.

It is apparent that our model raises important issues which will need to be addressed by further research. However, it also provides a hypothesis which in principle is capable of being tested immediately.

Type of Behavioural Response

A major issue, and one that is all too easy to miss, is that attracting power and holding power imply that there is some unique characteristic which an object (or label) should possess in order to attract and hold all visitors. In reality, exhibit developers should consider the characteristics of the visitor, and not the objects. It is another manifestation of 'beauty lies in the eyes of the beholder'.

The fourth point of the model was initially phrased as 'the type of behavioural response'. This has been adapted to fit an area that, so far, has not been addressed. Looking at the Science Museum's visitors as a whole can be highly misleading and inappropriate. It works against the provision of an accurate picture because it obscures the fact that visitors are not a homogenous group. It is therefore proposed that the following categories can be used to describe the Science Museum's visitors:

- The 'buffs' – the experts who know the location of every rivet on the Spitfire. They are often male, usually adult, often solitary visitors, usually with a professional or leisure interest in the topic of a gallery. They invest large amounts of their time in very specific parts of a gallery.

- 'It's for the children' – usually with children of ages 4–14, who implicitly or explicitly are a 'learning unit'. There may be two groups here: the focused learners and explorers and the 'we should do this for the children, but let's get it over and done with as quickly as possible'.

- 'I'm museuming' – often couples, often tourists, often older. Culture-vultures who know the international museum code, they tend to systematically work their way through the museum.

- School visits – in the UK these group visits are usually related to the national curriculum and range in age from 5–17.

Each of these groups is different, with different expectations, different reasons for visiting and, in general, different needs. What must be done next is to incorporate the needs of these groups into our model – or to ignore them if the targeting of the exhibition does not include a particular group.

Conclusions

It is believed that this paper presents the beginnings of a synthesis that can be of use to other exhibition developers. The model is an evolving one. There is a need to incorporate new findings, including the work of other visitor studies, and to test the validity of the above suggestions, as well.

The purpose of this paper is quite simply to help the authors to be more effective in the development of new interpretive projects. Our intent is to provide ourselves and our colleagues with a feel for the visitors who come to the Science Museum, come into the galleries, take part in programmes, attend lectures and so on. We want to provide a more tangible image than that ill-defined, nebulous term 'the general visitor'. We will continue to update this model and refine our understanding of our visitors. This paper is merely a beginning.

References

Bitgood, S C (1987). *Knowing when exhibit labels work: a standardized guide for evaluating and improving labels*, Technical Report 87–90, Jacksonville, Alabama, Center for Social Design.

Falk, J H (1982). 'The use of time as a measure of visitor behavior and exhibit effectiveness', *Journal of Museum Education Roundtable Reports* 7(4), pp. 10–13.

Griggs, S A (1984). 'Evaluating exhibitions', in J Thompson and D Prince (eds) *The manual of curatorship*, London, Butterworths.

McManus, P M (1987). 'It's the company you keep – the social determination of learning-related behaviour in a science museum', *International Journal of Museum Management and Curatorship* 6, pp. 263–270.

26 Comfortable Viewing Zones

Anonymous

Extracted from *The arts and 504: a 504 handbook for accessible arts programming*, National Endowment for the Arts, Washington, DC, n.d., pp. 61, 63.

Signs and Labels

For both standing and seated people, there is a comfortable viewing zone of 19 in. [48.3 cm] within which text can be displayed if printed in large type. This comfortable viewing zone is between 48 in. [1.2 m] and 67 in. [1.7 m] above the floor. 54 in. [1.4 m] to centre is a good height for mounting signs and labels on the wall.

Letters ⅝ in. [1.6 cm] high can be read comfortably by sighted people at a distance of more than 6 ft [1.8 m].

Smaller type sizes customarily used in exhibition displays can be read at a distance of 4 ft [1.2 m] if printed in maximum contrast. The visual zone reduces to 8⅓ in. [21 cm] when displayed 52 in. [1.3 m] and 60 in. [1.5 m] from the floor.

Display Cases

Display cases should allow short or seated people to see the contents or the labels.

If the sides of the case are transparent, the bottom of the case may be mounted as high as 36 in. [0.9 m] above the floor, but never any higher. Cases with transparent sides are usually wall-mounted or free-standing on a solid base.

Floor-mounted cases often have solid sides and can only be viewed from the top. These cases should be no higher than 36 in. [0.9 m] to the top of the case so short and seated people can see down into the case. It is more important that the top of the case does not exceed 36 in. [0.9 m] than that wheelchair clearance be provided underneath. However, all display cases must have enough clear floor space beside them for people in wheelchairs to pull up close to the display.

Labels should never be flat on the bottom of cases. Labels can be mounted vertically on the back wall or outside the case; two labels at different heights may be needed if the case is very large. For low, glass top cases, one label may be mounted flat on the top for standing people who are viewing the contents from above, and one label may be mounted on the vertical surface of the display.

27 Visitor Orientation and Circulation: Some General Principles

Stephen Bitgood

This article appeared in *Visitor Behavior* 8(3), 1992, pp. 15–16.

. . . General principles will be divided into three major areas: conceptual orientation, visitor circulation, and wayfinding. While the principles which follow are not meant to be exhaustive, research and experience suggest they include many of the important considerations from the visitor perspective.

Principles of Conceptual Orientation

1 Visitors tend to have a more satisfying experience and acquire more knowledge when they are given information about where to go, what to expect, how long it might take to visit, where to find rest rooms, etc. (e.g. Shettel-Neuber and O'Reilly 1981; Bitgood and Benefield, 1989).
2 Advance organisers that give pre-knowledge about the theme and content of the exhibit before entering the exhibit area are preferred by visitors and will usually facilitate understanding of the messages. However, these must be carefully designed and placed if they are to be effective (e.g. Griggs, 1983; Screven, 1986).
3 The only sure way to determine if visitors are adequately conceptually oriented is to obtain systematic input from a visitor study.

Principles of Visitor Circulation

Explicit cues: Some stimuli that influence visitor circulation patterns are explicit. The following principles relate to such cues:

1 People tend to approach landmarks, moving objects or animals, sound, and large objects. Thus, such factors can be used to attract visitors in the direction you wish to lead them; or they may function to distract visitors and lead them in directions you do not wish them to go.
2 Visitors tend to turn in the direction of the closest visible exhibit, all other factors being equal . . .
3 Spatial arrangements involving exhibit islands create pockets of low attention (apparently because the traffic flow does not place each object within the visitor's line-of-sight or because of no systematic way to see all of the exhibit objects in the space). (Shettel, 1976; Miles et al., 1982; Bitgood et al., 1991.)
4 People tend to approach an area containing other people, unless it is too congested in which case a crowd may have a repelling effect.
5 People tend to approach and exit a room when they encounter an open doorway even if they have not viewed all of the exhibits or objects in the room. (See Melton, 1935.)

6 Exhibits that are on the periphery of exhibition areas are less likely to be viewed than those in the centre or along the main path (e.g. Bitgood and Richardson, 1987).

Implicit cues: Circulation patterns are also influenced by more subtle cues:

7 People tend to remain on the same type of floor surface (carpet, wood) unless other forces draw them to another surface.
8 People tend to prefer the security of a main pathway and are reluctant to circulate off this pathway to areas on the periphery of the environment.

Internal cues: There are several internal cues that seem to influence circulation behaviour:

9 There is a tendency for people to continue walking in a straight line unless some force pulls them in another direction or stops them (the principle of inertia).
10 In the absence of explicit or implicit cues or inertia, visitors (when entering a room) tend to turn right (Melton, 1935). This is referred to as the 'right-turn bias.'
11 Objects/displays located along the shortest route between the entrance and exit receive the greatest amount of viewing (e.g. Melton, 1935).
12 If visitors are looking for some specific objects or areas, goal seeking behaviour may overpower any of the other factors described above.

Principles of Wayfinding

Placement of information: The following may apply:

1 Wayfinding information should be placed where it is needed – at critical choice points.
2 Wayfinding information should be placed so that it is not in competition with other stimuli.
3 Wayfinding information should be salient or easily noticed.

Simplified patterns: That are congruent with the way people form cognitive maps include:

4 Environments should be designed with a minimum number of choice points.
5 The easiest circulation patterns for people to form a cognitive map are simple geometric forms such as circle, square, or cloverleaf. Intersections with angles other than 90° make it more difficult to form a cognitive map. Therefore, pathways that form right angles should be preferred.

You-are-here maps: Following Levine's (1982) principles will make fixed maps more useful:

6 'Up' on the map should be associated with 'forward' in the environment; 'right' on the map should be 'right' in the environment, etc.
7 A 'you-are-here' mark should be provided on the map to let people know where they are.

8 Landmarks that are visible from the position of the map should be marked on the map so that the viewer can see where he/she is in relation to environmental features.

Hand-held maps: Hand-carried maps are preferred by visitors (e.g. Bitgood and Richardson, 1987) and are most effective if they consider the following:

9 Features on the map should be simplified as much as possible. Too much detail causes confusion.
10 The map should include easily identified landmarks in the environment.
11 As with other visitor aides, hand-held maps should be evaluated with actual visitors.

Other Principles

1 Provide redundant wayfinding cues. Some visitors prefer to ask for directions, some prefer to get it on their own. Having redundant cues will increase the chance that visitors will notice cues and give him or her a choice. Recurring cues also give a feeling of security to the visitor.
2 Give people choices (information desk, maps, direction signs, etc.).
3 The use of symbols (such as animal silhouettes) to indicate directions can be confusing if used without words and if the symbols are not easily recognised (Serrell and Jennings, 1985).

References

Bitgood, S and Benefield, A (1989). *Evaluation of visitor orientation at the Space and Rocket Center*, unpublished report, Jacksonville, Alabama, Center for Social Design.

Bitgood, S, Hines, J, Hamberger, W and Ford, W (1991). 'Visitor circulation through a changing exhibits gallery', in A Benefield, S Bitgood, and H Shettel, (eds) *Visitor Studies: Theory, Research, and Practice* 4, Jacksonville, Alabama, Center for Social Design, pp. 103–114.

Bitgood, S and Richardson, K (1987). 'Wayfinding at the Birmingham Zoo', *Visitor Behavior* 1(4), p. 9.

Griggs, S (1983). 'Orienting visitors within a thematic display', *International Journal of Museum Management and Curatorship* 2, pp. 119–134.

Levine, M (1982). 'You-are-here maps: psychological considerations', *Environment and Behavior* 14(2), pp. 221–237.

Melton, A (1935). *Problems of installation in museums of art*, New Series No.14, Washington, DC, American Association of Museums.

Miles, R, Alt, M, Gosling, D, Lewis, B and Tout, A (1982). *The design of educational exhibits*, London, Allen & Unwin.

Screven, C (1986). 'Exhibitions and information centers: some principles and approaches', *Curator* 29(2), pp. 109-137.

Serrell, B and Jennings, H (1985). 'We are here' in *1985 Proceedings of the AAZPA*, Columbus, Ohio, American Association of Zoological Parks and Aquariums.

Shettel, H (1976). *An evaluation of visitor response to 'Man in His Environment'* , Technical Report No. 90-10. Jacksonville, Alabama, Center for Social Design.

Shettel-Neuber, J and O'Reilly, J (1981). *Now where?: A study of visitor orientation and circulation at the Arizona-Sonora Desert Museum*. Technical Report No. 87-25, Jacksonville, Alabama, Center for Social Design.

Section Six   Exhibition Case Studies

Introduction

Section Six of this book contains six case studies. These have been selected as examples of exhibitions that have either used a variety of strategies to involve visitors in the production of the exhibition or tackle issues relevant to specific target audiences. Many of the case studies, such as the first one at the Laing Art Gallery in Newcastle, by John Millard, have built on and reacted to earlier visitor research in the museum. Consultation with appropriate experts is also described by Millard. Integrating specific sections of both the community and the intended audience into the planning and production process is discussed by Hemming and Carnegie.

Most of the case studies involved careful identification of the primary intended audience for the exhibition, and generally this was specifically targeted; for example at an age-group (children aged 3–8 years at the National Maritime Museum in London, or 6–13 years in Barbados), or a community group (the Chinese community in London). This does not exclude other groups, but enables detailed attention to be paid to the needs of the target group. Experience has shown that this is rarely a problem to other visiting groups.

Some of the museums in the case studies experimented with new approaches to interpretation. The Maryland Historical Society in Baltimore encouraged an artist to make radical additions to objects in display cases; having the audience select the artefacts and write the labels for the exhibition at Paisley Museum in Scotland meant that different kinds of paintings were shown, and very different labels were written.

Examples of exhibitions have been chosen because they relate to the more general points made by the writers Section Five. However, responsive models of exhibition production are still very rare in Britain.

28 Case Study: Catering for Varied Audiences

John Millard
This article 'Art history for all the family' appeared in
Museums Journal 92(2), 1992, pp. 32–33.

Art on Tyneside, recently opened at the Laing Art Gallery in Newcastle upon Tyne, brings together the Laing's collection of silver, glass, ceramics, paintings and costume to tell the story of art on Tyneside over some 300 years. The novelty of this art display is the use of ideas from other museum disciplines and even from Jorvik or Wigan Pier: it is the first art display to use scenic recreations, interactives, sounds, smells and models, not to mention a talking tug-boat.

To some, such techniques are inappropriate for high culture. One arts pundit was thrown into a fury when he visited with his family. He felt that the display debased the art. However, his children approved, and, if the gallery's comments book is any guide, visitors welcome the friendly approach of the display. 'Transformation! Glorious transformation!' wrote one.

The Laing has an imposing portico and marble halls, which were meant to create a hallowed atmosphere for art when it opened in 1904. This sort of intimidating architecture is familiar enough, but it now suggests to many that art and art galleries are 'not for the likes of us'. The Laing, as Newcastle's city art gallery, cannot afford to project such an exclusive image. Newcastle suffers from problems of inner city deprivation and unemployment, and saw riots last summer. The gallery runs the risk of being seen as marginal, or even unsustainable in a city with scant resources to deal with serious social and economic problems.

The area of the Laing now occupied by *Art on Tyneside* used to contain a shanty town of new and old cases which had been gradually installed over a 15-year period, giving rise to displays that were disjointed and lacked focus. There were separate sections for costume, glass, watercolours and so on. Art galleries often separate categories of objects in this way and, as any contemporary crafts person can tell you, there is a hierarchy of materials, with painting at its apex. Such displays may be useful to students or collectors, but they are not for a general audience. The new display shows that the range of media in the Laing's collection can be brought together in a coherent display in which they have equal status.

Research on a series of exhibitions at the Laing suggested that regional art was a good candidate for this multimedia approach. Newcastle was a flourishing centre for silver and glass production before the fine arts had even a foothold in the area. The wood-engraver Thomas Bewick, a major figure on Tyneside, emerged from an eighteenth-century craft workshop specialising in a variety of media; and Victorian woodcarving, glass and pottery were at least as exciting as the painting of the time.

A chronological narrative was constructed with a series of settings, which show works of art in a historical context and give an impression of changes that took place in the cultural climate. A significant proportion of the display is devoted to the present, with video and exhibition areas showing art and architecture in the local environment, and encouraging visitors to take part in art in the region.

The key target audiences selected for the display were 8–12 year olds and people with disabilities. Exhibitions at the Laing targeted at children had been successful, and a series of *Freedom to Touch* exhibitions had been pioneered by education officer Gwen Carr for people with special needs.

Contact with Equal Arts (the arts and disability agency for the Northern region) and teachers' advisers in Newcastle was essential to unlock these target audiences.

Equal Arts put together a team of consultants with experience of a range of disabilities, and they were shown the initial design. This included a model of the display, which proved to be an invaluable aid to the consultants, one of whom had difficulty reading plans and none of whom were museum specialists. They produced a report with a list of recommendations. Many could be carried out at no cost, but more costly aspects included, for example: non-reflective glass to help visitors with impaired vision; an induction loop in the video area for hearing-impaired visitors; and raised floor-track for blind and partially-sighted visitors. Eventually grants and sponsorship were found to finance all of the disability consultants' recommendations.

As the display team worked on catering for the target audience of 8–12 year olds, outside designers Redman Design Associates contributed crucial experience of using interactives and other non-verbal forms of interpretation from museum disciplines other than art. The education officer was asked to take a lead on producing a copy for the panels, and a small team worked on their wording and on cartoons to complement the storyline for younger visitors. Tensions arose among staff, particularly over the graphic panels for each area. Some curators worried about over-simplification, but encouragement came from an unexpected quarter. The text of the graphic panels was translated for leaflets in Gujarati, Urdu and Cantonese, the main languages apart from English used in Newcastle, and the translators were enthusiastic about the clarity of the story it told. The story of *Art on Tyneside* is told in about 1,500 words on around a dozen panels and the text was checked by local school advisers.

The key target audiences have responded well to the display and are visiting in increasing numbers. The focus of the display on younger children and people with disabilities has also signalled to a greater audience that the Laing is serious about access. As a visitor wrote in the Laing's comment book: '*Art on Tyneside* was brilliant and it was a very good idea to make it easier for blind and disabled people. It's good for children too.'

The attendants' uniforms were changed for the opening of the display, from the traditional navy blazer and tie with a blue shirt, to polo shirts and sweatshirts with a logo. Many visitors noticed and commented on the changes:

'A breath of fresh air compared to the usual image of art galleries.'

'About 300 per cent better than it used to be.'

'What a transformation from a year ago.'

'About time! I feel as though you've just reopened the Laing's doors – very enjoyable.'

During its first few months *Art on Tyneside* attracted about 70 per cent more visits than the same period in the previous year. It cost just over £300,000 including £75,000 from the Wolfson Fund. Only time will tell whether this will be followed with the further investment needed to develop the gallery. Early indications are that visitors, politicians, business-people and even many art enthusiasts recognise and welcome *Art on Tyneside*'s attempts to appeal to people who would not normally think of going to an art gallery.

29 Case Study: Designing a Gallery for Children

Wendy Donawa

Extracted from 'From digs to dolls: the pedagogical design of the Barbados Museum's Children's Gallery', *Journal of the Barbados Museum and Historical Society* 41, 1993, pp. 59–73.

Background

. . . The educational design of *Yesterday's Children*, the permanent exhibit of the Children's Gallery, opened in May 1992, was as consciously factored into the design process as the artefact selection or the construction materials. *Yesterday's Children* interprets the social history of Barbados for children. It is not intended merely to dilute the existing adult exhibits. Yet there must be links in both adult and juvenile exhibits that relate to and enrich one another. The exhibition was shaped, therefore, by the following criteria:

- *Yesterday's Children* to be an informal learning environment interpreting the social history of Barbados for 6–13 year olds.

- Exhibits to be physically, psychologically and intellectually accessible to this age group, as well as appealing to older, younger, mixed and special needs visitors.

- Exhibits to offer a variety of learning experiences that foster the skills of critical observation, inferential thinking and visual literacy.

- Exhibits to incorporate instructional modes that are participatory and interactive, and that encourage discovery learning . . .

The Design of the Gallery

Interpreting Social History for Children

The storyline, or thematic content of *Yesterday's Children* was an initial concern. In museums, as in academia, interpretation is a matter of ongoing debate and evolution. What message should the new exhibit send?

During the period of the slave trade, close to 400,000 Africans arrived in Barbados to serve England's appetite for sugar and its enormous profits. Much of Barbados' history proceeds from this irreducible fact, and there is no way of making it palatable. The turmoil and anguish of Caribbean history have made its interpretation a heavy responsibility. For the Barbados Museum's existing history exhibits, this responsibility has made the selection of artefacts and hammering out of text matters of seemingly endless deliberation; it has made scholarly objectivity at times frustratingly elusive.

Interpreting history for children brings added difficulties. The storyline (though not the underlying research) must be simplified and focused for young people. But it must not be edited into either simplistic sensationalism or safe picturesque blandness: neither the Scylla of Rambo nor the Charybdis of Disneyland.

It was decided to keep the social history child-centred, stressing the personal, the intimate and the domestic. In particular, the hands-on exhibits and the dioramas of family life were designed to encourage the kind of empathy that takes history off the dry printed page. The overall storyline leads from the pre-Columbian Amerindian culture to the changes brought about by settlement, sugar and slavery, followed by a history of transportation in Barbados. From here the young visitor enters a 'village', exploring traditional crafts, toys, school, work, and the varied lifestyles of children.

Accessibility

The thematic storyline needed translating into physical and spacial terms that would assist learning. The gallery space was unpromising raw material, its long narrow shape (13 ft 6 in. [4.1 m] by 87 ft [26.5 m]) seemed to offer only an aisle-like space along which display cases would back the walls.

However, even this narrow space proved workable. Individual exhibits were conceptually as well as spatially linked to 'read' clockwise from the entrance, although each exhibit was also designed to stand on its own. Focus for each exhibit was created by its own separate, alcove-like environment, which cut off sightlines to other exhibits. From no point can the entire gallery, potentially confusing in its variety, be seen. Thus, wandering from exhibit to exhibit is something of an exploration and discovery for the child. The 'path' of the exhibition is at all points wide enough for a wheelchair to turn.

Accessible exhibits also need to take into account the size of the viewers and the dimensions that would enhance their comfort and interest. Displays were designed using a 50 in. [127 cm] eye-level, a comfortable viewing height for most 8–12 year olds, and for wheelchair users. Some components were lower, encouraging children to stoop or kneel and peek. This constant change and movement encourages children's natural animation and allows them to set their own pace. It also does away with the fidgeting and tension so prevalent in many more traditional school group activities.

Emotional and cognitive accessibility was a primary concern. The printed word, unfortunately, signals failure and humiliation for many school children. To ensure that text be an aid and not hindrance to comprehension, a subset of criteria was developed.

First, text was used minimally or not at all if the storyline could be interpreted through artefacts, graphics, charts or any other non-verbal medium. Barbados' racial demographics, for instance, are presented in graph form, while some otherwise dry historical information is shown in cartoon bubbles coming from the mouths of historical figures. Second, text is large (up to 140 points), with a clear, legible typeface (Helvetica or Univers), and visually interesting in its relation to the overall exhibit design. Third, all major text is written at an 8–10 year reading level (using the Fogg and Gunn formulae). Fourth, language has been kept clear, direct and emphatic. It is used to explain or describe, not to enumerate. There is a virtual absence of names, dates and information that could tempt adults to impose rote-memory tasks.

Formative evaluation proved useful. At several points during exhibit development, text samples were tried out on both primary school pupils and adolescents of varying academic backgrounds. Their responses helped weed out ambiguities and misconceptions.

Varied Learning Experiences

Unlike the formal school curriculum [in Barbados], where a pupil must succeed in Form I in order to enter Form II, the museum fosters informal, self-paced discovery learning. A 7 year old and a graduate student can each bring individual experience and perception to an exhibit; each can leave with valid and successful insights.

This varied public has challenging implications for exhibit design. Very young children have a short attention span, little sense of historical time and no capacity for theoretical thought. They need to move around as they touch, identify, compare and learn. Older primary school children develop a more literal and judgemental outlook; they want facts and drama. They are inveterate collectors themselves – comics, model planes, dolls, marbles – and can take an intelligent interest in the museum's collecting function. Children in secondary school are developing the capacity for abstract thought, and can understand historical cause and effect, and relate social contexts from past and present.

A clear conceptual structure is needed to translate these needs into exhibit design. For *Yesterday's Children*, this structure was organised on a hierarchy of intellectual 'nodes'. Those nodes on the first level contain the basic minimum of information needed to interpret each theme. Nodes on two, three or even four subsequent levels develop the theme with increasing depth and complexity; they can lead the visitor, at selected points, to quite sophisticated insights.

The structure works like this: *The Children at Work* diorama presents a thatched, mud-floored agricultural labourer's dwelling from the early years of the century. Inside, a small boy on a khus-khus-stuffed mattress watches his mother, flambeau in hand, as she prepares supper on a glowing coal pot. Infants and young juniors enjoy the drama of the flickering light, and respond to the situation of the little boy near supper and bedtime (so much that a net has been installed across the door to stop them crawling in and climbing on the bed). They can be led to ask and answer: What is the roof/floor/mattress made of? What is the mother cooking on? Why don't they have lights? What are the tools for? . . .

Traditional Crafts is a hands-on exhibit. Set in an old workshop, it honours the artisans who practised these disappearing skills. The youngest children sweep enthusiastically with the yard broom, rock the little rocking chair, whirl the potter's wheel round and round. Older juniors want to know how and why. They use traditional planes on the workbench, tighten the staveholder, check the labels to identify tools . . .

But it is not only on varied intellectual levels that exhibits must function. Implicit in the exhibits are values intended to inculcate attitudes. Cultural respect and self-respect lead us to cherish that which makes us, and to value that which makes others, distinctive. Many colonial and post-colonial conditions have militated against the development of these attitudes, against a desire to understand the past and to link it fruitfully to the present.

Archaeology and Amerindians seeks to redress the romanticised stereotypes of peaceful Arawaks and war-like Caribs by focusing on the ingenuity required to wrest a living from the natural environment. This exhibit should also make children aware that history exists outside the (often dry) printed work, and that archaeology is an intriguing 'detective' art and science . . .

Participation and Interaction: Discovery Learning

Different mental and physical activities stimulate different parts of the brain. When the young visitor always has a choice of behaviours to observe, to compare, to read (or not), to discuss, to stand, sit, move about, anxiety and tension are removed from the learning process, which proceeds at the child's own comfort and interest level. In *Yesterday's Children*, each of the thematic units employs a different instructional mode from those preceding and following it. This avoids monotony and ensures that as the child chooses a new environment, his or her brain shifts into another learning mode. The change is emphasised by the changing colour of each unit . . .

Some larger displays combine a variety of learning modes. *Archaeology and Amerindians*, for instance, has didactic panels with small exhibits and accompanying text with questions. The questions help children discover basic archaeological concepts. With this information, they can move on to the diorama of the archaeological dig in a more self-directed mode, to observe and interpret for themselves the clues that have been left.

In designing for participation there were, unfortunately, two attractive models the exhibits had to bypass. The first is the high-tech wave of the present and future. Some wonderful interactive museum-orientated software exists, and certainly has its place in any museum fortunate enough to have the funding. However, even if funding had been found to purchase hard and software, there are no staff or financial resources for its ongoing maintenance and replacement, so this route was not even seriously considered. The second model was harder to give up – the discovery room format so successfully developed and used by the Smithsonian Institution, the ROM and many others. Discovery rooms function entirely to encourage hands-on, participatory discovery learning, without any didactic intervention. A discovery room format was in fact recommended for the proposed Children's Gallery in the Barbados Museum's 1982 Development Plan.

But research showed that discovery rooms, well done, are amazingly cost and labour intensive . . .

A [high] training and staffing commitment . . . was out of the question, but many of the discovery rooms' guiding principles were used where feasible. In any case, advanced technology and uninhibited hands-on contact are not the only ways to encourage participation. Interaction is not physical, but also mental and emotional, and can be stimulated by the sensitive use of traditional resources and technologies . . .

Conclusion

The exhibition has not been open long enough to carry out formal evaluation studies, so firm conclusions cannot be drawn on the effectiveness of the education design. However, the general impression has been favourable and enthusiastic, and has been accompanied by an increase in the number of visiting family groups. The multilevel format works very comfortably here, with parents often reading and commenting or guiding the children's attention. Several special needs groups have also visited and participated.

A flexible and exploratory format has been developed to expand the existing schools programmes, at present servicing 5000 children annually. Children and most teachers have been responsive and very positive, though a few teachers have been uncomfortable with the informal format.

A bonus has been the number of visiting adults, and the valuable comments offered by elderly visitors who enjoy checking for accuracy of detail. In fact, adults appear to visit and interact enthusiastically with or without children, giving credibility to the old adage:

I hear and I forget.
I see and I remember.
I do and I understand.

30 Case Study: Developing Historical Thinking Through an Interactive Gallery

David Anderson

This article 'Learning history in museums' appeared in *International Journal of Museum Management and Curatorship* 8(4), 1989, pp. 357–368.

All museums, no matter what their subjects, are museums of history. They are, therefore, agents for the education of visitors about the nature of history as a form of knowledge, as well as being interpreters for the historical significance of their own particular collections.

As individuals, and as members of society, we all need to be capable of thinking historically if we are to address the issues that confront us in our daily lives. History asks us to put ourselves in the place of other human beings, and by doing so to define our own values and beliefs. It enables us to think critically and independently and to make informed judgements. It encourages us to question and to evaluate conflicting interpretations on the basis of evidence. It helps us to identify bias when dealing with controversial and politically sensitive issues. It is the destroyer of myths. In the words of a Department of Education and Science (United Kingdom) publication, 'Thinking historically is not only one manifestation of an open society, it is also one of the guarantors of its continued existence' (DES, 1985). However, in order to think historically, it is necessary to develop, at some level, an appreciation of the process of historical inquiry, together with certain important concepts and skills. These can provide a framework for discussion of the possible role of museums in developing historical awareness in visitors. They are summarised here (DES, 1985, pp. 2–3, 18–19; Schools Council, 1976, pp. 16–18, 38–42).

There must be an appreciation of the process by which history is produced. The subject matter of history – the human past – is infinite in extent and has no accepted body of facts or agreed laws. When choosing to study an aspect of the past each historian brings to the task his or her own values and theory of history, and the resulting interpretation is subjective and may conflict with other interpretations. On the other hand, the historical method – the procedure used by historians to evaluate and interpret evidence – is, or should be, objective. There is ultimately no way to arbitrate between conflicting theories of history, but any historical interpretation can be judged on the objectivity with which historical procedures have been carried out.

There must also be an understanding of certain basic historical concepts. First, an awareness of the nature of historical evidence and of the incompleteness and diversity of the human record; that the historical judgements and interpretations which are based on this evidence are as a result necessarily provisional; also that primary sources should not be studied in isolation but in association with secondary sources containing the interpretations of professional historians. Second, historical thinking requires an appreciation of similarity and difference, and of change and continuity over time; that change is not constant; and that it can be progressive in some respects and regressive in others. Third, an understanding of cause and motivation: that causes are the product of historical thinking and interpretation, and do not exist independently in the historical record; and that events in history have multiple related causes. Fourth, an understanding of the concept of empathy: that historians in attempting to reconstruct the past try to reconstruct not only the externals of life and behaviour but also the thoughts, feelings, motives, values and attitudes of people in the past; that empathising is not the same as sympathising with the people who are studied.

A variety of skills is also required for historical thinking to take place: skills in chronology, including the ability to sequence artefacts and events; the ability to use historical terms and ideas; the ability to ask historical questions; the use and analysis of evidence including the ability to compare sources, to recognise gaps or bias in evidence; skills of empathy, using historical imagination disciplined by evidence; the ability to make deductions, inferences and to form hypotheses, recognising the kind of evidence necessary to support or test these; the ability to make judgements, clearly distinguishing whether these are made with reference to the beliefs and values of the period under study or to the historian's own point of view; and, finally, skills of synthesis and communication of historical themes and ideas to make a credible narrative.

. . . There is no reason in principle to believe that [museums] could not devise appropriate strategies to promote the learning of the process of history by visitors of all ages (not only children) in an informal museum setting. In the United States at least two institutions – the National Museum of American History in Washington and the Indianapolis Children's Museum – have established interactive history centres. Neither project, it seems, was concerned primarily with testing the development of historical thinking (in the way outlined above), although both are of interest for their use of interactive techniques in historical galleries. The *Mysteries in History* gallery at Indianapolis Children's Museum encouraged visitors to be 'Pathfinders' by using five types of clue: archaeological, written, visual, spoken and personal history clues, all in a series of mini-environments depicting selected aspects of life in the state of Indiana. By engaging in the various activities, visitors would, it was hoped, understand the message of the exhibition, which was 'Clues in objects and the surrounding environment allow one to discover information about the past' (Tymitz-Wolf, 1986).

In 1988 the National Maritime Museum, with the generous financial support of the Friends of the Museum and in collaboration with staff and students of Goldsmiths College, University of London, established two temporary interactive history centres on an experimental basis, both associated with major exhibitions. The first was *Armada Discovery*, which opened in July 1988 and is now closed. The second is *Bounty Discovery*, which opened as part of the exhibition on the *Mutiny on the Bounty* in June 1989 . . . These two centres were consciously established to test some strategies for promoting historical learning, *Armada Discovery* in a small room separate from the rest of the exhibition, and *Bounty Discovery* in a larger gallery as an integral part of the exhibition.

Armada Discovery was designed for children aged 3–8 years and their parents. This age group was chosen partly because their needs are rarely addressed by museums, and particularly because the area would provide an alternative for families who did not want to bring small children on a tour of a blockbuster exhibition. The activities were housed in a room approximately 7 metres [23ft] wide by 12 metres [39ft] long. They introduced children to the Spanish Armada through the story of the *Gran Grifon*, the flagship of the hulks of the Armada, which was wrecked on Fair Isle, off the northern coast of Scotland, in September 1588. Children visiting the area were booked in for sessions lasting 30 to 40 minutes, run at frequent intervals throughout the day, every day of the week, over the 5 weeks of the school summer holidays. It was revisited by a total of 5,000 children and adults during this period.

Children entered to find the room in darkness except for a rocky corner in which they sat to hear the story of the ship, as told to them by one of the two interpreters. At the point in the story when the ship reached Fair Isle and the crew escaped from the ship onto the rocks, the lights went up to reveal a 10 metre-long [33ft] reconstruction of part of the upper decks of the *Gran Grifon*, standing out from a painted seascape. The children were invited to explore the ship, looking for evidence left behind by the captain, Juan Gomez de Medina, and his men. This they did with enthusiasm, in defiance of the convention that small children always prefer activities with simple abstract shapes and bright colours.

One part of the ship was a reconstruction of the captain's cabin, with a table, chair and bunk, panelled walls with carvings, jewellery, a wooden comb, a small animal cage, a chart, a pair of leather shoes, a leather jerkin and some sheets of paper with brief extracts from the captain's diary giving a vivid description of the shipwreck. All of these artefacts were replicas of material recovered from Armada wrecks or other contemporary ships. The captain's diary was a translation from his manuscript version held in Simancas. Most of the originals were on display in cases in the main exhibition. On the open deck outside the captain's cabin there was a ship's pump mechanism and, out of reach but not quite out of sight, the only rat that had not managed to escape from the sinking ship. A gun was assembled in the forepeak complete with gun carriage, cannon balls of varying sizes, shot gauges, sponge and linstock. The gun could be loaded, once the correct ball was identified by using the shot gauge, but not, of course, fired. Elsewhere in the forepeak lay a barrel of salt fish to smell, and one of dried ship's biscuit, discovered by touch through a small hand-hole, also rough wooden bowls and spoons and a leather water-bottle used by the crew. Like the artefacts in the captain's cabin these were all replicas.

Once the children had explored the ship, they could measure daily rations of biscuit and chick peas with scales, or explore and play with other modern materials and equipment. The purpose of these activities was to develop basic scientific and mathematical concepts directly related to the replica material on board the ship. After these informal explorations and activities, each session ended as it began with a storytelling session back on the rocks – sometimes, at the children's request, the story of the Spaniards' rescue from Fair Isle and the dangers they faced on the journey home, or, on other occasions, a story from a book or a re-telling of a folk tale about a shipwreck from one of the nearby Scottish islands.

The popularity of *Armada Discovery* encouraged the Museum to provide a larger activity gallery for children and adults as an integral part of the next temporary exhibition on the *Mutiny on the Bounty* . . . Visitors to [*Bounty Discovery*] . . . unlike those to *Armada Discovery*, are not required to join scheduled sessions but can move in and out of the gallery freely during opening hours, mingling with school groups or other visitors. On account of this and the very much larger number of people visiting the space (sometimes over 1,000 per day) the one or two interpreters present have less opportunity to initiate visitors into the space than they had in *Armada Discovery*, and carry a heavier security and supervisory responsibility, which necessarily inhibits their educational role as interpreters and storytellers . . .

Armada Discovery and *Bounty Discovery* were both set in historical environments in order to establish a coherent context for the activities and to emphasise the story that each embodied. The result in both cases was an imaginative recreation based on sources, with many of the scenes and objects depicted chosen to illustrate or extend themes in the activities. As such, the environments were, in a sense, works of art, but deliberately not works of fantasy (which was certainly a danger when reconstructing the Tahitian environment).

It is asking much of visitors, adults as well as children, to expect them to move from a conventional gallery into an activity gallery without becoming uncertain about their own roles. Experience has shown that it is important to establish a psychological frame for such spaces, which do not conform to the pattern of the rest of the Museum. This frame has several purposes: to explain to visitors the theme and purpose of the activities, and to indicate its geographical limits if necessary; to make clear the conventions the Museum has used in constructing the gallery (for example, the use of replicas in place of originals); to explain what visitors must not do, for reasons of safety or to protect the activities; and to explain what they can do to make the most of the opportunities it presents for learning and enjoyment. All of this must be done immediately visitors arrive at the space so that they are reassured and fully understand the new frame in which they operate.

The frame need not be communicated by words only. Visual conventions, such as the colour black, used in *Bounty Discovery* to indicate historical anachronisms such as non-environmental gallery walls and wall furniture, can be equally effective. In *Bounty Discovery*, signs and notices were introduced to help interpreters establish the conventions with visitors. Experimentation has shown, however, that while signs can establish negative rules (for example, with respect to running or climbing), the role of the interpreter is crucial at the beginning of the visit to the space in encouraging visitors to make the most of the potential of the space. On one occasion, in *Armada Discovery*, when interpreters were not present, families were observed as they entered and left the room freely, unsupported and undirected. Both learning and enjoyment suffered noticeably as a result, and the duration of the visit was significantly reduced. However, when the interpreters were in the space and introduced the sessions, children and adults readily appreciated the frame within which they participated. Children's play could not occur if they were not capable of some degree of meta-communication to establish rule structure. Children also show a remarkable ability to distinguish the boundaries between play and reality, and to move confidently and creatively between them (Bateson, 1985). It is not surprising, then, that they have little difficulty in understanding the complex and unfamiliar frame required for an activity gallery, provided its rules are communicated effectively.

The interpreters have all been, with one exception, student teachers at Goldsmiths' College. All interpreters had teaching experience. Several were early childhood specialists, which was a particular advantage in *Armada Discovery*. The pedagogic skills in that room produced a relaxed and informal space, but one that was also secure and closely structured. This minimised any control problems that might have arisen if inexperienced staff had been employed. No attempt has been made to put the interpreters into costume, thereby avoiding diversionary games with visitors who might try to trick them into acknowledging an event which had not, for their costumed persona in 1588 or 1789, yet taken place. As themselves, and as representatives of the Museum, they have been able to interpret the facility with more historical honesty, and arguably with greater diversity and sophistication than would have been possible if they had been in costume. Many visitors are inexperienced at interpreting the artefacts and look to the interpreters for guidance. There is a strong impression that the enthusiasm of visitors, and their perception of the value of the experience, is closely dependent on the presence of skilled interpreters. They have given life to the galleries.

One of the aims of both *Armada Discovery* and *Bounty Discovery* was to provide a space where adults and children could learn together, as it was realised that parents, like the interpreters, would play a crucial role in the success of the venture. Some artefacts, such as the captain's logs, and many of the themes within both galleries were deliberately set above the conceptual level of the children to reward adults and encourage them to participate. Before opening *Armada Discovery*, the Museum was concerned that parents might keep to one side of the room and leave their children to explore and play unaided. This fear was groundless. Most parents and grandparents, of both sexes, joined their children in investigating the ship with great enthusiasm, clearly from their own interest as well as from a desire to encourage their children. Once this was done, some parents then preferred to join their children at the play activities only at intervals, being quite content otherwise to talk to each other or read some of the books provided for both children and adults in one corner of the room. These non-participators were, however, a minority.

... The use of replicas deserves brief discussion ... The decision to use replica material in the two galleries was debated at some length. Artefacts were selected because of their symbolic value as well as their aesthetic qualities and function. Some were included to illustrate themes in the galleries or to suggest comparisons with other artefacts, thereby revealing contrasts between classes and cultures, and underlying social or moral values. In *Armada Discovery* few children or adults appeared to be under the illusion that the artefacts were originals, despite the high quality of most of the replicas. It was clearly quite impossible to have used contemporary artefacts in such a situation and no visitor was seen to reject them because they were not original. Their value in stimulating investigation and discussion was beyond question. Nevertheless, doubts remained, at least in the minds of the staff of the Education Section of the Museum about using replicas to teach visitors about evidence. An activity which addressed this issue directly, perhaps by inviting visitors to explore differences between originals and replicas, would in retrospect have been valuable.

How much historical learning took place? *Armada Discovery* and *Bounty Discovery* were both established (among other objectives) to experiment with selected strategies for promoting historical thinking, but neither gallery attempted to provide visitors with a comprehensive introduction to the historical process, and they did not make any reference to historical skills or concepts, or any other aspect of the learning of history, in notices or labels. This purpose was left unstated ...

Armada Discovery used, in combination, two approaches to the learning of history that seem to have been particularly suited to younger children – storytelling and the exploration of first-hand tangible evidence. The telling of the story of the *Gran Grifon* was an essential part of each session in *Armada Discovery*. It enabled the children to absorb necessary information and to involve themselves in the predicament of the crew of the doomed ship, before they went on board to find clues left behind by the captain and his men. The artefacts on the ship, some of which were familiar and some not, provided them with a rich resource and stimulated their curiosity. The skills of observation of evidence, of asking questions and of making deductions must all be learnt through practice, and not all children possessed them. Some children took the initiative and freely discussed artefacts and asked questions such as 'Why are the teeth of the comb so close together?' or 'What kind of animal would have lived in a cage as small as that?' Others needed the intervention of an adult before they looked for answers to such questions. Many of school age noticed the similarity between the wooden comb and the nit combs they had seen used at school, and deduced that sixteenth-century sailors, like twentieth-century children, must have suffered from head lice. Artefacts like the comb and the cage, which were familiar and yet posed problems that made human sense to the children, encouraged many of them to make comparisons between past and present, and suggest Donaldson (1984) is right when she argues that children are capable of logical thinking from an early age. Fewer children, however, compared the lives of the captain and crew of the *Gran Grifon*, perhaps because few of the articles in the two areas of the ship were directly comparable.

Some of the deductions offered by children (and adults) were incorrect. The most common mistake concerned the bunk in the captain's cabin which, like the rest of the furniture (and unlike all the other replica artefacts), had been constructed to a reduced scale to make it accessible for very young children. As a result, many visitors deduced that the captain must have been much smaller than the average today. (We happen to know from contemporary descriptions that the captain, Juan Gomez de Medina was, on the contrary, quite tall.) In this case the fault lay with the Museum, not with the children's reasoning, and was a salutary reminder of the need for consistency within the psychological frame . . .

Observations suggest that many visitors make spontaneous comparisons between the replica eighteenth-century artefacts, such as the sailors' square wooden platters, and those they use today. Some also make comparisons between food, beds and other aspects of the material culture of the two groups, and most seem to understand that they have traded with one another. Most questions and hypotheses are concerned with the concrete and familiar, such as food ('How were yams/breadfruit/ship's biscuits cooked?') and the life of the sailors on board ship ('Why was Bligh's cabin so small?'). Few visitors hypothesise about the likely consequences of contact and trade for either the Tahitians or the sailors. As in *Armada Discovery*, these examples suggest visitors can appreciate historical concepts and use historical skills. However many visitors also come with historical stereotypes well established in their minds. Most believe eighteenth-century English ships were almost like floating prisons, with half-starved sailors and brutal officers. In truth, life on board ship was certainly hard but, by comparison with many landsmen, sailors on ships of the period (including the *Bounty*) were well fed, and were disciplined according to naval regulations almost universally accepted by officers and men alike. *Bounty Discovery* does not correct the stereotype (except by listing and showing the substantial rations each man received), but it does stimulate discussion between visitors and interpreters on this issue . . .

In future, with further research and the development of a wider range of techniques, it may then be possible to create a history centre that more truly reflects the nature of the subject. This is an ambitious objective, but it is one that goes to the very heart of the educational purpose of museums.

References

Bateson, G (1985). 'A theory of play and fantasy' in J S Bruner, A Jolly and K Sylva (eds), *Play: its role in development and evolution*, Penguin, pp. 119–129.

Department of Education and Science (1985). *History in the primary and secondary years: an HMI view*, London, DES.

Donaldson, M (1984). *Children's minds*, London, Fontana, pp. 17–30.

Schools Council Project, 13–16 Project, (1976). *A new look at history*, Edinburgh, Schools Council History Project, pp. 16–18, 38–42.

Tymitz-Wolf, B (1986). *Mysteries in history: a case study of an evaluation process*, Bloomington, IN, Indiana University Press.

31 Case Study: Reflecting African American History

Susannah Cassedy
This article 'The museum mine field' appeared in *Museum News* 71(4), 1992, pp. 12–14.

At first glance, the exhibit case looks like any that you might see in a traditional history museum. 'Metalwork 1793-1880' announces the label – the sort of title that makes youthful museum-goers dissolve into yawns. Take a closer look, though, and what you see might send chills down your spine. Resting in the midst of these stately silver goblets and decanters is a pair of rusted iron hand-cuffs. The adjoining label reads 'Slave Shackles, Maker Unknown, Made in Baltimore, *c.* 1793–1864'.

The shock value of this display is only part of the emotional experience invited by *Mining the Museum: An Installation by Fred Wilson*, currently on view at the Maryland Historical Society in Baltimore. An unusual collaboration between a historical society and a modern art museum – in this case Baltimore's The Contemporary – the exhibit urges museum professionals and everyday visitors to investigate their perceptions of race, history, and the role [of] cultural institutions in shaping our views.

As professionals from both the historical society and the art museum describe it, *Mining the Museum* was an answer to a question they had been grappling with for several years: how can museums involve the traditionally neglected minority members of a community? For The Contemporary, incorporated only three years ago, this issue had been in the forefront from the start and had led to exhibits dealing with such issues as AIDS and inner city violence. But for the Maryland Historical Society, founded in 1844 and to this point a fairly traditional institution, the challenge was greater.

The historical society and the art museum initiated a dialogue last year after The Contemporary, which always works in temporary spaces, opened a Soviet photography exhibit in an old bus garage neighbouring the society's headquarters. Society director Charles Lyle met with The Contemporary's assistant director, Lisa Corrin, and the two commiserated over the future of museums in general and discussed the Maryland Historical Society's concern about reaching a more diverse audience. 'He said he didn't know how to make Chippendales relevant to kids in the projects', Corrin says.

It wasn't long before Corrin came up with an answer: bring in Fred Wilson, a New York-based African American artist whose recent work had dealt with museum exhibition and race. Following a formal agreement between the two institutions, the historical society gave Wilson almost total licence to go through their collections, extract what he needed, and develop an exhibit that would confront head-on ideas that previously hadn't made much progress outside the meeting room.

For months, Wilson 'mined' the historical society, digging through its attic and archives, often coming upon objects that had never made their way into an exhibit hall either because of space limitations or because they were considered inappropriate. These he combined with art works and artefacts that had been displayed many times before to create an installation that is alternately jarring, saddening, and entertaining.

At each section of the exhibit, the visitor must spend several minutes taking in all the components involved before the proverbial mental light bulb goes on. A row of cigar store wooden Indians stands with their backs towards the observer. Edge your way between the wooden statues to take a look at the photographs under their empty gaze, and you'll start to see what Wilson is getting at. People with names like Nina Robinson, Louise Robinson, and Margaret Proctor, dressed in unremarkable middle-class leisurewear are standing in front of a building. The label reads 'Courtesy of the Maryland Commission on Indian Affairs'. Look again, and you'll see the Native American facial features on these people with their stereotypically Anglo names.

The neighbouring display case filled with arrowheads identified only as a 'Collection of Numbers 76.1.25.3 – 76.1.67.11' is Wilson's comment on how museums and society deny the identity of its minority community.

Much of the installation investigates how cultural institutions and the objects they display ignore African Americans. One section of the exhibit examines the treatment of blacks in eighteenth- and nineteenth-century painting. Many of these works are portraits of American white gentry – or so they seem until a spotlight suddenly illuminates black slave children practically camouflaged in the darkness of the periphery. From one such portrait, a recorded voice emerges, ostensibly that of a slave child: 'Who combs my hair?' she asks. 'Who calms me when I'm afraid? Where do I come from? Where is my mother?'

In allowing Wilson to do as he pleased with their collection, the historical society undertook an unprecedented and risky endeavour. Jennifer Goldsborough, chief curator at the society, says that objects like the shackles had never been displayed before because they were 'very unsettling to the general populace', white and black alike. In the case of the Ku Klux Klan hood that Wilson displays lying in a baby carriage, the anonymous donor had requested it not be exhibited immediately. She equates giving Wilson a free rein to the biblical proverb about a 'prophet without honour' in one's own home who is granted liberties family members would never receive.

According to Corrin, what made the whole project work was co-operation between The Contemporary and the Maryland Historical Society. 'A whole process of collaboration took place, which included self-study by both institutions', she says. Community members, staff, and docents attended workshops to learn about what Wilson was doing. 'We got to the point where everyone wanted to be involved', she says.

At first, there was some resistance from the society's docents, many of whom are elderly white women who had never witnessed history and museum exhibition treated in this way. Yet the longer the exhibit was up and the more the docents worked with visitors, Goldsborough says, the more their views changed. Some requested to speak to Wilson personally so they could apologise for their initial reaction and tell him they now understood what he was doing. 'Some said they will never face a group of fifth-graders from the inner city again,' she says. 'He has reached many people on a personal, gut level'.

As for the visitors, the response has been similarly positive. 'Everyone seems to find it very powerful', Goldsborough says. A local high school for the arts used the exhibit as a vehicle for students to express their feelings about the Rodney King verdict and aftermath this spring in Los Angeles, and a university professor teaching a course on home and family life assigned a visit to the society as the focus of his final exam. The installation has been extended to

February 1993 to allow for more development of educational programmes and documentation.

32 Case Study: Working with Women's Groups

Elizabeth Carnegie

This article 'Women's pictures' appeared in *Scottish Museum News* 8(1), 1992, pp. 8–9.

Figure 32.1 'Self-portrait', Eve Thompson, living artist (*Paisley Museum*)

'She looks like one of these Hillhead, West End types – she never got over being a student . . . she's a vegetarian and she goes on these CND marches.' 'Cruel lips.' 'She seems to know her mind – we need her in our women's group, I think!!' (Comments on 'Self Portrait', Eve Thompson, a living artist, from Northend Women's Action Group.)

There is a tendency to self-consciousness which surrounds art, a fear of seeming foolish and ignorant or of admitting a sneaking liking for the fashionably despised. (I personally love Stubbs' pastoral scenes and have collected all the stamps.) *Women's Pictures*, an art exhibition at Paisley Museum and Art Galleries, set out to challenge these assumptions.

The aims of the *Women's Pictures* exhibition were two-fold: to show that the museum's pictures really belong to the ordinary people of the district and to give a special presence to a part of society which does not normally have very much say in museums or in art. Under the guidance of Fine Art Development Officer, Jane Kidd, local women's groups were given unrestricted access to the Museum's stores which are normally out of bounds to the members of the public. The women were at once both visitors and serving a curatorial function in that they were deciding what should be displayed and why. The groups – Ferguslie Women's Action Group, Ferguslie Single Parents' Group, Renfrew WEA Women's Branch and Paisley Northend Women's Action Group – chose 46 paintings representing women or girls for the exhibition which ran from 12 July to 31 August 1991.

The theme of women and girls was chosen so that the women would be able to relate to the subject matter. Each group spent a morning in the stores. Their comments as they chose the paintings were recorded to form the labels. Using the women's own words on the labels helped to demonstrate that everyone's comments and thoughts about a picture are important. As they were not art critics, they did not think to condemn a painting on grounds of quality though they did tend to look for naturalism. 'I like her left hand – I don't like the right hand, it's like one of these Sistine Chapel paintings, really posing, whereas the other one's dead natural.' (Well, we all know how difficult it is to paint hands, Michelangelo.)

This approach meant that many so-called 'duds' in the collection were brought to view and this raises an important point about the way the art world functions. In the main, the women saw the subject matter rather than the brush-work to be the key. This surely is the way art should be viewed.

Out of the 46 paintings finally chosen, only two were by woman artists. Therefore this exhibition could effectively be subtitled 'Women Looking at Men's Pictures of Women' and this was reflected in the women's comments.

> 'It's called "Asleep"?' 'No there's no way . . . lassies don't sleep like that.' 'Do you think it's a male fantasy on the artist's part?' 'Oh aye, he'd wish it was him she was thinking about.' 'It looks quite modern for 1930s, she looks quite young. But I think that's probably because she's nae claes on . . . I think it's a male fantasy.' (Comments on 'Asleep' (1935) by David P Ramsay (1888–1944).)

If the paintings had been chosen by men they would have been very different.

The women were quite literally choosing works to reflect their own lives and made natural comparisons between the women in the pictures and themselves. There was a tendency towards smaller works which would fit on the walls of their houses. Although the tone of the exhibition was celebratory, there was some social censure and a quite marked class distinction. They were moved by the poverty implicit in the face of the unnamed woman in 'The Paisley Shawl' (1915) by Fra Newbery (1855–1946).

> 'She looks as if she's had a hard life . . . Aye look at her face . . . but women then

Figure 32.2 'The Paisley Shawl', Fra Newbery (1855–1946) (*Paisley Museum*)

Figure 32.3 'Mrs Thomas Watt', James Wallace (1871–1937) (*Paisley Museum*)

did have hard lives. It's real. It shows in her face dinnit, no even her face, look at her hands. It looks as if she's been scrubbing – they'd nae washing machines – scrubbing board and . . . I think she represents every old person that's had a hard time.'

'Mrs Thomas Watt' (1918) by James Wallace (1871–1937) was compared with her. 'She's got a stern face, you feel as if she's got a lot of power in her. She looks like one that would walk by a' the poor weans . . . she looks as if she would go "hmph" and walk past them.' 'I think she really looks dead stern . . . see the one with the Paisley shawl – she would probably look like her and as young as her if she'd never had the life she'd had. She's probably about the same age as that old dear . . . she's been well fed, she's had all the stuff to make her complexion look alright.'

Figure 32.4 'Dawn', James Elder Christie (1847–1914) (*Paisley Museum*)

Poverty, wealth, vanity and leisure (or the lack of it) were recurring themes. 'Midnight' by Charles McCall (born 1907) was chosen to illustrate women's vanity from a possible range of works because she looked 'really vain'. Vanity was viewed as the product of having time and money to indulge yourself.

'She had money . . .' 'She looks very proud.' 'A proper lady, she would call herself.' 'She looks as if she's giving her hair a hundred brushes.' 'Well, it's a different image from the working woman.'

The women were constantly highlighting the fact that they had little time for leisure. 'The Apple' by James Elder Christie (1847–1914), showing mother and child, brought the response 'It's like a walk or . . . leisure time – you never see women doing that, they're dragging them out of Presto or that . . .'. Yet 'Dawn' (also by James Elder Christie) depicting a highly stylised, idealised view of womanhood rising naked and swirling from the water was chosen because 'she was the way we would like to see ourselves'. A series of weekend workshops was held to coincide with the exhibition whereby women were encouraged to produce two self-portraits doing exactly that. One was to show how we view ourselves, and the other, as others see us. The results were on display in the gallery.

Women's Pictures showed the potential for emotional involvement with art exhibitions and argued that it was possible to break down the barriers associated with art. The groups involved were given total control over the final product and everyone came to see it at least once. Although with projects of this kind there is a very real danger of exploiting or manipulating a response, it was sensitively handled. Jane Kidd's starting point was a very simple one. It does not matter why you like a picture – and you don't have to know a lot about it. If you like it, that's enough!

33 Case Study: Working with the Chinese Community

Steve Hemming

This article 'Chinese homes' appeared in *Journal of Education in Museums* 13, 1992, pp. 33–34.

The exhibition *Chinese Homes* ran in the spring of 1992 at the Geffrye Museum and was developed out of a community education initiative. The first contact the museum had with the Chinese community was when a group of Chinese elders visited the museum two and a half years ago. It was fairly obvious that they didn't get much opportunity to visit museums and that it was a very new experience for them. It was obvious too that they were really taken with their visit. It was also a new experience for the museum, which up until then had very little contact with this particular community. At this early stage there was no plan to have an exhibition looking at Chinese culture, the only objective was to increase access to the museum for this particular group.

During their visit many points of interest had emerged surrounding the cultural differences between life and home in the Far East, in China and also Vietnam, and life and homes here in Britain. To look at these further a small personal history project was established in which the elders could tell their stories: where they had come from, what their homes had been like, what they used to eat, did at school and so on, but also, very importantly, what they thought of England and adapting to life here and how they had managed to do this.

It was a very positive exercise and many of the stories used in the exhibition came from the project. It was also very good for the elders involved who talked to each other about their experiences, something many of them had not done before. Some of them even found out that they came from the same town or had other experiences that were common but hadn't come to light before. The project also started to build up a sense of trust between the museum and this group, which is vital for any kind of long-term community development.

At the end of the project it was apparent that there were many ways of relating the subject matter to the museum's theme of English interiors and that there was scope for developing some kind of exhibition.

This was discussed with members of the Chinese community to see what they thought of the idea and what themes they could suggest. Only one theme really interested them and that was Chinese New Year. They chose this because they felt it was most expressive of their culture and by far their most important festival. They also felt that it was an element of their culture that not many western or non-Chinese people knew about. Lion dances in Gerrard Street may be familiar, but not what goes on in the home, so it was something that they very much wanted to show.

It became the starting point for the exhibition. Other elements such as the influence of Chinese art and design on English interiors, and the arrival through trade of the first Chinese communities in Britain, came later. What was essential was that what was culturally important to Chinese people came first.

The Chinese community was involved from start to finish in the exhibition, from correcting the catalogue and panel texts to approving the poster image. The two Chinese rooms in the exhibition were set up by the Chinese elders from the community centre in Hackney. They chose the artefacts and arranged them.

The exhibition was very much a collaborative initiative between the Chinese community and the museum, and one from which both have gained. The Chinese community had, through its involvement, shown aspects of its culture that were not widely known amongst the ethnic majority and hopefully it has gained in stature from raising this awareness. The museum has found new ways of working with the community and interpreting a very Eurocentric display to show its wider roots which can be developed in further exhibitions.

Section Seven   Text

Introduction

There is a widely held belief that the majority of visitors rarely read much of the text on panels and labels in exhibitions. Paulette McManus' research demonstrates clearly that not only are many of the labels read, but that they set the agenda for discussion in the exhibition space. The first extract in this section is drawn from her research at the Natural History Museum, London, where she found that visitors talk back to interpretive panels, as though they are holding a conversation with the writer. The more conversational the style of writing, the more this is likely to happen. It is important then, in writing exhibition texts of all sorts, to visualise a couple, or a group of people, in a social situation, reading the words, sometimes to each other. The texts will only be incorporated into the mutual social interaction of visitors if it is easy for this to happen. If texts are, for whatever reason, too taxing, they will be ignored as people concentrate on their visit on their own terms.

Hirschi and Screven point out some of the many reasons why exhibition texts may be ignored. These include poor positioning, poor writing, and failure to anticipate accurately visitors' existing levels of knowledge of and attitudes to the subject. Their research showed how reading will be increased if labels are produced in a more effective way.

Coxall analyses two pieces of writing from two different exhibitions. Both concern the same subject, the artist Francis Bacon, but the approach to the information given and the style of writing used are very different. Through her analysis, Coxall shows how these texts will be accessible to people with different levels of knowledge about art and art history. It is up to the text writers to decide who they are writing for, and to work out, perhaps through audience research, what these people know about the topic, and write accordingly.

There are several ways of assessing exhibition texts through the use of standard tests. Carter describes two of these, the Fry test, which measures complexity of language, and the Cloze procedure, which helps measure understanding. Neither of these has been developed especially for museums, and both have their limits, but nonetheless, they can be useful in preliminary assessments. Coxall's second article discusses more complex ways of assessing the meaning of language which addresses social, cultural and ideological implications. She shows in her discussions of exhibition labels how biases and value judgements can creep into a piece of writing unnoticed by the writer. The article also reviews the tests described by Carter. Coxall's aim is to make text writers more aware of the way language structures work from a linguistic point of view, so that writers can raise their awareness and communicate more effectively. The Geffrye Museum has addressed some of these points in the re-assessment of the collections and displays made recently.

Finally in this section, we address the pragmatics of production. The excerpt from *Writing on the wall: a guide for presenting exhibition text* by Kentley and Negus discusses a labelling system which shows how the written information in an exhibition can be split between introductory panels, group captions and didactic panels and object captions.

Adults normally read at a rate of 250–300 words per minute. A point which is vital and made strongly by Hooper-Greenhill (*Museums and their visitors*, Routledge, 1994, p. 127) is that if this reading speed falls below 200 words per minute, comprehension is lost.

Two books that cover the production of exhibition texts are Serrell (1985) *Making exhibit labels: a step-by-step guide*, American Association for State and Local History, Nashville, Tennessee, and Dean, D (1994) *Museum exhibition: theory and practice*, Routledge. Both of these are useful practical guides.

34 Label Reading Behaviour

Paulette M McManus

Extracted from the article 'Oh yes, they do: how museum visitors read labels and interact with exhibit texts' in *Curator* 32(3), 1989, pp. 174–189.

'Look! Can you read? It says something.'
'Well what it says, it lived on the Isle of Wright.'

This fragment of a conversation between a 10 year old schoolgirl and her teacher was radio-recorded as they stood in front of an *Iguanadon* skeleton in the Natural History Museum. The visual observation made of them at the time indicated that they did not read or attend to the exhibit label beside the skeleton. Yet the recording shows that reading and the label's content were the subject of their exchange (McManus, 1985).

'People don't read labels' is a comment frequently voiced at gatherings of museum professionals, and the idea is almost a part of museum folklore (Borun and Miller, 1980). Some professionals even disparage the role of words in exhibit communications when they claim that the everyday ability of humans to negotiate shared meanings through the symbol system of language is a less comprehensible and a more abstract activity than communication through an unexplained 'non-verbal language of real things' (Schouten, 1987). This report indicates that such judgements have been made because it is difficult to assess accurately whether visitors are reading by use of visual observation methods. It also shows that most museum visitors read, depend upon, and use exhibit texts, and it describes the place of these texts in museum communications. The report is based on findings from a survey of communications with and between 1,571 individuals in 641 visitor groups at five exhibits in the Natural History Museum (McManus, 1987a).

Observed Behaviour

Visual observation of the reading behaviour of 583 visitor groups was made at the five exhibits. Singletons – 144 of the 583 – were considered as groups of one. Almost half of the groups (48.4 per cent) were observed as not having any member seen to read an exhibit text (Table 35.1).

Table 35.1 Reading behaviour observed at five sites

Behaviour	N	%
Not seen to read	282	48.4
Brief glances at text	228	39.1
Comprehensive attentive reading	73	12.5
Total	583	100.0

Recorded Conversations

Extremely significant statistical relationships were found between visually-observed reading behaviour and the use of interactive exhibits, duration of conversations, duration of visits, and group type (McManus, 1987b). For this reason, further investigation of the visitor as a communications processor was made by examining 167 transcripts of recorded conversations. The recordings were made at the time of observations at four of the sites (Lucas, McManus and Thomas, 1986).

Despite the high percentage of groups visually observed as not containing readers, the transcripts indicated that more than expected were, in fact, reading groups and that despite appearances people do read exhibit texts. In many groups, one member read segments of text aloud for his or her companions. This behaviour was noted in all-adult and child/adult groups and has also been reported in an American study (Hirschi and Screven, 1988). Some visitors closely paraphrased texts and used phrases from the texts in their utterances. All repetition of texts in conversations was dubbed 'text-echo'.

The Text-echo

When visitors echo text, they bring the writer's words to life in their conversations and thoughts about the exhibit – the writer is introduced as a partner in their discourse. The following examples illustrate the phenomenon. The first is from a family observed not to be reading; the second is from a family observed as attentive readers. Both conversations took place at the interactive *Sorting Game* exhibit. The following key is used to enable the readers to reconstruct the flavour of the conversations.

( )   untranscribable words due to recording problems
(.)   a micropause: e.g. for intake of breath, to think
(n.0) the duration of a pause in seconds: e.g. while thinking of or waiting for an answer
boldface type: words from exhibit text

In this conversation between a father and his young son, the text was read aloud in order to establish what to do.

Father: Different species? There's the human species (3) **press the button to clear the board (.) slide the discs up to make three groups (.) one group (.) in each disc do your groups contain the same kinds of living thing** ( ) (.) let's try this let's OK? This is (.) three groups OK that's a frog that's amphibian right?

In the second example, parents paraphrase and read text both to explain the game and to 'read' the meaning of the photograph beside the exhibit to their children. This text was on a panel to the left of the game and above a photograph of a person dipping a net into a pond.

How we recognise species. Sorting living things . . .
If you search a pond you will find many different living things. How would you sort these things out?

Mother: You start by (.) it says there (.) if you want and put a big (.) rod (.) you put a big net into a fishpond or swamp (.) and **how you would start to sort out the different**

Father: **the different things** which you would get out of your net

Text-echo and Visually-Observed Reading Behaviour

. . . When visitors process an exhibit communication as a group, one member may take on the reading task for them all. (It would be odd if everyone *did* read individually!) This practice gives more visitors access to texts than might appear to be the case from a cursory glance around the museum or even from a survey of visitor studies, which commonly focus on individuals without taking the social context of museum visits into account (McManus, 1987b, 1988). The majority of visitors obviously attend to exhibit texts. More than 8 out of 10 groups show direct evidence of having a member or members read exhibit texts, and 7 out of 10 groups voice the exhibition team's words so that the team is present by proxy in their conversations.

Visitor Interaction with Exhibit Texts

Visitors interpret texts in an interactive manner – just as they interpret each other's utterances; they approach the exhibit within a communicative framework that includes the exhibit team. This situation is examined below through illustrations from the conversation transcripts and then placed in a theoretical framework.

Someone is Talking

When visitors process labels, they feel that 'someone' is talking to them. This attitude is independent of reading-behaviour category. Fragments from conversations follow.

'What's the name of it? Does it say?'

'Andrew, look at this one here, this tells you all the animals that eat things in the house.'

'No! It says it's a mammal.'

'Right, Sal. It says what about you.'

'Eighteen seventy-eight. That's what it says here.'

'No! It says you can do the ones that move and the ones that don't move.'

'It didn't say so. Sort them into three groups?'

'There's a game! It says, look, have you read it?'

Visitors Talk Back

In some conversations, visitors respond verbally to the Museum 'someone' who is communicating with them. Here, reading from text is in bold type; the visitor's acknowledgement, reply, or query is capitalised; conversation addressed to companions is in ordinary type.

WHAT'S THAT? **Bread beetle.** Look at that.

Are you a primate? Yes, you are a primate. NO I'M NOT.

What about you? Are you a primate? YES! I'M A PRIMATE AS WELL.

Look! **Start with a clear board. Press the button below to do this.** I'VE GOT IT. It's just bringing the discs down to the bottom. THANK YOU, DOCTOR. **Slide the discs upwards to make three groups.**

When you have made your groups, do your groups contain the same class of living things? SSS? WHAT BOBS AND SNAILS AND ER.

Can you give your groups names? I DOUBT IT.

Visitors Keep to the Text Topic

Conversations were about the topics established by label writers. Instances where visitors shifted from the exhibit topic to introduce an unrelated topic were exceedingly rare in the transcripts. One cannot introduce a topic without being a party to the discourse, and the leading role visitors assigned to the exhibit team indicates the high status given to the team within their communicative framework. Brown and Yule (1983, pp. 68-83) discuss the topic introduction and control aspects of conversational interactions.

To summarise: visitors react as if the team is talking to them through the exhibits, and they vocalise their interaction with the team. Teams exert considerable topic control over conversations through label texts, and groups are very likely to voice segments of the team's messages, activating the words as parts of conversations. Thus consideration of the relationship between visitor and exhibit team as close and conversational is justified.

Theoretical Framework for the Conversational Relationship

. . . The intent to avoid specialised language registers and to design texts for general readers is bound to lead to a close conversational relationship between author and reader, especially when the reader is inclined to form such a relationship anyway. This tendency is further developed in the museum setting; here, text language – like oral language – can be interpreted and its meaning verified within a relevant context. For everyday spoken language, verification is simple: look around. Using Cambourne's (1981) example, the meaning of 'I'm waiting on the table' can be verified by checking to see if the speaker is dressed as a waiter or waiting for a table to appear on a computer printout. In the museum, the visitor has the same verification option – to interpret the meaning of texts by referring to the rest of the display.

The closer the conversational relationship between the museum writer and visitor, the more likely is successful communication. Visitors are likely to work toward such a relationship. The difficulty appears to be persuading text writers – who work without seeing their readers face to face – to try to communicate within such a framework and assumed relationship. Rand (1985) describes progress toward this goal and points out that once such an approach is accepted, we still have to explore how to 'keep up our end of the conversation'.

What Visitors Require from Exhibit Texts

Satisfaction of the Visitor's Interrogative Framework

Visitors employ an interrogative framework to prescribe the boundaries of a label communication. This first step, 'outlining behaviour', is then followed by predictive processing of the text message. A woman's questions as she approached the *Sorting Game* exemplify the interrogative framework. (The communicative meanings are shown in italics.)

'What's this?' (*What is the discourse topic?*)
'What's going on?' (*Where lies the action? What is being said about the discourse topic?*)

The visitor is asking for clear establishment of reference to topic and an easily perceivable, cohesive explanation that can be followed, engaged with, and evaluated. The questions reflect fundamental concerns apparent in all visitors' conversations – they are eager to find out, and indeed need to know, broadly, what is being said before they can engage mentally with the communication . . .

Adherence to Topic

The two fundamental rules for dealing with what is being said in a label text – establish reference clearly and explain simply – may appear obvious, but they are often not followed. Failure to attend to them affects the path of communications fundamentally. The chief tendency is an unconscious shifting of the area of reference. Texts about diet shift into discussions about dentition; texts about the impact of new technologies slide into descriptions of the equipment's mechanical functioning; and texts about an artefact's aesthetic or design qualities move on to its creator's life history . . .

Establishing Orientation to Topic: The Conversational Frame

. . . Analysis revealed only three instances (0.2 per cent of all discourse acts) of visitors relating exhibit content to past personal experience with phrases such as 'I remember those kinds of moths as well'. The comments were all made at Site 1, *Household Pests* exhibit – of all the exhibits investigated, the one most related to everyday life. This relationship appears to have induced the behaviour. Apparently visitors do not commonly seek to anchor their understandings in their mundane everyday experiences. The conventional wisdom is that communicators should anchor new material in the everyday experiences of those they are communicating with. Since visitors do not do this very closely themselves, maybe we should concentrate on the importance of clear introductory explanations as orientation to new topics – backed up, perhaps, by localisation of the themes discussed.

Readability and Conciseness of Texts

Visitors are not likely to attend to the entire text of a label for two reasons.

1 Visitors in groups want to enjoy and maintain their social relationships so they are likely to get what they can take rapidly from the exhibit message and feed it quickly into their conversations. The text writer will not be permitted to dominate the language situation in the way that a teacher does in the classroom.
2 Fluent reading for comprehension does not require attention to an entire text. Visitors will scan and sample segments of it to confirm that the meanings they have already predicted are there. The surer visitors are of the topic and content of a text and the more familiar with the syntax used, the less they need to read.

If the topic is not established or the style is unfamiliar (too formal or academic) or jargon is used or there is any other kind of 'noise' in the presentation, visitors will have to slow down and attend more to the text if they want to find out what it is about. If the reading rate drops below 200 words a minute, their comprehension will be severely hampered (Cambourne, 1981, p. 93). Exhibits are often rated as 'successful' if visitors are visually observed to spend a lot of time at them. If this time is taken up in painstaking reading that blocks both understanding and visitor conversations, 'holding power' estimates can be very misleading signs of success.

An Appropriate Conversational Tone

The way things are said affects the path of communications. Helpful clues about the way things *should* be said can be discovered by looking at the way visitors talk to each other. The way things are said also covers the way things are *not* said, so we are also interested in the ways visitors do not talk to each other. The analysis of the discourse acts in 41 conversations (McManus, 1989) showed that closed questions are not favoured in naturally-occurring small-group discussions where people obviously prefer to keep their talk open and exploratory. Closed questions had a very low frequency (2.7 percent of 1,382 discourse acts); replies to them had an even lower frequency (1.9 percent) . . .

An Appropriate Social Tone

The discourse-act analysis also showed that directives such as 'Look at this!' had a low frequency (2.2 percent), indicating that authoritarian forms of interaction are not acceptable to small groups. They were very likely to be challenged with a response asking for the reason for the directive rather than obeyed unquestioningly . . .

References

Borun, M and Miller, M (1980). 'To label or not to label?' *Museum News* 58(3), pp. 64–67.

Brown, G and Yule, C (1983). *Discourse analysis*, Cambridge, Cambridge University Press.

Cambourne, B (1981). 'Oral and written relationships: a reading perspective', in Kroll, B M and Vann, R J (eds), *Exploring speaking-writing relationships: connections and contrasts*, Urbana, IL, National Council of Teachers of English.

Hirschi, K D and Screven, C G (1988). 'Effects of questions on visitor reading behavior', *ILVS Review* 1(1), pp. 50–61.

Lucas, A M, McManus, P M and Thomas, G (1986). 'Investigating learning from informal sources', *European Journal of Science Education* 8(4), pp. 341–352.

McManus, P M (1985). 'Worksheet-induced behaviour in the British Museum (Natural History)', *Journal of Biological Education* 19(3), pp. 237–242.

McManus, P M (1987a). 'Communications with and between visitors to a Science Museum', unpublished PhD thesis, University of London.

McManus, P M (1987b). 'It's the company you keep . . . the social determination of learning-related behaviour in a science museum', *International Journal of Museum Management and Curatorship* 6, pp. 263–270.

McManus, P M (1988). 'Good companions . . . more on the social determination of learning-related behaviour in a science museum', *International Journal of Museum Management and Curatorship* 7, pp. 37–44.

McManus, P M (1989). 'What people say and how they think in a science museum' in Miles, R S and Uzzell, D (eds), *Heritage interpretation, Vol. 2, The visitor experience*, London, Belhaven Press, pp. 156–165.

Rand, J (1985). 'Fish stories that hook readers: interpretive graphics at the Monterey Bay Aquarium', *American Association of Zoological Parks and Aquariums Annual Proceedings*, pp. 404–413

Schouten, F (1987). 'Psychology and exhibit design: a note' *International Journal of Museum Management and Curatorship* 6, pp. 259–262.

35 Effects of Questions on Visitor Reading Behaviour

Kent D Hirschi and Chandler Screven

Extracted from an article in *ILVS Review* 1(1), 1988, pp. 50–61.

Label reading is an important aspect of whatever educational benefit visitors receive from attending a museum. If, therefore, such visitors fail to read a particular exhibit label, they are not experiencing the full impact of the exhibit. In fact, in many cases, it is only through the information contained in the labels that visitors can have any true understanding of the exhibits they are observing. Researchers have found that throughout an entire museum visit, visitors will read about 18 per cent of the labels with which they come into contact (Borun and Miller, 1980).

The reasons why visitors ignore many labels are numerous. Foremost among these are problems with the labels themselves. Label location, physical make-up, length, wording, and appropriateness all play a part in the 'do or don't I read' decision (Screven, 1986). Label development which supports label reading also supports the educational impact of the exhibit. Some methods for creating more readable labels include the use of questions, the use of interactive flip labels (which ask leading multiple-choice questions with feedback to choices), information mapping, and information layering. The use of questions posted at exhibits is the subject of this study.

Questions can be embedded as part of new labels and integrated with text (e.g. the flip label). In addition, apart from their integration in label systems, provocative questions can simply and economically be added to existing labels as a motivational tool. If such a step is taken, with the question being the only variable changed in the exhibit, visitors may be more motivated to read an adjacent label and thereby obtain useful interpretive information from the exhibit. This study undertook just such a step. The goal was to determine if a question can motivate visitors to read existing, unaltered exhibit labels.

Other than the motivational problems associated with labels, a further challenge concerning the visitors themselves presented itself. The visitors selected for study were family groups. Family group reading tends to be brief in character (McManus, 1987). Improvement in the time devoted by family groups may increase the value of their exhibit experience. If questions increase reading behaviour among these visitor groups, they could prove to be an economical method for facilitating learning from exhibits.

Method

Subjects

The study focused on family groups defined as groups of at least two individuals and including at least one adult and one child (estimated to be below 18). Only groups which appeared to be made up of related individuals, i.e. parents or grandparents with children, were observed. School groups and club groups were eliminated from the study. Groups were chosen at random and were overheard to speak English before they reached the first exhibit area under study. Previous label reading was not considered as a criterion for selection. A total of 40 groups contributed to the final results. The average size of the tested groups was 4.3 people. In all, 172 individuals were tracked.

Exhibits and Materials

Five exhibits were selected in the Milwaukee Public Museum. The exhibits were located in one section of the museum and were chosen for their variety and attractiveness. They included two dioramas, a glassed-in display, and two spatial areas accessible to visitors . . .

Discussion

Under the NQ condition [exhibit areas without question panels attached], there was a very poor level of label reading present. The levels (only 1.32 seconds per exhibit) were even lower than might be expected compared with other studies on groups containing children (Borun and Miller, 1980; McManus, 1987). If groups and/or individuals do not read labels, they are unlikely to get the full educational benefits of many exhibits that depend on label information to enhance interpretation and to correct misinterpretations of exhibit content. In the case of the target exhibits used in this study, label reading was critical for the non-expert museum visitor. Families in the NQ group were overheard referring to walruses as seals, Japanese exhibits as Chinese, etc. The exhibit labels would have at least corrected such misconceptions if they had not been ignored.

So why was label reading at the unaltered exhibits so low? When one looks at the particular labels used in the five exhibits, many reasons of the sort listed by Screven (1986) are found:

- The labels are poorly located. The polar bear diorama's label is located on the wall past the diorama. The Japanese house and garden label is located behind the visitors as they view the exhibit.

- Most of the labels are not located next to or on the objects they describe.

- In some cases the labels are difficult to read due to poor lighting.

- The labels are long and crowded, ranging from 100 to 336 words.

- The labels, especially in the Samurai exhibit include technical terminology.

- Most labels do not directly relate to the objects in the exhibit.

The purpose of this study was to examine the possibility that simply adding questions linked to existing exhibit labels would encourage the reading of these labels. Results were statistically significant between the 1 per cent and 5 per cent level in three of seven cases and between the 5 per cent and 10 per cent (borderline) level for the remaining four labels, all of which were in the expected direction. Given the small N [number] of 20 family groups and considerable within-group variability, the sizes of these increases are surprising and, with larger Ns, would probably be higher.

The large increase in mean reading time for Q groups [groups using exhibit areas with question panels attached], over reading time for NQ groups seems to support the hypothesis that adding label-directing questions to existing exhibits can attract visitors and increase reading times to varying degrees. Questions that directed attention to labels appeared to increase the likelihood that the labels would be read. The only label unread throughout the study was the one deliberately left without a question.

However, the effect of the questions on reading differed among exhibits. These differences reflected differences in interest in the questions themselves as well as label formats, length, vocabulary, crowding, location, and other characteristics listed earlier. The *least* read question-enhanced label was poorly located and overly technical. The *most* read question-enhanced label had two questions referring to it, was less crowded, and was the only label with a two-part format. Furthermore, the content of the eight labels tended to be abstract and overly technical, ignored direct references to the exhibit, and lacked integrating concepts that related to display objects or to visitor experience. Most label content was superficial, factual, and textbook-orientated. This meant that under the Q condition, questions had to be directed to trivial or technical topics. It should not be surprising, therefore, that labels were seldom read completely (which required 352 seconds for all labels), but instead were either read to the sentence containing the answer (which required 113 seconds) or skimmed until the answer sentence was located. Given the deficiencies in label content and format, label reading probably would be further improved with improvements in label content, vocabulary, and format.

If one believes that the more time visitors spend at individual exhibits, the more educational benefits they receive, the correlations of total time spent at exhibits and time spent reading are encouraging . . . Once the questions were in place, the visitors tended to spend more non-reading time in the exhibit areas, as well as more time reading; i.e. increased exhibit time is not accounted for by increased reading time alone.

Another observation was a phenomenon one might call the 'designated reader'. In most of the family groups in the Q condition, only one person would read the label while the others observed the exhibit. This finding was similar to that of McManus (1987) where parents did the reading in family group situations. The designated reader, almost always an adult, would read through the label until he or she reached the answer to the question. At this point, it was common for the reader to read aloud the sentence or sentences which answered the question. If this answer was not forthcoming, other members of the group would ask the reader for the answer. This method allowed each group to benefit from the information in labels without each individual having to invest reading time and effort.

The results of this study suggest that, while questions increased reading, they also encouraged visitors to focus on a narrow range of label information related to the specific question. There is no direct evidence to determine if in this process visitors learned anything else from the labels. General observation and group conversations suggested that the families paid little attention to other label information. If so, the potential educational value of the improved reading activity generated by the questions was very limited. When labels provide a basis for understanding exhibit content, questions alone probably are not enough. Labels must provide meaningful and relevant information rather than trivial, technical, and abstract information.

If labels focus on concepts, rules, or generalisations that connect to existing visitor knowledge and experience and are exemplified by exhibit content, then the present study provides some evidence that questions can encourage reading and useful educational outcomes. If rules are also applied to labels concerning their readability, spacing, organisation, lighting, location, and direct links to exhibits, then reading effort will be reduced and the likelihood that labels will be read will be further increased.

While there are many questions raised by the investigation of the factors that encourage label reading on the one hand and understanding label (and exhibit) content on the other, the results of the present study support the role questions can play in this process. The addition of questions which refer to existing labels significantly increased visitor attention to the previously ignored labels. One can only wonder what levels label usage could reach with the proper integration of questions and improved labels.

References

Borun, M and Miller, M (1980). 'To label or not to label?', *Museum News*, 58(4), pp. 64–67.

McManus, P M (1987). 'It's the company you keep . . . the social determination of learning-related behaviour in a science museum', *International Journal of Museum Management and Curatorship* 6, pp. 263–270.

Screven, C G (1986). 'Exhibitions and information centres: some principles and approaches', *Curator* 29(2), pp. 109–137.

36 Readability Tests

James Carter

This article 'How *old* is this text?' appeared in *Environmental Interpretation*, February 1993, pp. 10–11.

Do your readers really understand you? Readability – the measure of how easy a text is to read and comprehend – depends on many factors. The reader's motivation is a major one. For example, an 8 year old will work hard to understand a complex or poorly translated computer game instruction book, but wouldn't attempt a financial report of the same complexity. Typeface and layout also affect how fluently you can read text. But the complexity of the language is a factor too, and reading age tests can be a useful check on whether your writing is likely to be understandable or not (Gilliland 1972).

Reading age tests have been developed in the education sector, where it's obviously important to match the abilities of children who are learning to read with the style and complexity of the books their teacher gives them.

There are many different methods, some of which rely on involved mathematical formulae. The Fry test is easy to do and relatively quick.

1 Select at random three passages of 100 words. If your text isn't this long (and often it shouldn't be!) use just one passage.
2 Count the total number of sentences in each passage and take the average of these numbers.
3 Count the total number of syllables in each passage and again take the average. It's easiest to do this if you go through the text writing the number of syllables in pencil above each word.
4 Plot these two averages on the graph (Figure 36.1).

If you want a benchmark to aim for, try writing for a reading age of 12 for panels in an exhibition for the general public. If that seems low, just think about your readers. You can't rely on them being highly motivated: most interpretation is about provoking interest, not satisfying a desire for detailed knowledge. They're likely to be standing up, perhaps outdoors, with distractions including wandering children, low-flying jets and ice-cream stalls. It's not that you're writing for people who have a reading age of 12, just that you need to make your text as easy to read as possible.

It's important to recognise that reading age is not related to physical age or mental age. The method above is simply a measure of how complex the word and sentence structure is, and therefore of how easy it is to read. A recent test on a copy of *The Sun* (popular tabloid daily paper) and on a feature in the *Independent on Sunday* magazine (colour supplement to serious broadsheet) gave reading ages of 11/12 and 15/16 respectively. *The Sun* isn't written for people who are stupid, just for those who prefer something easy to read (whatever else you may think about it!).

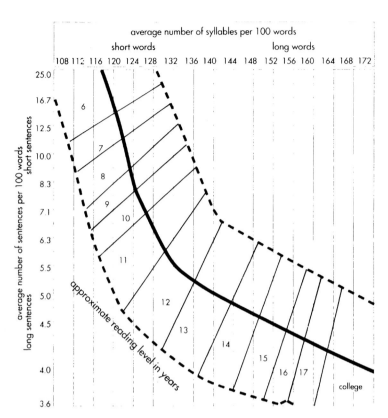

Figure 36.1 The Fry test for reading age. This graph has been redrawn from the *Journal of Reading*, April 1968: the dotted lines indicate the boundary of the region of maximum reliability of the test

Mind the Gap

The Fry test only measures complexity of language. It's quick and easy, but it can't tell you whether your intended audience actually understand what you've written. Cloze procedure gives an indication of how your readers interact with your text, and how much they really understand it (Rye 1982).

The name comes from *closure*, a concept in Gestalt theory which suggests that we will mentally complete any incomplete pattern. For example, a diagram of a circle with gaps in it will still be perceived as a circle. As applied to readability and comprehension tests, the procedure has many possibilities and variants, but the version which follows is appropriate for interpretation intended for adults.

1 Select a passage from your text and prepare a version of it in which every fifth word is replaced by an equal-sized blank. The passage should start at the beginning of a paragraph. A length of about 250 words is recommended, but not essential. Leave the first and last sentences intact, and ensure that you don't remove proper nouns unless they have already occurred.
2 Show this prepared text to a representative sample of your audience, and ask them to guess the missing words. Allow as much time as necessary. The equal-size blanks prevent guesses on the basis of word length.

3   Calculate the score as a percentage. Count an answer as correct only if it is exactly the same word as in the original, though you can allow minor misspellings. Numbering the gaps interferes with the readers' flow, and makes it more difficult for them, so find some other method of checking the completed passages.
4   Scores below 40 show that your readers may have real difficulty with your text. The following table shows the relationship between Cloze scores and comprehension.

Comprehension level	Frustration	Instructional	Independent
Cloze score	0–39%	40–59%	60–100%

Table 36.1 Correlation between comprehension and Cloze score. (From Rye [1982])

These comprehension levels indicate how well readers might do in a multiple-choice questionnaire based on a full version of the text.

'Independent' is equivalent to a score of 90 per cent or better – complete understanding. 'Instructional' means a score of between 75 per cent and 89 per cent – in a classroom setting, enough for full understanding with some assistance. This should be acceptable for most interpretation: you're not aiming to equip visitors for an exam. Visitors are often in groups, and their companions will fill in gaps in any individual's understanding. They can also pick up clues from other text, or from objects on display.

'Frustration' level, however, means that the text is too difficult even with some help. It's time to go back to the drafting stage!

Pass the Salt

There are many other tests for readability, some of them available as computer programs. But perhaps they all need to be taken with a healthy pinch of salt.

They can mask real difficulties – a poorly-written short sentence can be less comprehensible than a well-written long one. They can draw attention to apparent faults which would cause no difficulty, especially if they involve comparing text with lists of 'familiar' words. One computer package, for example, rejects 'Brighton', 'Royal' and 'dragons' in a children's guide to the Royal Pavilion in Brighton. It's worth remembering that some 'familiar words' lists were compiled in the United States in the 1930s!

Above all, tests like these are no substitute for writing with feeling and power. Writing solely to match a particular reading age could easily be dull: the trick is to write simply, but with an enthusiasm that makes your writing worth reading.

References

Gilliland, J (1972). *Readability*, London, Hodder and Stoughton.

Rye, J (1982). *Cloze procedure and the teaching of reading*, Oxford, Heinemann Educational.

37 Writing for Different Audiences

Helen Coxall

This article 'Museum text: accessibility and relevance' appeared in *Journal for Education in Museums* 12, 1991, pp. 9–10.

> All too often present-day museums are regarded by their curators as providing lessons for a homogenous but perhaps a non-existent public, a public that exists mainly in the curator's mind: a group of well-bred, culture-hungry, beauty-loving, logically minded people, with plenty of time to spare, inexhaustible physical stamina and, above all, at least an arts degree. (Hodge and D'Souza, 1979)

Since Hodge and D'Souza wrote this, communicating with the museum visitor in general, and providing audience-appropriate museum text in particular, has become a topical issue that is of scant interest to some and considered boring or even irrelevant by others. What is it about language that causes so many of us to blanch at the thought of trying to write museum labels that are more 'user-friendly'? And what is it about the term 'user-friendly' that causes the reaction that such practices are not appropriate in the museum setting? Perhaps memories of tedious grammar lessons at school forbid investigation into appropriate linguistic style, while connotation with 'user-friendly' technology creates instinctive resistance. It is, after all, easier to ignore the unfamiliar than to address it. But is it really so difficult to write text that is appropriate to a museum's audience?

Several articles and books have been written on how to write museum text. Those that advocate reliance on readability formulae to test the appropriateness of language are in danger of causing us to produce texts that are readable but boring. It is even possible to produce a so-called readable text that is also incomprehensible. This is because readability formulae, in the main, measure language style in the form of sentence and word length, not comprehension. It is true that long, complex sentences and polysyllabic lexicon (long words) can cause difficulty to readers. However, so can unknown, unidentified, technical terms (often derived from Latin) and untranslated foreign words. These are just two examples of the many things that readability formulae cannot identify.

There are, however, other more empirical ways of assessing the appropriateness of texts to particular audiences, that attend to different ways of saying. The easiest way to demonstrate this is with examples. Here are two main information panels taken from two different galleries. Both discuss the same artist, although not the same exhibition. The first appears to be aimed at a specialist audience, whereas the second is clearly aimed at a non-specialist audience.

Francis Bacon

Bacon is widely considered to be the most important British painter of his generation. Greatly struck in the 1930s by a painting by Picasso in which the human figure is radically, even savagely reconstructed, he has stated that he hopes to 'unlock the valves of feeling and therefore return the onlooker to life more violently'. Drawing inspiration, too, from the power of observation and of emotion in masters of past centuries, his own work is deeply traditional in its ambition and grandeur. But Bacon's images are of specifically modern man. Despite (and in a sense, because of) their distortion of form, they are essentially realist.

Bacon's imagination is triggered by photographs, ranging from film stills to medical text book illustrations. At the same time he wants his paintings to spring as directly as possible from the unconscious. For this reason, he makes extensive use of chance in the painting process. The result is pictures in which intensity of emotion is fused with the insistent material presence of paint itself. On the tension between abstraction and realism in his work Bacon has commented that 'the paint is the image and the image is the paint'.

As there were no accompanying leaflets available, this information panel is densely packed with information. It has to be concluded that it is for a specialist audience for the following reasons. First, it is written in a formal, impersonal, academic register. It takes the form of an art history critique rather than a personal address to the museum visitor. The language is technical, employing such complex noun phrases as: *the insistent material presence of paint, intensity of emotion, valves of feeling*, and *distortion of form*. Few of these terms would be familiar to the uninformed and none is explained. Furthermore, out of a total of 32 nouns used, 20 are abstract as opposed to concrete nouns (they refer to abstract concepts) which is a very high proportion. Abstract language such as *grandeur, realism, the unconscious, inspiration, abstraction, material presence* etc. inevitably result in difficulty for the uninformed reader.

Second, some of the sentences are rather long. Sentence two and three are 40 and 27 words long respectively. Furthermore the longest sentence contains three embedded subordinate clauses, (three additional 'asides' slipped into the main concept being expressed by the sentence). Subordinate clauses always cause difficulty as they make the reader work harder to follow the meaning.

[(Greatly struck (in the 1930s) by a painting by Picasso) (in which the human figure is radically, even savagely reconstructed)] he has stated that he hopes to unlock the valves of feeling and therefore return the onlooker to life more violently.

The whole qualifying subordinate clause (indicated by the square brackets) has been placed, somewhat unusually, at the beginning of the sentence, in front of the subject *he*. This clause contains three further subordinate clauses (identified by rounded brackets). As a result, there are four separate ideas being pressed together into the space of one sentence, each one relying for comprehension upon the former. This style of writing complicates the meaning. It is of interest to note that although readability formulae identify the length of sentences as causing difficulty, they are not able to identify the difficulties caused by subordination and abstraction.

Third, the complexity is further increased by the use of evaluative language. Thus, in the same sentence, we read that the human figure is not only reconstructed, but *savagely* and *radically* reconstructed. Also the viewer is not only returned to re-look at life, but to do so more *violently*. These polysyllabic adverbs further modify and therefore further complicate the multiple layers of meaning in this sentence. It is of course true that artists and art historians would not have difficulty with a passage like this, being familiar with both the subject matter and the terminology.

Francis Bacon

Francis Bacon was born in Dublin in 1909 of English parents. In 1925 he left home for London, where he took work as an interior decorator, but from 1931 devoted himself increasingly to painting. After destroying his early work Bacon resumed painting around 1944 with 'Three Figures at the Base of a Crucifixion', on display here. His paintings first entered the collections of the Museum of Modern Art in New York in 1950. From this period onwards he has had several one-man shows in Europe and the United States. Bacon is inspired by several arts: by poetry, both classical and modern; by painting and sculpture, particularly the Old Masters; by cinema and photography. Both scientific and popular photography have always fascinated him. Throughout his career, even when abstract art was most fashionable, Bacon has believed in painting the figure: 'I think that great art is deeply ordered. Even if within the order there may be enormously instinctive and accidental things, nevertheless I think that they come out of a desire for ordering and returning facts onto the nervous system in a more violent way.'

This text covers some issues that the first one refers to and some that it did not refer to. It identifies itself self-consciously as an information panel in a gallery by referring specifically to the work on show and recording when Bacon's paintings were acquired by American and British galleries. Although both texts quote the artist, the selected quote here is of a more concrete nature. Generally the passage dwells more on the career of the artist than on an evaluation of his work. However, the gallery did provide alternative sources of material. There was an information pamphlet available that gave more detailed information, and a catalogue for the better informed. The information panel and leaflet were clearly aimed at a lay audience. There were also short statements made by the artist on the walls of the exhibition. These provided viewers with a way into looking at the work, without being in any sense didactic.

The longest sentences in this text are of 24 words as opposed to 40 in the previous text. Only two separate subordinate clauses are used in nine sentences as opposed to the five used in the previous nine sentence text. Out of a total of 35 nouns only eight are abstract, putting the percentage of abstract to concrete nouns at about a quarter, instead of the previous text's total of nearly two-thirds.

This text contains several context-sensitive words and phrases. These are words that are normally used in speech rather than in academic writing. They enhance the cohesion of a statement by virtue of their self-referring nature and give the impression of a direct address to the reader. In this case they refer directly to the actual circumstances of the exhibition, such as: *on display here*, *from this period*, and create the impression that the artist is actually talking to the reader e.g. *I think that*.

There are several polysyllabic words in this text, but they are all familiar ones that would be included in conversational speech (they are not peculiar to the field of art discourse), for example: *increasingly, interior, collections, destroying, photography, particularly.*

Thus, to summarise, it is clear that these two texts were written for very different audiences. Their different approaches can teach us something about the importance of providing different texts for different audiences. They can also teach us something about how to assess our own museum texts. The relevance of these observations is certainly not confined to art gallery texts. The same principles apply in all museums, whether they be concerned with science, technology, natural history, ethnology, social history, design, archaeology or anything else.

It is of interest to note one of the conclusions drawn in research conducted in the USA by Funkhouser and Maccoby (1971). Their research investigated the communication of science information to a lay-audience and revealed that although the scientists themselves were quite able to understand complex technical texts, they actually preferred reading more accessible ones.

It is obviously vital for a writer to be very clear at the outset exactly who they are writing for, and exactly what they are trying to communicate. Writers should ask themselves: is this particular text (be it information panel, exhibition guide, catalogue or label) appropriate and relevant to its specific audience? Most writers experience little difficulty in writing for their own specialist peers. More difficulty is encountered, however, when trying to write for an audience that, although motivated, has no prior knowledge. If one of the audiences that you write for in your museum is a lay-audience it might be useful to keep the following points in mind:

- Avoid a formal, impersonal, academic register. (Beware of transposing the academic prose of your source documents, which were written to be studied at a desk, to an informational panel, written to be scan-read on foot.)

- Use familiar words wherever possible.

- Use context-sensitive words wherever appropriate.

- If possible, relate the text directly to the exhibited objects.

- Where technical terms are needed, define them.

- Avoid sentences becoming too long or too heavily subordinated.

- Don't include too many abstract concepts.

- Limit the use of evaluative language.

- Where possible, restrict one idea to one sentence, one subject to one paragraph.

- Start with the most important points; don't leave them to the end.

- Try not to overload the reader's short-term memory with too much information. Remember that a few key points, clearly put and re-enforced for emphasis, are more likely to be remembered than numerous ones referred to only once.

- Again, ask yourself what you are trying to say, who you are writing for and whether it is accessible and relevant to that audience.

References

Funkhouser, G R and Maccoby, N (1971). *Report of study communicating science information to a lay audience: Phase 2*, NFS GZ–996, Institute for Communication Research, Stamford University.

Hodge, R and D'Souza, W (1979). 'The museum as communicator: a semiotic analysis of the Western Australian Museum Aboriginal Gallery, Perth', *Museum* 31(4), p. 255.

38 Writing Label Copy

Eric Kentley and Dick Negus (compilers)
Extracted from *Writing on the wall: a guide for presenting exhibition text*, National Maritime Museum, 1989 pp. 4–6.

Technique

There can be no single style of exhibition writing . . . The style should reflect the display.

However all writing should be:

Clear: Avoid or explain any term you couldn't reasonably expect a 15 year old to understand. Don't assume that the visitor has read any previous statement in the exhibition. Be unambiguous. Within reason, use colloquial English. With complex subjects, move from the familiar to the unfamiliar, from the concrete to the abstract, or consider alternatives to text.

Concise: Keep it briefer than you thought possible. Limit the number of ideas in each sentence. Use short words and sentences. Don't overwhelm the visitor with information. Never state what can obviously be seen. But use sentences, not notes.

Relevant: Be certain that all writing is directly related to the exhibition's aims and as far as possible to the visitor's experience.

Consistent: Stick rigidly to your panel and object caption formats, forms of abbreviation, etc.

Enthusiastic: Visitors will only be excited by an exhibition if you can convey that you are. Don't be dry. Use the active rather than the passive whenever possible. If people are mentioned, flesh them out. Try to make the text memorable. But use superlatives and other adjectives sparingly.

In exhibitions with a strong educative aim, occasionally address visitors directly. Tell them what to look for, rather than just inform them what can be seen. Questions – if they are worth answering – are not only good for achieving an educative aim, they can also reduce visitor tiredness. They are most effective when placed just after the relevant exhibit.

Humour can be appropriate but needs very careful thought. What seemed funny at the start of an exhibition may be an embarrassment by the end. A surprisingly large number of people are hostile to puns . . .

Do not ask for italics or underlining for emphasis. If there is a vital point that must be stressed consider scrapping the rest of the text. Similarly, if you feel that a particular point you are making requires placing in brackets, it is probably not relevant enough to be included.

Information Structure

Once the exhibition's aims are clearly defined, the storyboard can be sketched out. This defines the order of the objects and what needs to be said where.

As far as the written word is concerned, the basic types of information carriers are:

- Titles – main and section
- Introductory panels – main and section
- Group captions
- Didactic panels
- Object captions
- Multi-object captions

An exhibition may not require all of these and some may be merged, for example section titles and section introductory panels. The number of each type of information carrier and the purpose and location of every one should be mapped out as part of the design process.

Titles

The exhibition title must be a clear indication of what the exhibition is about, stated as crisply and memorably as possible. Section titles should do the same for the sections, a section being as large as a gallery or as small as a case. Clever and witty titles work only rarely.

Introductory Panels

The exhibition introductory panel is the most important piece of writing in the exhibition and every display must include one.

It must tell visitors:

- what the exhibition is about
- how it is organised (e.g. chronologically)

Otherwise visitors must work these out for themselves. They may have neither the inclination nor the ability to do this and the exhibition will appear to be a random collection of isolated objects.

The panel should also motivate visitors by telling them:

- why the objects are worth displaying
- why visitors should be interested in the exhibition
- what they can learn from it

Section introductory panels should do for each section what the exhibition introduction panel does for the whole exhibition: explaining the theme, organisation, importance and value of the section.

Group Captions

Where several closely-related items are in a single case or hung together on a wall, a group caption can accommodate text that might otherwise be repeated on each of the individual object captions. It should have a heading and a short text, explaining the relevance of the objects and the links between them.

Didactic Panels

Detailed but essential background information is given on didactic panels when it cannot be included elsewhere. These panels can also be used to ask questions. They need headings and, if they are of any length, subheadings (up to a maximum of four). If illustrations are included, keep their captions to a minimum. Any graphs and charts should be very simple.

Avoid straight bibliographies: they are unreadable. If certain books must be acknowledged, mention them in a sentence.

Object Captions

A caption identifies an object, or if it is a picture states what it shows. It may give a certain amount of production data – who, when, where, of what – and explain how an object works and its historical significance. It states who the lender is and the object's reference number.

However, there is no standard formula for ordering this information: one must be devised which is appropriate to the exhibition and capable of consistent use throughout it.

All object captions must have a heading and this should at least implicitly answer the question, why is this object in this exhibition? Titles of paintings and books do not always make apt headings but must be mentioned. A footnote may be the appropriate place. A common caption formula is to follow the heading with a subheading giving production data, such as a painter's name, followed by a short text. Think carefully before perpetuating this. If the text is an elaboration only of the heading, the subheading is an interruption: the production data would be better positioned in a footnote.

Text is not compulsory on object captions. Include it only if it adds to the storyline. Do not rely only on the text to make the storyline clear: this is the primary job of the heading.

It is obligatory to acknowledge lenders of objects. However, as the source of objects is of little interest to most visitors, lenders' names are put on the bottom line of the caption.

Similarly, object reference numbers are useful only to us and the very few visitors who want specialised information or photographs. Numbers clutter captions. Quote only one – ideally the item number – on the bottom line. In general exhibitions, do not prefix it. If there is a catalogue accompanying the exhibition, quote only the catalogue number, prefixed with Cat.

Multiobject Captions

A multiobject caption forces visitors to turn their heads between the caption and the objects and at the same time work out which line refers to which object. They are thus not ideal but with small objects they are unavoidable. They should be well keyed, with a number adjacent to the object or, where the objects differ clearly in shape, with a silhouette diagram. A maximum of six objects a caption is recommended.

Copy Lengths

There are no minimum lengths for panels and captions. The following figures should be treated as absolute maxima. If you exceed them, you are trying to put across too much information in a single chunk. The Smithsonian Institution recommends text word counts of about half the figures given.

	Heading	Subheading/footnote	Text
Exhibition and section titles	5		
Intro and section intro panels	8		150
Group captions	8	8	100
Didactic panels	8	5 (× 4)	200
Object captions	8	8	40
Multi-object captions	8	8 (× 6)	100

Siting

In planning a piece of copy, it is essential to know where it will be displayed. Visitors spend a large amount of their time near the entrances to exhibitions. This may mean that your text will have more chance of being read here. It could also mean that the area will be crowded. A 200-word didactic panel in a narrow alleyway will be walked past. So will a lengthy caption near the end of a long exhibition.

39 Issues of Museum Text

Helen Coxall

Extracted from 'How language means: an alternative view of museum text' in *Museum languages: objects and texts*, Kavanagh, G (ed.), Leicester University Press, 1991, pp. 85–99.

My research in museum text is primarily an exploration into how the use of language in museum labels, information panels, guide books and catalogues conveys meanings. A large part of the research consists of critical linguistic analyses of texts from selected galleries and museums, with regard to social and ideological implications. Assumptions that are embedded in language are all-pervasive and cannot be ignored. Madeleine Mathiot makes this point in the preface to her collection of essays on the sociology of language, saying that 'referential meaning manifests itself as a culture's categorisation of "the world" through language' (Mathiot, 1979). My interest is in the way that a writer's choice of language, and the issues that he or she chooses not to address in the final text, transmit both the official policy of a museum and the personal 'world view' of that writer . . .

Several people have already written upon the general subject of museum text. Although Beverly Serrell's well known book *Making exhibit labels* concentrates specifically on legibility, readability and design, rather than on semantic implications, she does make a rather disturbing observation in her introduction which has direct bearing on this issue.

> Museum labels have small amounts of copy compared with books, yet people expect them to last for years, often under adverse conditions. Museum labels are also unique, unfortunately, in that although the number of people expected to read them is large, the amount of time spent on their preparation is often very brief and the amount of editing very little. With an annual attendance of 10,000 visitors, a museum exhibit on display for 5 years may draw at least 25,000 potential readers. A book prepared for such a market would undergo far more rigorous and numerous editing stages than the average exhibit label. (Serrell, 1983, p. 1)

This alone points to a very valid reason for the need for more investigation into museum text. It is an accepted fact that not every visitor reads the texts provided, or reads them to the same extent. There has been a considerable amount of valuable study devoted to visitors' responses to text, and to methods of increasing the percentage of those who read the information provided. A substantial amount of this work has been done by Paulette McManus, who has published papers about visitor reading behaviour in Natural History and Science Museums (McManus, 1988; 1989a; 1989b; 1990). However, while acknowledging this work and always bearing it in mind while doing my own work, this aspect is not the focus of this paper.

Other professionals in the field of museum communication have advocated the use of readability formulae in order to ensure that language is aimed at a specific age group's level of reading ability. To mention just a few: the Communication and Design team of the Royal Ontario Museum have, in the past, recommended that museum staff use the Fog index (Gunning, 1952) or the Flesch readability formula (Flesch, 1948) to match the language with the reading ability of the target audience. In this country, Sorsby and Horne's article in the *Museums Journal* (1980) discussed the advantages and limitations of the applications of the Fry test (Fry, 1968) to museum texts. In 1989 the National Maritime Museum in London published a book by Eric Kentley and Dick Negus called *The writing on the wall*, in which they described and recommended the use of the Fry test and the Cloze procedure (see Bormuth, 1966) as measures of language that aid accessibility.

There are three problems with this line of approach. The first is the difficulty of targeting a specific group when the majority of large museums are visited by a cross-section of the public including schoolchildren, students, family groups, adults, specialists and visitors to whom English is a second language. The second is that even if a museum considers its collection sufficiently specialist to justify targeting only one of these groups, by aiming its interpretive labels at a correspondingly restricted audience they will automatically exclude a wider potential audience, who although not specialist, would visit if the presentation was accessible to them. The third and most fundamental problem caused by relying primarily on readability formulae to assess museum text, is that they are measures of style rather than content. Readability formulae are almost exclusively concerned with such restricted features as word and sentence length, but not with meaning.

George Klare, who is probably the greatest authority on readability formulae and who has written extensively on the subject, still feels unable to recommend any of them to writers in general. He comments rather wistfully: 'I wish I could be more certain of how to tell writers what to do to change readability effectiveness' (Klare, 1976, p. 148). However, although it is obviously of undeniable importance that texts should be comprehensible to visitors, this should not be permitted to exclude the issue of how the text communicates its message and whether or not this approach is both appropriate and relevant to the potential audience. As Norman Fairclough points out in his book *Language and power*:

> We ought to be concerned with the processes of producing and interpreting texts, and with how these cognitive processes are socially shaped and relative to social conventions, not just with the texts themselves. (Fairclough, 1989, p. 19)

Accessibility and Relevance

The following text has been taken from Oxford University's Natural History Museum to illustrate the issue of accessibility.

> Primates may be described as plantigrade placental mammals, primarily arboreal, typically with nails or claws on some of the digits, possessing clavicles, having the orbits encircled with a bony ring and usually directed somewhat forward; the innermost digits of at least one pair of the extremities opposable; radius and ulna not fused, allowing free supination and pronation of the manus; separate centrale almost always present in adult; brain well developed with some hypertrophy of the neopallium and reduction of the olfactory lobes typical.

This text was obviously written for zoology scholars as it contains nineteen technical Latin terms, unaccompanied by definition. It takes the form of a factual list of descriptive features presented as one extremely long sentence. The sheer length (83 words) of this sentence and the fact that after the first semicolon the syntax changes abruptly to verbless phrasal forms, makes it extremely difficult to follow. It could be argued that, as this text would be accessible to the specialist academic audience for whom it was written, there is no necessity to alter it. However, first it is debatable how accessible this text would be to first year undergraduate students and second, the assumption that specialists prefer reading highly complex text has been contradicted by research. Funkhouser and Maccoby found in 1971 (quoted in Klare, 1976) that although knowledgeable scientists found little difference in the comprehensibility of more and less readable versions of science articles, they disliked the less readable versions. Third, this line of argument completely disregards the fact that the museum is visited daily by the general public and subsequently has another, non-specialist audience.

Inevitably, it is necessary to employ technical terminology in science museums. However, there is no reason why technical terms could not be defined, sentences shortened, lists presented as annotated points and unnecessarily complex language modified. All this could be achieved without losing the intended meaning. It is also worth pointing out that textual complexity sometimes results when factual information has been transposed from source documents, without due regard to the different nature of the original reader and that of the museum audience.

Another obvious way to ensure that a text communicates with a wider audience is to provide translations into languages other than English. This is not only applicable to the large national museums whose visitor numbers are boosted by an annual influx of tourists from overseas, but to the local community museums where English is a second language to many of the local people.

The next text has been selected to foreground the issue of textual relevance. This example also illustrates the importance of taking care when choosing evaluative words to qualify meanings and when deciding which information to leave out. Such choices have caused the writer unconsciously to create rather than to relate history. The text is taken from the eighteenth-century section of the Geffrye Museum, a decorative art museum whose aim is to record and show the history of urban home life, interiors and the development of English furniture from 1600 to the present day.

> Expensive oil paintings could now be copied and mass produced in a variety of ways such as engraving or etching. These prints were cheap and widely available. By the late Georgian period it was fashionable to have an overall decorative scheme. Yellow silk damask was a popular fabric for curtains and chairs.

This is an apparently objective, authoritative-sounding statement of fact – but what does it mean? The three adjectives *expensive*, *cheap* and *available* are at once evaluative and relative terms. Whose opinion, therefore, is being expressed? Is this intended to imply that they were considered cheap by people of the time who could afford silk damask furnishings, or that they were considered cheap by the whole population? As the majority of the population at the time could not even afford furniture, how accurate is the qualifying adverb *widely* in 'widely available'? If the availability was restricted to the middle classes (who numbered less than 25 per cent of the population at that time) whose history is being related here? If it is only that of 25 per cent of the population should that not be made clear?

The *Oxford English Dictionary* defined *popular* as 'liked or enjoyed or used by many people; of or for the general public', and *fashionable* as 'in a currently popular style; used by stylish people'. Thus *fashionable* would appear to be an élitist word reserved for 'stylish people', which would seem to be more correct in the context of a wealthy home. However, *popular* (i.e. of the general public) is hardly an appropriate word with which to describe a taste for silk damask.

In view of the fact that the museum claims to record and show the history of urban home life from 1600 to the present day, the writer could easily have explained the very legitimate reason why they only have access to examples of the kind of furnishings owned by the most wealthy quarter of the population. Because this was not done, the impression given is that the ignored three-quarters of the population have no domestic history at all.

This situation has considerable implications for the museum's audience. After all, anyone who is not used to elegant living could easily feel excluded by this history and feel that it had no relevance to them or their predecessors. This is not to suggest that people cannot appreciate things that are not within their own realm of experience – in fact quite the contrary is true. The issue here is that this text is not just relating an apparently objective message about Georgian urban life; rather, it is implicitly creating a history in which the whole working-class section of eighteenth-century society (over three-quarters of the population) has been marginalised into extinction. If this section of society was not even worth acknowledging by the writer, what is the same section of society looking at the exhibits and hearing this message going to assume?

Ways of Seeing

The text from the Geffrye Museum also illustrates that the choice of language can reflect the writer's, often quite unconscious, socially-constructed way of looking at the world. This process of social conditioning continues unnoticed by the majority of us. In their book *Language as ideology*, Kress and Hodge make the following observation:

> The world is grasped through language. But in its use by a speaker, language is more than that. It is a version of the world offered to, imposed on, enacted by someone else. (Kress and Hodge, 1979, p. 9)

They go on to make a claim that the grammar of a language itself is a theory of reality. Initially this may sound a little far-fetched. Nevertheless, social structures not only determine discourse but are themselves produced by discourse. As Catherine Belsey points out, our system of communication – our language – is already in existence before our children learn it and in learning this language they learn words that stand for concepts which are taken as natural, 'commonsense' concepts but are actually socially determined ones (see Belsey, 1987, pp. 1–67).

For example, the word *tree* (setting aside the obvious difference if the word is translated into different languages) carries different connotations for different cultures. It would have a very different meaning to a current inhabitant of the Brazilian rain forest threatened by exploitation, than it would to a current inhabitant of Ethiopia where dead trees are symbols of drought, or to a current inhabitant of Scandinavia where pine trees are grown as a trade commodity. Hence *tree* is not such a straightforward, 'commonsense', term as it first appears to be.

It does not automatically follow that because our language is socially determined, we are unable to escape the unconscious articulation of underlying ideologies. However, it becomes imperative that we are clear as to the nature of these underlying assumptions if it is not our wish to perpetuate them. It also does not follow that each of us has a fixed perspective that can be quickly identified. As Roger Fowler cautions in his book *Linguistic criticism*, 'it would be incorrect to think that each individual possesses one single monolithic world view or ideology encompassing all aspects of his or her experience; rather the (representational function of language) provides a repertoire of perspectives relative to the numerous modes of discourse in which a speaker participates', (Fowler, 1986, p. 149).

If writers are articulating perspectives that have hitherto been regarded as commonsense concepts, they may be implying meanings of which they are unaware. Critical linguistic analysis can serve as a valuable tool with which to uncover a text's hidden agenda in order to 'see reality in a new light' (Halliday, 1971, p. 333). Furthermore, with its assistance it should be possible for a critically-aware writer to draw on other discourses in order to create a new perspective. And this applies as much to writers of museum text as to any other writers. This is not meant to imply that complete impartiality is possible, as this would not be realistic. Nevertheless, a greater awareness of the way all discourses are socially constructed would be of great benefit to any writer involved in the publication of so-called facts . . .

To summarise, the choice of language and the avoided subjects in museum text are closely associated with implicit or mediated meanings, but the interpretation of a collection is also indirectly influenced by other forces, such as the museum's policy, the socio-political climate and the funding bodies.

The Museum as Myth

Objects in a museum's collection need interpretation in order that the public may fully understand their significance. Although some may be records of the past, meanings do not reside within objects and they cannot speak for themselves. Their meanings are re-ordered by their method of display and interpretation. An exhibition and the accompanying information form an explicit message to the public about the objects on display, whatever they may be. However, this message is determined by the way the information has been selected and carries an implicit message about the values of the museum and the staff who curated the exhibition. And value is a judgement, not an inherent property.

The issue of evaluative judgement has implications about the responsibility museums have to their public. After all, a museum is not just a preserver of precious relics but an information link with these objects and the world. The preferred 'truth' of the objects in a collection is constructed by an exhibition team's selection of objects, by what they choose to say and particularly what they choose not to say about them, as well as by the viewer's reinterpretation of what they see. The display and interpretation of collections not only educates and fascinates, but influences and, in some cases, reinforces current stereotypical attitudes. Museum staff, therefore, have a responsibility to be very clear about which message they are trying to communicate, and the implications that these might have for their visitors. As has already been observed, it is sometimes difficult to ascertain exactly who the museum audience consists of. It is, however, very important that staff have some idea about the potential audience, because it is not just the museum and the writer that determine the meaning of an exhibition but the interpretation made by the audience which will vary greatly according to who that audience is.

Thus, with their objects and their audience in mind, and the knowledge that the choice and combination of words is crucial to the preferred meaning of the text, writers of museum texts have to question whether or not they are unconsciously perpetuating any stereotypes or myths through their choice of language. They would be well advised to question this because museums are generally regarded by the public as centres of excellence and objective learning, their collections being accepted as assemblages of authentic objects. In other words, the museums *themselves* have acquired a status of 'myth'. Texts accompanying their permanent collections are automatically imbued with a received aura of unquestioned truth – in Roland Barthes' words they are 'innocented'. However, no text can be entirely innocent or objective, for the construction of language is itself a construction of reality.

Why is it assumed that museum text is unquestionably objective, and why is the validity of its viewpoint not examined more closely? I think the answer to this lies in the assumption that the object, like the camera, 'cannot lie'. In his essay *The photographic message* (1977), Barthes explores this very idea by focusing on the way that a photograph of an object, though obviously not itself the same as the original object, is usually taken as a truthful reproduction of it, and this apparently unmediated, objective photograph transmits its 'innocence' to any text accompanying it. This occurs even though the text may misrepresent the image, take it out of context, or even deliberately mislead the reader (as is common practice in certain kinds of news reporting) (see Hartley, 1982, pp. 26–37). If this is the case with a photograph of an object, it is obvious how much more easily the same assumption can be made of the authentic object itself. In the same way, objects in the museum's collection authenticate their texts. This obviously has far-reaching implications which Jeanne Cannizzo articulates very clearly as follows:

> Museums are carefully created artificially constructed, repositories; they are negotiated realities. We need to examine the ideology and cultural assumptions which inform our collection policies, which determine our display formats and influence the interpretations placed upon the objects which we designate as the essence of our cultural and historical identity. In short, museums are amenable to analysis as visual [and spoken] ideologies. (Cannizzo, 1987, p. 22)

It is understood that all museum staff, whether teachers, designers, conservators or curators, are committed to a set of values that have been formed through years of training and experience. These commitments are further reinforced by established criteria for professional evaluation and advancement. If curatorial professionalism, for example, is judged on the basis of peer evaluation, it is natural that a curator's primary audience will subsequently be his or her peers. However, unless a public audience is identified and catered for as well, the result will be a 'carefully created, artificially constructed repository' that is neither accessible nor relevant to the visiting public.

Thus, the aim in examining texts to discover the writer's official and personal philosophies is not in order to threaten the museum's staff and their code of practice, but to enable the staff to become aware of their implicit assumptions so that these may be more fully understood . . .

The intention is to suggest alternative ways of saying that are appropriate, relevant and that avoid unintentional bias. The method employed is an observation-based approach to the investigation of referential meaning through critical linguistic analysis of text which involves an examination of lexical and syntactical choices and combinations in museum text. The approach is appropriate to all kinds of museums and galleries, whether local or national, independent or publicly funded, with any type of collections from science and natural history to history, ethnology, archaeology, technology and art.

Having said this, it is important to acknowledge that as nobody is free from socially-constructed thought the analyst's own ideological bias will of necessity mediate the way in which such analyses are conducted. However, provided the issue of the analyst's own reflexivity has been sufficiently explored it will be possible to conduct a valid investigation into the linguistic implications in the text, as long as it is not claimed that these are the only possible interpretations (see Hammersley, 1983, pp. 14-23).

The last sample text deals with the subject of immigration in the nineteenth century and provides a good demonstration of the process by which a writer's choice of language can result in an unconscious projection of prejudice. The following social history text from the Museum of London was accompanied by photographs and newspapers but no artefacts:

Immigrants

1 For centuries London had provided a home for immigrants.
2 From 1880 onwards thousands of Jews, driven from Russia and Eastern Europe by religious persecution, settled in the already established Jewish community in Whitechapel and spread into the hitherto predominantly Irish districts of Spitalfields and St George's in the East.
3 Since over 4000 Jews were arriving every year in London, a large area of the East End was soon a clearly defined 'ghetto' with its own synagogues, religious schools, shops and street markets.
4 Numerous Russians and Germans also found lodgings in the courts and alleys of East London while other Germans settled in and around Tottenham Court Road.
5 Down in the docks were colonies of Lascars, Malays, and Chinese who had themselves arrived originally as sailors, but who now made a living looking after domestic needs of the crews of ships and port.

Initially, the most striking thing about this text is the title: *immigrants*. Had the abstract noun *immigration* been used instead, it would have served to describe a process rather than a state of being of persons. As it stands, however, this title acts as a label for all groups of people who were not native to the country, and thereby could imply they were intruders.

The first sentence implies that London's attitude to these people was paternalistic by the use of the verb *provided*. After all, it could just as easily have said 'London became the home of these people'. Also, the use of *London* in a humanising metaphor actively providing a home for these people reinforces the idea that a favour was being granted to them because they did not really belong.

In the second sentence the vague use of the quantifier *thousands* in 'thousands of Jews were arriving every year' has the effect of maximising the number. An identified number would have made it sound less like an invasion. *Thousands* could mean 2,000, but could also mean 900,000. The number is left to the reader's imagination, and therefore the implicit suggestion is that it is a very large number indeed. The emotive adverbs *already* and *hitherto* add to this impression by their implicit suggestion that enough people lived there already and that the area had belonged to someone else before they came; thus implying a take-over.

The invasion idea is furthered by an unfortunate use of the verb *spread* which is also commonly used in connection with disease or plagues of vermin. It has been pointed out in the introduction that the meaning of a text is dependent upon the choice and combination of the language used by the writer. If the second sentence were re-written omitting or replacing the words mentioned above, the result would be a less value-laden message:

> From 1880 onwards 30,000 Jews, driven from Russia and Eastern Europe by religious persecution, settled in the Jewish community in Whitechapel and also moved into the predominantly Irish districts of Spitalfields and St George's in the East.

In the third sentence the maximiser *large* achieves the same effect as *thousands* did. A large area could be 1 square mile or it could be 10 square miles, depending on whose point of view is being taken. This line of criticism leads to the conclusion that this text was written from the perspective of a current inhabitant rather than from that of a dispassionate historian.

The *clearly defined ghetto* cannot pass without comment. By whom is it clearly defined? The word *ghetto* is problematic as it is uncommonly used nowadays, except in connection with racism. It should be pointed out that this text was written thirteen years ago and would undoubtedly be handled differently now, but that does not change the fact that it is currently still there for all visitors to see. The *Oxford English Dictionary* defines it as 'Ghetto 1611. [It.]. The quarter in a city, chiefly in Italy, to which Jews were restricted'. This feature of European society which dates back to the 1600s, was re-created during the Second World War as a preliminary to genocide. As a result, it has now come to be directly associated with suffering. The writer is therefore projecting an anachronistic term on to these people, who lived in 1880, with unfortunate results.

The fourth sentence deals with the area of London that Germans and Russians moved to. The fifth talks about Lascars, Malays, and Chinese. The outdated names *Malays* and *Lascars* are again the result of the date of the text, but what is the significance of the phrase *down in the docks*? Apart from being reminiscent of an old music hall ditty – 'Down in the jungle' – it also makes it sound as if they lived underground. The noun *colonies* further adds to the feeling that these people were subhuman, being a term also associated with monkeys or ants.

For those readers who are unconvinced by this line of enquiry, let me conclude by asking a question of this text. What kind of accommodation did the different immigrant groups live in? The answer is that the Jews lived in ghettos; the Lascars, Malays and Chinese lived in colonies; and the Germans and Russians lived in lodgings. I think the inference is very clear.

References

Barthes, R (1977). 'The photographic message', in *Image music text*, essays selected and translated by S Heath, pp. 15–31, London, Fontana.

Belsey C (1987). 'Critical practice', in Hawkes, T (ed.), *New accents*, London, Methuen.

Bormuth, J R (1966). 'Readability: a new approach', *Reading Research Quarterly* 1, pp. 79–132.

Cannizzo, J (1987). 'How sweet is cultural politics in Barbados', *Muse*, Winter, pp. 22–7.

Communication and Design Team, Royal Ontario Museum (1976). *Communicating with the museum visitor: guidelines for planning*, Toronto, Canada.

Fairclough, N (1989). *Language and power*, London, Longman.

Flesch, R (1948). 'A new readability yardstick', *Journal of Applied Psychology* 32(3), pp. 221–33.

Fowler, R (1986). *Linguistic criticism*, Oxford, Oxford University Press.

Fry, E B (1968). 'A readability formula that saves time', *Journal of Reading* 11, pp. 513–16, 575–8.

Gunning, R (1952). *The technique of clear writing*, New York, McGraw-Hill.

Halliday, M A K (1971). 'Linguistic function and literary style', in Chapman, S (ed.), *Literary style: a symposium*, New York and London, Oxford University Press.

Hammersley, M (1983). *Ethnography: principles in practice*, London, Routledge.

Hartley, J (1982). *Understanding news*, London, Methuen.

Kentley, E and Negus, D (1989). *The writing on the wall*, London, National Maritime Museum.

Klare, G R (1976). 'A second look at the validity of readability formulas', *Journal of Reading Behaviour* 8, pp. 129–52.

Kress, G and Hodge, R (1979), *Language as ideology*, London, Routledge & Kegan Paul.

McManus, P M (1988). 'Good companions . . . more on the social determination of learning-related behaviour in a science museum', *International Journal of Museum Management and Curatorship* 7, pp. 37–44.

McManus, P M (1989a). 'Oh yes they do: how museum visitors read labels and interact with exhibit texts', *Curator* 32(3), pp. 174–89.

McManus, P M (1989b). 'What people say and how they think in a science museum', in Uzzell, D (ed.), *Heritage interpretation Vol. 2, The visitor experience*, pp. 156–65, London, Belhaven Press.

McManus, P M (1990). 'Watch your language! People do read labels', in Serrell, B (ed.), *What research says about learning in science museums*, Washington DC, Technology Center.

Mathiot, M (1979). *Ethnolinguistics: boas, sapir and whorf revisited*, The Hague, Mouton.

Serrell, B (1983). *Making exhibit labels: a step-by-step guide*, Nashville, Tennessee, American Association for State and Local History.

Sorsby, B D and Horne, S D (1980). 'The readability of museum labels', *Museums Journal* 80(3), pp. 157–9.

Section Eight   Evaluation

Introduction

We are increasingly conscious that evaluation is important, but what is it and how do you do it? Much of the early research was carried out in America, but there is now a fair amount of work being done in Britain. Papers from a conference at the Science Museum, published as *Museum visitor studies in the 90s* (1993), indicate the state of the art at the present time, and include contributions from Britain, North America and Europe. The work carried out at the National Museums on Merseyside over the past decade is summarised in Sudbury and Russell (eds) (1995), *Evaluation of museum and gallery displays*, Liverpool University Press. A comprehensive evaluation using a range of methods at Birmingham Museum in 1993 is described in Peirson-Jones, (ed.) (1993), *Gallery 33: a visitor study.*

In the first article Borun introduces the fundamental principles of exhibit evaluation and discusses the main stages of evaluation – summative, formative, and front-end – giving examples of the value of each. The second extract briefly lays out some of the main methods that can be used, and discusses their strengths and weaknesses. Which methods to use and in which combination depends on what you want to find out. More information on methods, especially qualitative methods, and further references are given in *Environmental interpretation: the bulletin of the Centre for Environmental Interpretation*, July 1990, a special issue which focuses on evaluating interpretation.

Serrell discusses some possible approaches to evaluating exhibitions and proposes an approach which is easy to carry out using a set of criteria based on watching and talking to visitors. This could be applied in any museum without too much difficulty. Hein describes a case study that shows how evaluation in a natural history gallery before and after fairly simple gallery modifications affirmed the value of those modifications. The main purpose of the changes was to improve access for people with disabilities, but the effect of the changes was to improve the visit for everyone. In the next article Stevenson concentrates on the long-term effects of museum visiting and describes a case study where tracking and follow-up post-visit interviews were combined. It is rare to find studies that research the memories of visits, although this was one of the methods used in the Gallery 33 study at Birmingham.

The final extract describes a long, and personal, haul through a range of approaches to exhibition evaluation. The moral of the story is that without a commitment to evaluation on the behalf of museum management, resources will not be committed, and exhibitions will be less effective for visitors. A commitment to evaluation should be built into the exhibition policy.

Exhibit evaluation is now in a process of transition. Many of the methods in current use were developed for science centres in the USA. Whilst there is no reason to question the validity of the main conclusions of the resulting studies, the scarcity of comparably sophisticated work on arts and humanities exhibits here in Britain is striking. This lack is the more problematic because it is precisely in these disciplines that differences between the USA and Britain in academic traditions and wider culture are likely to be most significant. The research of the Department of Museum Studies at the University of Leicester to develop new methodologies for evaluation, as yet unpublished and hence not included in this book, is, therefore, particularly welcome.

40 The Stages of Evaluation

Minda Borun

This article 'Assessing the impact' was published in *Museum News* 68(3), 1989, pp. 36–40.

Whatever the goals of a museum exhibit – imparting information, stimulating interest in a subject, changing or reinforcing opinions, providing aesthetic experiences – you must become aware of the public's response to know if the exhibit is achieving its goals. Learning what visitors like, learn, and feel about exhibits can guide decisions about what to keep and what to change, what works and what needs improvement.

Museum visitors are part of a special communications system, receiving messages from the museum staff through the medium of the exhibit. To know if the message has been received and understood, the museum can complete the communication process by listening to visitor response.

Evaluation is the process of finding out to what extent a programme produces the intended impact. Museum professionals evaluate exhibits, tours, films, or educational programmes. I will focus on exhibits, but similar procedures can be applied to other museum offerings.

Evaluation: Peaks and Valleys

. . . Two distinct yet concurrent trends support the re-emergence of museum evaluation. First, there is a renewed interest in accountability. Moving beyond simply displaying a rare and valuable collection, museums are increasingly concerned with their educational mission. And they are becoming interested in the teaching effectiveness of their programmes.

Second, evaluation makes sound marketing sense. No serious business would put a new product on the market without conducting market research and field-testing and revising prototypes. Now that earned income through admission and other fees is a significant factor in a museum's operating budget, customer satisfaction should be a serious concern.

The first steps in an evaluation project are to consider the time, money, and personnel available and set priorities.

Appropriate evaluation of a visitor's museum experience is difficult. Often what is called evaluation consists of measuring what is easy and accessible (such as the number of visitors) rather than dealing with the many dimensions and goals of the museum visit from the exhibitor's and the visitor's point of view.

The most frequent kind of evaluation study is summative evaluation, which measures the outcome of a completed project. Summative evaluation sometimes is required by or conducted for a project sponsor to demonstrate how well things turned out. Summative evaluations take place, by definition, after-the-fact and too often are buried in filing cabinets.

On the other hand, formative, or process, evaluation is part of the development of an exhibition. In this situation, visitors are exposed to mock-ups or prototypes – early stages of an exhibit – to assess the impact. The information gained allows the project team to decide how to change and improve the exhibit before its public debut. This occurs several times; with each round of evaluation and revision, the exhibit achieves a closer fit to its audience and to project goals.

Ask These Three Questions

Formative evaluation is most useful when it becomes an ongoing part of the process of exhibit-making. It begins with three questions: (1) Who is the audience for this exhibition? (2) What impact do you want to have? (3) How will you know you've had this impact?

Before you can define the goals of a new exhibition, you first must know who the audience is likely to be. Knowing the different age groups of museum visitors and their educational backgrounds should influence the level of sophistication of the exhibit. If, for instance, most visitors come in family groups and have an interest in, but little specialised knowledge of, the proposed subject, a series of technical exhibits with complex labels would be neither effective nor enjoyable.

An important part of defining the audience is front-end analysis, in which visitors are interviewed to find out what preconceptions, misconceptions, and understandings they bring to the subject of a planned exhibit. This procedure can be extremely helpful in outlining the exhibit's scope and content. Front-end analysis can ensure that the prototypes used in formative evaluation will start off closer to achieving their goals.

A display at my museum, the Franklin Institute in Philadelphia, provides an example of how useful front-end analysis would have been. One exhibit requires an understanding of the principles of gravity. Through interviewing visitors we found the widespread misconceptions that gravity is air pressure, that air is the medium through which gravity works, and that things will float in a vacuum. Nearly 40 per cent of the people we interviewed held one or more of these views. We are now working on supporting displays that teach the basic concepts people need to know to understand the main exhibit.

Once you identify your audience, you can decide what to say and why you think it's important. The exhibition staff – curator, designer, researcher, educator, and evaluator – can analyse the intended effect on the visiting public. What are the goals of the exhibition? Are they simply to please and entertain? Or do you want to teach something? Do you want to create a sense of awe? Or spark an interest in a particular topic? Do you want to introduce visitors to new information to reinforce and extend their knowledge and experience?

Most museum exhibitions, of course, have multiple goals. For an exhibit to be successful, the critical goals must be identified. Through the process of goal clarification, conflicting notions held by different members of the project team can emerge and be resolved. And some common design flaws can be avoided.

For example, if the main goal of a display is to present a beautiful object for aesthetic appreciation, care can be taken not to obscure the visitors' view with lengthy printed labels or glaring glass. If an object is being used to illustrate a stage in a developmental sequence, the printed text used to explain the sequence should not be hidden at the top or side of a display case or typed inconspicuously in tiny muted print. A lever-operated participatory device for a science exhibit aimed at audiences age 8 and older should not require a body weight of 120 pounds [54.5 kg] to depress the lever, and its instructions should not employ 200 words of polysyllabic prose.

These examples are extreme, but not uncommon. Too often exhibits fight with visitors instead of welcoming them. In the course of exhibit design, fabrication, and installation, it's all too easy to lose sight of the people who will see the exhibit. Obviously, this is less likely to happen if you identify audiences and define goals.

Once the audience and goals have been specified, you can approach the third question: how do you know whether you've had the desired impact? What would you like the visitor to do? General goal statements must be translated into a set of specific behavioural objectives. A behavioural objective specifies that you want certain kinds of visitors to do or say something with a particular level of frequency or competency.

Scholars and museum professionals might regard an exhibit as an eloquent expression of familiar concept. It is often difficult for these experts to understand that a display embodying a principle does not necessarily explain that principle to the uninitiated. Collaboration between evaluators, curators, and exhibit designers can result in exhibits that bridge the gap between embodiment and explanation.

Exhibit evaluation requires an objective measure of success. By setting behavioural objectives for an exhibit as a whole and for its major components, you are defining things that can be measured.

Objectives tend to cluster around these main concerns: (1) *Attracting power* – What percentage of visitors of which age range do you expect to stop at the exhibit? (2) *Holding power* – How long does it take to see the display, and what percentage of the people who stop at it stay this amount of time or longer? (3) *Proper use* – How many visitors who stop at a display use it correctly and observe the intended effect? (4) *Instructional power* – Do people understand what the display was designed to teach or demonstrate? (5) *Affective power* – Do people like the exhibit?

Matching Impact with Expectations

Formative evaluation begins by creating a mock-up. Generally, you can choose inexpensive materials so that modifications can be made and tested before the display is produced in final form. Then observe a sample of visitors and consider each objective in turn. If the display falls short of its goal on any measure, modify and re-test until all of the objectives are met. This is an iterative process, gradually narrowing the gap between the impact of the display on its audience and the expectations of the curators and designers. The result: an exhibit you know visitors will understand and appreciate.

An example from the Franklin Institute: one display that features a giant lever had to be modified when the evaluator found children were not using it properly. The original display had 10 ropes hanging from the lever. One child at a time was supposed to pull on each rope in turn to determine which made it easiest to lift a 500-pound weight [227 kg]. What the evaluator found was that children were treating the lever like a playground device: as many as 25 children would grab the ropes at one time, defeating the purpose of the exhibit. As a result, the number of ropes was reduced to four, side guard rails were erected to narrow the entrance to the display, and a sign was placed on the display that asks: 'Can you lift 500 pounds by yourself?' In addition a docent was stationed at the display to encourage one child at a time to test the ropes.

Many evaluation techniques are available, including formal interviews, open-ended discussions, written questionnaires, quizzes, rating scales, projective tests, and unobtrusive observation. Each technique yields a specific type of information, and each has its limitations. Techniques used in visitor observation and interviews derive both from the nature of the exhibit and from its goals. For example, attracting power and holding power require quantitative measures using methods such as counting, tracking, and timing visitors at the exhibit. For qualitative goals such as how visitors relate this exhibit to their personal experience, unstructured, open-ended or naturalistic interview techniques are appropriate. By combining data from observation, interviews, and questionnaires, you can cross-check findings to create a more reliable picture.

Museum professionals sometimes avoid statistical procedures and tend to be more comfortable with naturalistic interview techniques. But it takes more skill and training to get useful information through unstructured probes than through a questionnaire. It's important to select a representative sample of the museum's audience to guide your decision-making process. Usually, in formative evaluation, 25 randomly selected visitors can give you a good idea of what's going on. In fact, in the beginning of the process, you might determine that a modification in the prototype is necessary after speaking to only a few people.

Test an Entire Installation

Too often, formative evaluation is carried out on a display-by-display basis. Such piecemeal evaluation does not permit the assessment of the impact of the display in the context of the whole exhibit. When time and funds permit, I recommend testing an entire installation, allowing evaluation of introductory and summary labels and general themes as well as individual displays.

The *Mechanics* exhibit at the Franklin Institute was developed with the aid of full-scale formative evaluation. First, prototypes of major exhibit devices and displays were tested; then, a preliminary version of the whole exhibit was installed. All of the explanatory text was written on brown wrapping paper with felt markers, allowing us to continue testing and revision. We explained the process to visitors through signs at the entrances to the exhibit. Although the design department had to overcome its initial horror at this idea, visitors responded favourably. They liked being able to contribute their ideas to the exhibit and said that the brown paper gave it an informal 'laboratory' look appropriate to the content.

Optimally, further evaluation is carried out after an exhibit is installed. In practice this may be difficult to arrange. Once the exhibit is installed, the press and public quickly follow, and attention tends to turn to the next exhibit. If, however, some funds have been reserved for final evaluation and revision, significant improvement can occur.

Museums have great potential for communicating with visitors in a stimulating and delightful way. Yet current museum practice does not fully realise this potential. All too often, exhibitions embody rather than explain. For the informed visitor, these exhibits are inspiring in their elegance. But for the public at large, they often can be hard to comprehend.

Funding from public and private sources is becoming more difficult to obtain, and attention in the museum community has begun to shift from the educational ideal to the real need to increase earned income. Evaluation can lead to educationally effective exhibits that create visitor satisfaction, favourable word-of-mouth publicity, and increased attendance. It's worth a try.

41 Monitoring and Evaluation: The Techniques

Gillian Binks and David Uzzell

This editorial was published in *Bulletin of the Centre for Environmental Interpretation: Evaluating interpretation*, 1990, pp. 16–17.

Most of the techniques used [in evaluation] are established techniques in the field of marketing, social survey and educational psychology, which are applied and modified to suit the particular situation about which the interpreter, interpretive planner or facility manager is concerned.

Regrettably there is not yet a British handbook of evaluation techniques for interpretation facilities and services. There are, however, useful guides to recreation site surveys and accounts of surveys and evaluation studies of individual interpretive media and facilities which are worth consulting. They offer valuable information, for example on planning and designing surveys, using questionnaires, observation, group and depth interviews and some deal with techniques of measuring learning and attitude change. Many of them include examples of questionnaires which provide a useful basis for devising your own.

It is possible with the help of some of the references [at the end of this article] to devise, carry out and analyse your own survey. Alternatively you may decide to use an off-the-peg survey, some of which have been devised for museums, or you may decide to bring in outside help. It usually all depends on the size and complexity of the evaluation you wish to undertake and your budget. Market research companies, university and polytechnic marketing, tourism and social science and educational psychology departments and individual recreation and interpretation consultancy firms can usually offer tailor-made surveys and evaluation packages on a consultancy basis. Many polytechnic and university departments have staff who are willing to advise you informally on aspects of your survey if you decide to do it yourself. Some may supply student help and some computer services departments also offer help with questionnaires, design and processing. Below are described the main techniques, with their strengths, weaknesses and likely costs.

Questionnaire Surveys

Strengths

- Lots of experience around among people who have carried out questionnaire surveys in other nearby museums, visitor attractions, etc. You may be able to use, with minor modification, questionnaires they have designed – provided they answer the questions you want answered. Be careful.

- Quite cost effective. You can produce a large number of questionnaires for the price of the print run. However, the more you produce, the more you will have to analyse. Also a larger sample may not mean a more accurate sample.

- Again easy to train people to give out questionnaires, or administer them.

Weaknesses

- While there may be expertise available locally in the design and production of questionnaires, it does not mean that it is going to be good expertise. There are many badly-designed questionnaires around. Poorly-designed questionnaires give you inaccurate, unreliable and therefore useless results. Questionnaire design is a skill.

- Large sample needed for reliable and representative results.

- May require the use of computer to analyse results: see comments on structured interviews.

Likely Costs

- Considerable staff time to plan, supervise, analyse.

- Specialist advice as necessary . . .

- Printing of questionnaires – depending on length and print run.

- Off-the-shelf questionnaires, e.g. DRS Museum Scan . . . standard questionnaires printed and processed; or . . . questionnaires designed for your site with analysis and customised report.

- Interviewer's fees – ranging from student rates, staff time or professional interviewers. 20–40 questionnaires per interviewer per day depending on length.

- Computer processing costs.

In-Depth Interviews (With a Small Sample of People)

Strengths

- Detailed qualitative information, very revealing and 'true'.

- Enables exploration of issues both guided and in response to respondents' concerns and agenda.

- Useful for initial exploration of issues prior to a more representative survey.

- Does not require sophisticated technology to analyse data, although there are advanced computer programs which will, after content analysis, analyse the findings.

Weaknesses

- Time consuming.

- Typically only feasible with a small sample, therefore difficult to make representative. This may not matter – depends on purpose.

- Needs skilled interviewer.

- Difficulty of interpreting information – content analysis is typically used.

Likely Costs

- Staff time to plan, supervise and analyse.

- Specialist advice (training of interviewers as necessary) . . .

- Skilled interviewers' fees . . . maybe four interviews per day per interviewer.
- Interviewers' travel costs if interviews are home based.
- Costs of computer processing if appropriate.

Structured Interviews

Strengths

- Can deal with a larger sample than in-depth interviews.
- Allows respondents to elaborate their answers, perhaps unlike a questionnaire.
- Not too difficult to train interviewers.
- Can also be useful for initial exploration of issues prior to a more representative sample survey.
- Can use data in a qualitative or quantitative way.

Weaknesses

- Labour intensive and therefore expensive.
- Large sample needed (like a questionnaire survey), if they are to be regarded as representative of a larger population.
- May require the use of a computer to analyse results, with consequent necessary understanding of statistics and computer programs. There are now many off-the-shelf computer programs available, but they still require an understanding of the statistical analysis, and the assumptions on which the statistics are based.

Likely Costs

- Staff time to plan, supervise and analyse.
- Specialist advice . . .
- Printing costs of interview schedule/questionnaire.
- Interviewer fees ranging from student rates . . . to professional market research interviews . . . 15–20 interviews per interviewer per day.
- Computer processing.

Behavioural Mapping or Observation

Strengths

- Direct measure of the public's behaviour. What the public say they do and what they really do are often two very different things. Enables you to see how they actually use your exhibition, country park, etc.
- Useful complement to other techniques such as questionnaires or interviews, as it enables you to check or corroborate responses.
- Low technology – pencil and paper.
- Inexpensive.

Weaknesses

- Time-consuming. Following or observing one person around an exhibition may take 30 minutes, therefore limited number can be completed in a day.

- Does not provide you with the visitors' account of what they were doing or why. You have to interpret their actions: in some cases it is not always clear what people are doing. They may spend 5 minutes looking at an exhibit – this could be because it is fascinating, or because they are having great difficulties understanding it.

Likely Costs

- Staff time to plan, supervise and analyse.

- Specialist help if necessary.

- Observers' fees: student rates or equivalent staff time.

- Computer analysis as appropriate.

References

Lee, T R and Uzzell, D L (1980). *The educational effectiveness of the farm open day*, Countryside Commission for Scotland.

Miles, R S et al. (1982). *The design of educational exhibits*, London, George Allen & Unwin.

Stansfield, G (1981). *Effective interpretive exhibitions*, CCP 145, Countryside Commission.

Tourism and Recreation Research Unit (1983). *Recreational site survey manual: methods and techniques for conducting visitor surveys*, London, E & F N Spon.

Uzzell, D L and Lee, T R (1980). *Forestry Commission visitor centres: an evaluation package*, Report to the Forestry Commission, Edinburgh.

42 Using Behaviour to Define the Effectiveness of Exhibitions

Beverly Serrell
This paper appeared in *Museum visitor studies in the 90s*, Bicknell, S and Farmelo, G (eds) Science Museum, 1993, pp. 140–143.

There is no accepted definition of exhibition success, and there are no standards for making comparisons between exhibitions. What makes an exhibition 'good' tends to be based on subjective opinion rather than concrete, easily applicable criteria. Specific educational objectives are sometimes used as a measure, but documenting visitor achievement of narrowly defined cognitive goals is a disappointing and restricted view of the whole museum experience. Thus, to answer the question 'What makes a good exhibition?' one must first define 'good'. I offer three criteria, which, if met, are evidence of a 'good' exhibition. By measuring museum visitors' informal social behaviour and their immediate recall of and reactions to an exhibition, that exhibition's effectiveness can be judged objectively. Survey methods used to gather information about visitor behaviour are empirical, not particularly technical and affordable. Data include the speed at which visitors move through the exhibitions; the number of elements to which they attend; and their ability to recall specific facts, ideas, attitudes or concepts that are related to these elements and to the messages put forward by the exhibition developers. In this paper I will present and discuss . . . some measurements and data . . . and look at the characteristics that successful exhibitions may have in common.

Problems with Defining Exhibition Success

How can the success of a museum exhibition be measured? Are there any standards to follow? How can you tell if your evaluation data mean that your exhibition is 'good'? These questions beg answers that can embrace the diverse nature of museum audiences and the wide range of exhibition sizes, budgets, topics and locations. Harris Shettel (1973) has proposed a three-factor model that includes audience demographics, ratios of actual time and required time spent, plus pre- and post-test data on visitors' knowledge and attitudes. Shettel's model has not been widely adopted, possibly because it relies on data collection and analysis techniques that are too complex for many museums. Few comprehensive, objective, measurable criteria have been suggested by others.

What makes an exhibition 'good' tends to be a subjective opinion and depends on the idiosyncratic eye of the beholder. To counteract the influence of subjectivity, criteria for success have been measured against objectives specific to the exhibition, as defined by the exhibition developers. Traditionally, these have consisted of the visitor's achievement of narrowly defined cognitive goals – a very limited measure of the whole museum experience. Criteria more reflective of voluntary, informal, social experiences are needed.

Marketing Studies Are Not the Answer

Demographic and psychographic audience profiles may provide information about who the visitors are, where they come from and what their interests are, but they do not usually illuminate how visitors experience an exhibition. Audience surveys conducted as self-reported interview data give inflated exaggerated accounts of the amount of time spent in an exhibition, or the amount of label text read.

Comment Books Are Not the Answer

Comment cards or books are widely used in all types of museums these days, especially in controversial exhibitions. Usually placed at the end of an exhibition, they give visitors a chance to express their views, opinions and suggestions, and also provide a good opportunity for visitors to conduct a dialogue with the museum and with other visitors who have commented before them.

Can comment books tell you if the exhibition is good? Not really. Comment books can serve as an evaluation tool for staff, but they have limited validity and are not statistically reliable, making them one of the most unscientific ways to measure visitor responses. Although they are a source of qualitative feedback for museum staff, they should never be used as the sole method of evaluation. Comment books are primarily for the benefit of visitors, giving them a voice in the exhibition.

Criteria Based on Visitor Behaviour

This paper offers a definition of 'successful' that is based on visitor behaviour. Visitor experience, expressed through empirical behaviours, involves time spent, use of exhibition elements and outcomes such as new or confirmed knowledge, attitudes or skills. All of these criteria are objectively defined and results can be systematically collected.

Analysis of behaviour taken from a random sample of visitors to the exhibition will indicate if a majority of the sample meets the following three conditions:

1 Visitors move through the exhibition at a rate of less than 300 ft^2/min [28 m^2/min].
2 Visitors attend at least 51 per cent of the exhibition elements.
3 Visitors can correctly quote or recall specific facts, ideas, attitudes or concepts related to the exhibition elements and the exhibition's objectives.

If these three criteria are met by the majority of your sample, the exhibition can be considered successful, or 'good'.

This formula can be used to evaluate any kind of exhibition: temporary or permanent, large or small, big budget or shoestring, art, science or natural history, from complex or technical exhibitions with extensive labels to exhibitions with few words and visual or aesthetic goals.

Watch What Your Visitors are Doing

The first criterion deals with time and how visitors spend it. Time data are quantitative, objective and easy to gather. 'Tracking and time' involves unobtrusively observing and recording visitors' movements through an exhibition from the moment they enter until the moment they exit, regardless of how much time they spend.

When visitors move through the exhibition at a rate of less than 300 ft^2/min [28 m^2/min], it probably means they are stopping and paying attention, not just strolling slowly, glancing at things. Studies have shown that the amount of time spent is positively related to the frequency of behaviours that indicate contemplation, involvement and learning.

The second criterion deals with the number of exhibit units at which visitors stop out of the total number available. 'Units' can be defined variously: as a group of graphic panels, a video, a diorama, a case of objects, a large artefact, etc. These data are collected during tracking and timing by keeping a record of those exhibit units at which visitors stop.

When half of the sample use less than half of the exhibition, the exhibition is under-utilised according to this criterion. That means it was successful with fewer visitors. Perhaps more importantly, it may have been unsuccessful for more visitors. When more than half the visitors use more than half of the exhibition's elements, the exhibition environment is probably not overwhelming and contains an appropriate mix of modalities, such as reading, listening, watching and touching. Studies have shown that in exhibition halls with fewer elements, visitors tend to use a higher proportion of what is available. Popular elements within exhibitions tend to be used by a cross-section of the total audience.

Get Visitor Feedback

The third criterion has to do with what visitors are getting out of the exhibition, that is, 'learning', broadly defined and not measured in traditional ways. While tracking and timing can reveal what visitors do, other methods such as interviews and questionnaires are needed to investigate what visitors think and feel about the exhibition.

Visitors have a wide variety of ways of referring to their own 'learning' outcomes, which can be classified as both cognitive and affective. Open-ended questions are the best prompts for seeking this kind of feedback, such as: 'I didn't know that . . .', 'It made me think that . . .', 'I found out that . . .', 'I never realised that . . .', 'It reminded me that . . .', 'I felt that . . .', 'I was surprised that . . .'.

If the majority of visitors complete these kinds of statements with specifics that relate well to the goals of the exhibition (or at least are not counterproductive to them), then the exhibition was probably successful in communicating and connecting to their own needs and goals. If visitor feedback is general and not related to many of the specific exhibition elements, then there is little evidence that the exhibition was useful. That is, it probably did not serve most visitors' motivational and intellectual needs by relating to their interests, expertise, priorities or values . . .

The criteria outlined in this paper are useful for planning purposes as well as summative evaluation. They can be used to determine how well an exhibition is working and what changes might be needed to correct low use by visitors . . .

Successful Exhibition Behaviours Are Not Correlated to Budget

Success according to these criteria of time, use and visitor understanding are not related to an exhibition's budget. It costs no more to make a successful exhibition, and may perhaps cost less. Smaller exhibitions with fewer elements and simpler communication goals are often used more thoroughly by visitors than large ones. When there is less to do, visitors tend to do more.

Good Exhibitions Are Visitor-centred

Few exhibitions have so far actually met all three criteria, but the ones that do seem to have several important characteristics in common, all centred on the audience's needs:

- The exhibition developers' goals have been clearly stated in terms of visitors' experience – what they will do, feel, say and know – and not just in terms of how the content will be presented.

- Visitors are able to orientate themselves quickly and consciously. The layout of the hall or gallery is apparent, and visitors can make choices and budget their time accordingly.

- Labels are not long, and they speak to visitors in non-technical terms. Developers do not try to say too much or cover too many topics, either in a single label or in the exhibition overall.

Are smaller, temporary, or travelling exhibitions more successful? Are the criteria too stiff for big, permanent exhibitions? Maybe. Could large exhibitions be changed in relatively inexpensive ways to hold more visitors' attention longer? Yes, and they will have to be if museum professionals are serious about wanting their exhibitions to be 'client-centred', that is, appealing, appropriate and accountable to a broader range of audiences. Museums in the future should be filled with more good exhibitions as defined not by their creators, peers, or academic critics, but by their users.

Reference

Shettel, H (1973). 'Exhibits: art form or educational medium?' *Museum News* 52(1), pp. 32–41.

43 Evaluating a Display Adapted for People with Learning Difficulties

George E Hein

Extracted from an article 'Assessing the hands-on learning process' in *ECSITE Newsletter*, August/September 1990, p. 3.

The project

Background

The Boston Museum of Science carried out an accessibility audit in 1985, inviting three experts on the needs of blind, deaf and physically-handicapped visitors to describe accessibility to the Museum. As a result, the Museum set about making its premises more accessible. One project, supported by the National Science Foundation, was to change the exhibits in the New England Life Zone, a large room approximately 10 m by 20 m [33 ft by 65 ft] containing six dioramas of animals native to New England. We have studied the impact of these changes on both handicapped and 'ordinary' visitors.

Gallery Changes

Modifications consisted of three major components plus some additional materials. All the dioramas received new and expanded sign panels. These panels included information which could be accessed in several ways. The labels were re-written and the manner of their display altered, so they were easier to read and easier to understand. In addition, a panel was erected in front of each diorama. This panel was approximately 60 cm [about 2 ft] off the ground and contained an audiotape and earphone with descriptive material about the diorama, a 'smell box' which, when turned on, fanned an aroma associated with the animal habitat to the visitor, and, on most of the panels, something to touch, such as deer antlers or a moose hoof.

A second component consisted of three-dimensional presentations of some of the species in the diorama, set out so that visitors could touch them. This included two bird models made of metal, and mounted specimens of a beaver and a bear.

The third new component consisted of three free-standing hands-on displays related to the exhibits.

Our Evaluation

My graduate student Candace Heald and I carried out three types of evaluation activities. First, we provided formative evaluation information to the staff as various exhibit additions were placed on the floor and visitors had an opportunity to interact with them. Second, we carried out a systematic study of 'ordinary' visitors' behaviour at three times: before modification (base line), about half way through (interim evaluation), and after the modifications were complete (final evaluation). Finally, we did some special case studies of groups of handicapped visitors after there was something displayed with which they could interact.

Results

Time in Gallery and Flow Pattern

Our results from the systematic study of 'ordinary' visitors demonstrate that they spend significantly more time in the gallery after modifications and that the fraction of visitors who spend 1 minute or less in the gallery has decreased. More important, the visitor flow pattern is different. Before changes, the flow pattern consisted primarily of in-and-out visitors and of others who circulated either clockwise or anti-clockwise round the sides of the gallery. After the changes visitors – when viewed as a whole – appear to follow a random pattern wandering through the exhibition. But, if individual visitors are observed, the random pattern dissolves into a series of purposeful paths. We can distinguish categories of visitors who make use primarily of one sensory mode: there are touchers, listeners, smellers and seers among them. Also, we can detect a 'physical dialogue' between visitors and components of the exhibition, as they go back and forth between related components. These findings suggest that the apparently chaotic flow patterns observed in some science centres may mask purposeful behaviour on the part of many visitors.

Attracting Power

Before the changes, the moose diorama was the strongest attractor. Approximately 60 per cent of visitors stopped there, while some of the other dioramas attracted less than half that many visitors. After the changes, all the dioramas attract an approximately equal percentage of visitors, all in the 60 per cent range. The interactive labels have made all the dioramas attractive, without any change in the exhibits themselves. In addition, the new hands-on elements attract visitors without decreasing the attracting power of the dioramas.

People still like the dioramas, and, even when they compete with other newer exhibit components, they attract significant numbers of visitors through the addition of expanded interactive labels. I believe that some science and natural history museums, in their eagerness to add new kinds of exhibits, sometimes remove popular and informative traditional displays.

Learning Outcomes

From interviews with visitors we noted that in answer to a question about whether they read labels, the changes decreased the 'no answer' and 'no' categories from around 70 per cent (combined) to less than 15 per cent and raised the 'yes' answer category accordingly. More important, a significantly larger fraction of visitors responded 'yes' and were able to provide an example of something they remembered from the labels. Visitors provided us with information they had obtained from the whole combination of explanatory materials: written labels, recorded messages and other sources.

More powerful evidence for the learning potential of the expanded labels and hands-on components comes from a question we asked visitors about their knowledge of the message that the gallery was intended to deliver. We asked visitors before and after the changes whether they could name an adaptive animal feature which allowed it to live as it does. For the beaver and the moose alone, we had a great increase in the fraction of visitors who could name some adaptive feature and a four-fold increase in the different features mentioned.

Our simple probes suggest that providing visitors with more modalities to interact with exhibits dramatically increased the potential for learning from the exhibition.

Formative Evaluation

In this evaluation, as is usually the case, we learned that exhibit components need to be tested on the floor to avoid some components that do not work well for visitors. Even maximum accessibility does not mean access for all. Unless a museum has infinite space and resources, all exhibition areas require some compromises; what makes exhibits more accessible and more interactive for some audiences will make it less so for others.

Redundancy/Consistency

One of the many benefits of working with handicapped groups was that they reminded us of the importance of both redundancy and consistency in setting up interactive learning environments for them and for all visitors. The handicapped visitors were particularly sensitive to changes in presentation format and needed multiple, redundant clues to suggest how they might interact with an exhibit. But their needs only emphasise the basic requirement of redundancy and consistency for all learners. Some new interactive science centres make high demands on their visitors by varying the nature of the visitor interaction from exhibit to exhibit and by employing inconsistent signage. No wonder visitors find the settings difficult!

Conclusion

By instituting changes intended to make an exhibition more accessible to a special population, the museum made it more accessible to all. By expanding accessibility, we can increase both the enjoyment and the potential for learning for all our visitors. In examining this unique exhibition designed for accessibility, we have added to the general knowledge concerning learning from hands-on interactive exhibits.

44 The Long-term Impact of Interactive Exhibits

John Stevenson

Extracted from an article in *International Journal of Science Education* 13(5), 1991, pp. 521–531.

Introduction

There has never been greater interest in interactive exhibits or in interactive science-and-technology centres (ISTCs). The growth in numbers of ISTCs in the UK has been high over the 6 years since the *Launch Pad* gallery opened at the Science Museum in June 1986. Also, there is increasing interest from researchers in establishing what really happens in these centres . . .

This paper examines whether there is indeed a long-term impact on visitors in family groups when they visit *Launch Pad*. In particular the research is concerned with how memorable the experience can be.

Background

. . . The *Launch Pad* Sponsorship Brochure produced in 1983 stated that the aim for the creation of *Launch Pad* was:

> . . . to provide a place where people of all ages can discover that exploring and experimenting in technology can be a satisfying and worthwhile experience.

The aims or hopes for *Launch Pad* were further elaborated and set out in Stevenson (1987a):

> The emphasis is unashamedly on enjoyment, and *Launch Pad* is biased strongly towards technology rather than pure science. However, the experience is also designed to be subtly educational; visitors learn without being aware that they are learning. A visit to *Launch Pad* is also intended to be inspirational; to act as a stimulus and to introduce young people to technology and science and encourage them to pursue these subjects further . . .

Professional Views about ISTCs

The literature, especially related to ISTCs and what goes on in them, is insubstantial, scattered and diverse so it was necessary to collect informally 'professional views' about them in order to define relevant research issues. A 'professional view' was considered to be the collection of theories, opinions and ideas which an ISTC professional (i.e. someone working in an ISTC or closely involved with one) forms as a result of their experience and intuitive assessment of ISTCs. 'Views' relating to what professionals think actually happens in an ISTC will not be reported here, only those relating to a possible long-term effect.

Views about what visitors may actually take away with them are many and varied, and are summarised below:

1   *A set of 'experiences' (or memories)*. These memories can be considered to
    be divided into three categories: what they did; how they felt; what they
    thought.
2   *A set of 'effects'*. If a visitor notices, for example, that when spinning around
    on a turntable a person goes slower when leaning out, then the visitor is
    considered to have discovered 'effect'.
3   *A set of 'explanations'*. These are explanations for the effect which the visi-
    tor has observed.
4   *A set of 'applications'*. Some of the effects which a visitor observes may be
    seen by him or her to have a practical application.
5   More *'understanding'* in a general sense.
6   *A change in attitudes*. It is generally hoped that a visitor may feel positively
    disposed towards science after a visit to an ISTC.

Research in Museums and ISTCs

. . . As the importance of informal education (Lucas 1983) becomes more widely
known the value of the family in teaching and facilitating learning for its
members has been recognised (Butler and Sussman, 1989).

We know that visitors talk about the exhibits whilst they are in front of them,
and it is not unreasonable to suppose that they might talk about them
afterwards. The museum visit is only a part of their total experiences; how do
they relate the visit to what they already know, their experiences in school or at
work, television and radio programmes, newspapers, etc?

A Study of Visitors to *Launch Pad*

Museums are generally thought of as being memorable places – people not only
remember the visit as a special event but also remember much of what they saw
and did. Also, as the role of a museum is to collect, conserve and display
material of historical significance its purpose could be said to be to keep certain
memories alive in people's minds. Research on visitor behaviour in museums has
indicated that visitors only spend a minute or two in front of each exhibit and
that after about 30–45 minutes 'museum fatigue' sets in. This suggests something of a paradox. Why do visitors find a museum visit memorable considering
the short time during which they are involved with the museum and its exhibits?
Research on visitor behaviour has not indicated that visitors are showing a great
degree of surprise, or other behavioural signs which might make an experience
particularly memorable.

Considering that a visitor on average spends so little time with each exhibit
then it seems unlikely that much cognitive processing will take place. If this is
so then we would expect that most visitors' memories of their experiences
would be episodic rather than semantic (a distinction first made by Tulving
(1972)). Episodic memories consist of autobiographical information about
events in one's own life, whereas semantic memory results from some kind of
cognitive processing and consists of facts about the world in general.

The memory of a person's first visit to a museum will be a unique episodic
one. After several visits to different museums a person will form a general idea
of museums as places where there are objects of historical significance, staff to
look after them, etc. This generalised knowledge, or 'schema' (Bartlett, 1932) or
'script' (Schank, 1982; Rumelhart and Norman, 1983), helps guide a person to

the behaviour appropriate to a museum. There are also 'scripts' for how to behave at the dentist or in a restaurant, for example.

Schema theory, however, is not very good at explaining why certain events can be remembered in vivid detail. The 'levels of processing' approach can explain this aspect. Craik and Lockhart (1972) argued that perception, attention and memory are interdependent. Therefore, the more processing that takes place at the time of encoding the memory trace, the better the memory of the event. Deep, distinctive or elaborate processing can also affect long-term memory. It is not just the processing which takes place at the time of encoding which may be important. Memory seems to be reconstructive, or constructive, and therefore processing can take place after the initial encoding.

What should one expect to find when looking at the memories of visitors about *Launch Pad* over 6 months after their visit? It would be rather disappointing for the originators of *Launch Pad* and supporters of ISTCs if little was remembered, especially if it was of a purely episodic nature. *Launch Pad* has an educational aim. Although it is implausible to expect much learning, as 'teaching events' only last a few minutes, is there any evidence to suggest that episodic memories are subsequently processed into semantic ones?

My study was designed to investigate in more detail the outcomes of a museum visit by conducting a long-term study of visitors. The study has concentrated on family groups and the data were collected in four main stages:

1 Tracking of one member of a group in *Launch Pad*;
2 Questioning all the members of a group immediately afterwards;
3 Sending each member of the group a written questionnaire several weeks later; and
4 Interviewing, at length, the same group about 6 months later.

Since a large part of the data collection involved visitors recalling what happened many months ago it was important to have an appreciation of the current understanding of how memory itself works. I provide a review in Stevenson (1987b) where its relevance to this study was argued for. In the field of psychology there is now much interest in the study of 'everyday' memory (Cohen, 1989) or research that has 'ecological validity' (Neisser and Winograd, 1988) . . .

Summary and Conclusions from Findings

The tracking data indicate that visitors to *Launch Pad* do attend to the exhibits for a considerable portion of their time in the gallery, and do not support the view that children spend a large part of their time rushing around. No real evidence for 'museum fatigue', as it is popularly termed, was found in this study of visitors to *Launch Pad*. Analysis of the tracking data revealed few differences in the way that males and females interacted with the exhibits, which provides encouraging news to those who hope ISTCs provide equal opportunities for both genders.

This study provides evidence of how individuals in an ISTC interact with and observe exhibits, mostly in association with others. For example, of time spent interacting, on average 81 per cent is spent with members of the family group or with other visitors.

The results from the post-visit interviews and the follow-up questionnaires show that immediately after their visit, everyone is able to talk about the exhibits in detail and to choose between them. The vast majority stated that their visit had been enjoyable and that they had been impressed by *Launch Pad*. A further indication of this is that 99 per cent stated that they had talked about *Launch Pad* after their visit, often to other family and friends.

The follow-up interviews provide clear evidence of the long-term impact of *Launch Pad* on visitors. Several months after their visits, people are able to recall in vivid detail much of what happened. Visitors recall not only what they did with the exhibits but also how they felt and thought about them – and much of this recall is spontaneous. When asked whether their feelings about *Launch Pad* had changed since the day of their visit, all visitors replied that they had not. This suggests that visitors' experiences are stable and not likely to change when they are reflected on.

There was evidence that visitors thought about what they were doing in *Launch Pad*. Most of this thinking was concerned with 'effects' rather than 'explanations' or 'understandings', although quite often visitors related their experiences to what they knew already or had seen on television. A large proportion of visitors' thoughts were accurate or appropriate, and this, together with the fascination that the exhibits provide for the visitors, suggests that cognitive processing does take place. The FUIs [Follow-up Interviews] also provided evidence that visitors do talk about their experience to the rest of their group and others after their visit.

As expected, most of the recalled memories were episodic in nature. However, the FUIs also contained material that was not episodic, indicating that memories of the visit had been processed subsequently.

This study has shown that many of the aims of ISTCs are being achieved, particularly as the experience is very interactive and generates interest and enthusiasm. Although no direct attempt was made to measure changes in attitudes, some visitors made it quite clear in the interviews that their attitude to science and technology was now more positive. Several adult females, who had no formal science education, had found their experiences in *Launch Pad* to be non-threatening and stimulating – they found they were able to learn along with their children without any bad feelings.

The approach taken in this study has produced rich and varied data which have shown that it is a useful way of investigating visitor behaviour in an ISTC, and illustrates that a visit to an ISTC is highly memorable and of lasting impact.

References

Bartlett, F C (1932). *Remembering*, Cambridge, Cambridge University Press.

Butler, H B and Sussman, M B (eds) (1989). *Museum visits and activities for family life enrichment*, The Haworth Press, New York and London.

Cohen, G (1989). *Memory in the real world*, Hove and London, Lawrence Erlbaum Associates.

Craik, F I M and Lockhart, R S (1972). 'Levels of processing: a framework for memory research', *Journal of Verbal Learning and Verbal Behaviour* 11, pp. 671–684.

Lucas, A M (1983). 'Scientific literacy and informal learning', *Studies in Science Education* 10, pp. 1–36.

Neisser, U and Winograd, E (eds) (1988). *Remembering reconsidered: ecological and traditional approaches to the study of memory*, Cambridge, Cambridge University Press.

Rumelhart, D E and Norman, D A (1983). 'Representation in memory' in R C Atkinson, R S Hernstein, G Lindzey and R D Luce (eds), *Handbook of experimental psychology*, Chichester, Wiley and Sons.

Schank, R C (1982). 'Reminding and memory organisation' in W G Lehnert and M H Ringle (eds), *Strategies for natural language processing*, Hillsdale, New Jersey, Lawrence Erlbaum.

Stevenson, J (1987a). 'The philosophy behind *Launch Pad*', *Journal of Education in Museums* 8, pp. 18–20.

Stevenson, J (1987b). 'Memorability: a new approach to understanding the outcomes of visits to interactive centres and museums', Paper presented at the Nature of interactive exhibits and exhibitions: towards defining objectives conference, University of Liverpool, pp. 23–33.

Tulving, E (1972). 'Episodic and semantic memory', in E Tulving and W Donaldson (eds), *Organization of memory*, New York, Academic Press.

45 Quest for the Perfect Methodology: A Tragi-comedy in Four Acts

D D Hilke

Extracted from a paper in *Museum visitor studies in the 90s*, Bicknell, S and Farmelo, G (eds), Science Museum, 1993, pp. 67–73.

Introduction

When Sandra Bicknell called to ask me to present a paper on evaluation methodology, she found me in my new offices at the Maryland Science Center. The phone was answered 'Director of Exhibits'.

Only a few years earlier, her calls had reached me at the Smithsonian and the voice answering the phone had intoned 'Office of Audience Research'.

To Sandra, placing the call to the new location was a minor inconvenience. However, the new telephone number was important. The change in positions was not irrelevant to my perspective on evaluation methodology. The methods one chooses – indeed the methods that will be valid and cost-effective in a given situation – are very much influenced by the context of the evaluation and the relative positions and expectations of all parties involved including the evaluators and evaluation advocates.

Act One: Basic Research

In 1981, I was in the final throes of pursuing my PhD in cognitive psychology. The job opening at the Smithsonian Institution offered an opportunity to study the spontaneous learning strategies of groups of mammals co-operatively exploring a novel context. For those who have not guessed yet, I am not talking about a longitudinal study of baboons at the zoo. The actual populations under study were tourists to the National Museum of Natural History, Smithsonian.

To the psychologist in me, the fact that the research site was a museum was the least interesting part of the equation. There were human families here, there was novelty here (something we all knew would elicit exploratory behaviour), and there were interesting variations in the kinds of exploratory behaviour that were supported. In some rooms, visitors were able only to look, read, talk and move. In others, they were able to touch, manipulate and juxtapose. There were the beginnings of a controlled study here: traditional halls versus discovery rooms. It was a delightfully complex context in which to undertake some basic research (Hilke, 1989a).

The primary goal of the study was to contribute to basic research. To this end, there were three factors that constrained the research methods chosen: a desire to address basic issues which could contribute to the general understanding of human behaviour; a desire to produce findings replicable by other researchers; and an abhorrence of what statisticians call type one error: a mistake made by saying that something is true when it is, in fact, false.

This third factor often leads to large sample sizes, controlled or randomised variables, tests for statistical significance, and many, many qualifiers in how the data can be legitimately interpreted.

The utility of the research to the creation of better exhibitions either at that time or in the future was not really considered in constructing the research programme. The criteria for success were those of an academic. Although I and other museum professionals would ultimately find the results interesting and provocative, only much later did such perspectives begin to shape the analysis and interpretation of the data (Hilke, 1987; 1988a).

I begin with my former life as a research psychologist because many of the evaluators working today are, or at one time were, academic researchers. To the extent that these professionals still filter their evaluation methodologies through these academic constraints, the field of visitor research will slowly but surely accrue verified facts and theories regarding visitor behaviour. Long-held rules of thumb (such as the fact that a visitor will turn right on entering an exhibition) may be validated, systematically qualified or repudiated. Little by little a science of visitor behaviour will begin to emerge. This is good. However . . .

Act Two: Evaluation Research

But I get ahead of myself. In 1985, I left the ivory tower of the Smithsonian's Office of Educational Research and founded the Office of Audience Research at the National Museum of American History. The office was named Audience Research instead of Visitor or Museum Evaluation mostly to assuage my own fears that the work I was to do as an in-house evaluator might be petty and site specific (museum professionals may want to substitute the phrase 'immediately useful') instead of fundamental and generalisable (museum professionals substitute 'interesting but of little immediate practical value').

One of the first projects I embarked upon was a summative evaluation of the effectiveness of a computer interactive in a small travelling exhibition jointly created by the National Museum of American History and the Smithsonian Institution Travelling Exhibition Service (Hilke, 1988b; Hilke, Hennings and Springuel, 1988). At that time, there was little research on the impact of the computer interactive in museum settings, and I was determined to rectify the situation.

Like a cancer that begins small and eventually transforms its host, thoughts about all of those factors that might possibly affect visitor behaviour in the exhibition infected the research design. The research was to be conducted at two different museums to control for museum and population effects. There were to be computer 'on' sessions and computer 'off' sessions to ensure that differences in behaviour or learning could be explicitly attributed to the computer. There were to be measurements of behavioural patterns throughout the exhibition recorded separately for hands-on, static and other types of exhibit displays, so that behaviours elicited at the computer could be compared with behaviours at other types of exhibition media.

Only an accountant could have had more columns of data to make sense of at the end of a day's work! What could have been a simple evaluation of visitor reaction to one exhibition unit became the King Kong of visitor studies.

Actually, the study was quite a success and so was the computer interactive. The curator was happy to learn that the computer had a positive impact not only on visitor learning, but also on visitor affect and behaviour in the exhibition at large. I was happy as a clam – learning more about the complex relationships that could exist amongst various exhibition media and merrily plotting strategies for future studies. Unfortunately, I was simultaneously learning how very, very difficult and time-consuming such evaluation *research* is, and my boss, who was a key player in running the museum, was wondering why this simple evaluation was dragging on and on.

Evaluation research is not without its costs. The careful, methodical and highly focused studies that meet research criteria are expensive, time-consuming and, of necessity, address only a limited set of relationships. The controlled focus that gives these studies their validity and generalisability can mean that other important variables and relationships are literally discounted. To the museum professionals who need information for decision-making quickly, evaluation research may seem to take too much time and money for too little return.

All of this came to a head when I joined 'the team' (Hilke, 1989b).

Act Three: Formative Evaluation

By 1987, it was clear to me that the exhibition developers in my museum just did not understand how evaluation research could help them create better exhibitions. Our discussions were friendly, but our perspectives diametrically opposed. The developers suggested that I simply did not understand the constraints of actually doing an exhibition: there was little enough time to do background research, assemble the artefacts and create a communicative design, without throwing audience concerns and evaluation studies into the mix.

I countered that exhibition developers persisted in making the same mistakes over and over again, that they should actively consider and assess the visitors' reactions at every step along the way, and, in my less tactful moments, that exhibitions that did not work for their audiences were worthless anyway since their entire *raison d'être* was that visitors would experience them.

In a strategic ploy that could have been described at the time as 'know thy enemy', I decided to infiltrate the ranks of the developers, get myself placed squarely on a team developing a major exhibition, and prove to them once and for all that . . .

To cut a long story short, we were both right. Working together for three years during the creation of *Information age: people, information, and technology* led us all to recognise the validity and importance of visitor-orientated development and of formative evaluation. However, this experience in crafting immediately practical evaluations forced me to re-evaluate my criteria for what makes a good evaluation, and broadened the set of evaluation tools I use on a day-to-day basis.

From the perspective of an exhibition team member, the major factors constraining the evaluation were quite different. They included timeliness, importance, persuasive power and expense – not necessarily in that order.

The information acquired through the evaluation effort needed to be available at a time when that information was able to affect the course of exhibition development. If available too soon, the information was seen as distracting and irrelevant. If available too late, the information was not able to affect the decisions to which it was relevant with the result that either the evaluator was left feeling useless or the team members were left living with a decision they regretted even before the exhibition had opened its doors.

The evaluation needed to address issues of visitor behaviour and experience that were both critical to the achievement of the goals of the exhibition and critical to decisions that would be made in the course of the exhibition's development. There were too many assumptions being made daily regarding what visitors would do *vis-à-vis* the proposed exhibition to waste evaluation resources on issues that were not highly design or content dependent or that would not have broad and lasting impact on the visitors' ultimate experience of the exhibition.

Finally, the evaluation method chosen needed to make available data, interpretations and explanations which would be seen as valid and relevant to the decision-makers and decision-influencers on the team. For some team members, visitor quotes and anecdotes were far more persuasive than charts and graphs; for others, the opposite was true. There is an art to presenting an evaluation report so that each power broker hears the information in a form she or he finds persuasive and valid. However, it was not always a matter of presentation. The most rigorous evaluation method would be of no avail if the ultimate power brokers did not believe in the validity of the method or in the relevance of the information it acquired to the decision at hand.

The evaluation needed to be possible with the money and staff resources at hand. Obviously, this had always been a factor in devising an evaluation, but it had never been a major factor for me before. An academic could always glance fleetingly at the PhD on the wall and simply say: 'Well then, it just can't be done because it can't be done right.' As a member of the exhibition team, I knew it had to be done somehow. Decisions would be made eventually with or without the evaluation results. The question was never as simple as 'Can I do it right?'. The question became 'Can I do something cost-effective that will give more valid information and the chance of a better decision than would be available if I did nothing?'.

Since my experience on the *Information age* team, I have tried to summarise, in simple checklist form, the various factors that came to influence the methods chosen for various evaluations throughout the project . . .

Now Playing: Act Four: Museum Management

What happens when you *are* the decision-maker? What happens when it is up to you to decide whether to invest in evaluation, when to trust the opinions of the team without audience feedback, and whether to spend $30,000 on a salary, a contract or exhibition fabrication? Can you ignore that inner voice that says 'This is where you always wanted to be, right? The power is yours. What are you going to do with it?'. After a year as Director of Exhibits, this question still reverberates in my mind. I arrived on the job on 10 August 1992 and discovered that the Exhibits Department had exactly 10 weeks to create and install a 5,000 ft^2 [465 m^2] interactive exhibition that would house six animatronic dinosaurs. A brainstorming session a few weeks before had come up with the working title *The Great Dinosaur Game*. Nobody really knew exactly what we meant by the title, but it sounded right and the Marketing Department was already refining its hyperbole with the slogan 'The game too big to fit in a box'. We had a lot of work to do.

As a dutiful evaluator turned exhibits director, I mumbled suggestions regarding audience testing and feedback at least twice a day over the next 10 weeks as my exhibit developers came to me with sketches, scripts and prototypes for approval. In the end, the decisions were theirs and mine, based almost entirely on professional feedback we gave each other or elicited from staff around the museum.

In the mad rush to get the exhibition on the gallery, the only visitor data we collected concerned the choice of materials for our game paths. As the exhibition opening neared, I wondered how I was ever going to admit to my colleagues that the sum total of evaluation work we had done for the exhibition was to place two squares of plexiglass next to the museum's ticket booths to see if we really got fewer scratches with the vastly more expensive scratch-resistant plexiglass. It was not a pretty thought.

October came. The exhibition opened. Word of mouth was great. And I finally found some spare staff time that could be allocated to see if visitors were actually behaving in the exhibition as we had intended. A staff evaluation was designed, data were collected, and just as one of my chief developers was summarising the data, another exhibition descended like a tornado, sweeping up every staff member that crossed its path.

The evaluation data would be valuable one day, but at that moment we had an exhibition to create. Without a thought, I told my developer to stop evaluating and start developing. Our deadline was much too close to waste any time on anything that was not essential.

It was only at the weekend that I stopped to realise how much I was beginning to sound like the exhibition developers that I had argued with at the Smithsonian. I still believed deeply that the primary criterion for evaluating the success of an exhibition was the ways in which visitors reacted to it. But without exhibitions appearing regularly, the museum would soon have no visitors to react.

When resources were scarce, I, like any manager, cut back to the bare essentials. I began to realise that I was experiencing a conflict in resource management that was naturally biased against visitor evaluation. Exhibitions can be created without any input or consideration of the visitor. All that is needed is some content, a design and the resources to get it implemented. These three factors do not guarantee a good exhibition, but, if managed well, they are sufficient to produce an exhibition that opens its doors both on time and under budget.

Power and opportunity naturally arise for those criteria-for-success related to each of these three areas. There is no such protection for visitor interests, at least none until it is too late.

The manager who sees an exhibition's *raison d'être* as the provision of a meaningful experience for its visitors must create schedules, budgets, milestones and staff positions that enforce visitor-oriented criteria-for-success and provide the means to work towards and evaluate them. In this way, the manager will bring balance to the exhibition development process and ensure that valid and appropriate content becomes informative and memorable for visitors, that safe and creative design becomes accessible and engaging, and that the exhibition still opens on time and under budget because the plan provided for both the time and money necessary to ensure that visitor feedback and visitor advocacy were an integral part of the process.

Was my work at the Maryland Science Center proving that such visitor-oriented management was impossible for me? Well, not entirely. Upon my arrival, I had also discovered that we had another exhibition development project on the books. This project had a time line of nearly three years, a budget of over a million dollars, and would result in two mathematics exhibitions which might in their life-span serve more than five million visitors.

Using the visitor-orientated philosophy outlined above, I re-wrote the schedule. Opening dates were pushed further into the future to allow for extensive periods of formative evaluation. Budgets were re-written to support front-end, formative and summative evaluations. Public space was reserved on the exhibitions schedule for prototype galleries. Expert advisors were created in physical accessibility and cultural accessibility. All new and old staff positions had evaluation written into their job descriptions.

On 10 August 1993, as I looked back on my first year at the Maryland Science Center, *The Great Dinosaur Game* had come and gone and the formative evaluation was still unfinished. Another original, temporary exhibition, *All Sorts of Sports,* had been created and no evaluation was planned despite the fact that many topics in the exhibition overlapped with many of our long-term exhibition development goals. I was frustrated.

But on the same day, I walked through our *Our Plans/Your Views: Mathematics,* a 1,400ft^2 (130m^2) prototype gallery for a permanent exhibition that would not open for nearly 2 years. Here, my staff, visitors and an outside evaluator were busy exploring the potential of the prototype interactive units to engage, excite and teach visitors. The final report from our front-end study for this exhibition was due any day, and our physical accessibility expert would be giving us a critical appraisal of the prototypes the following week.

As I looked back over the year, I could see many opportunities for visitor feedback that had been missed because of inadequate planning, time or money. But I also saw progress in creating a management environment in which those opportunities would be more likely in the future. What will that future hold? Will I ever find the perfect evaluation methodology or the perfect exhibition philosophy? Unlikely. The pressures which kept my colleagues at the Smithsonian focused on issues tangential to visitor concerns, I now recognise as intrinsic to the development and management of museum spaces. As a museum manager, I will never again escape these pressures; I can only hope to manage them in ways that complement rather than compete with visitor-orientated needs. To date my record as a visitor-oriented manager is mixed. But Act Four has only just begun.

References

Hilke, D D (1987). 'Museums as resources for family learning: turning the question around', *The Museologist* 50(175), pp. 14–15.

Hilke, D D (1988a). 'Strategies for family learning in museums', in Bitgood, S, Roper, J T and Benefield, A (eds), *Visitor studies: theory, research and practice* I, Jackonsville, Center for Social Design, pp. 120–34.

Hilke, D D (1988b). 'Computer interactives: beginning to assess how they affect exhibition behavior', *Spectra* 15(4), pp. 1–2.

Hilke, D D (1989a). 'The family as a learning system: an observational study of families in museums', *Marriage and Family Review* 13(3/4), pp. 101–30.

Hilke, D D (1989b). 'Joining the team: reflections of a social scientist turned exhibition developer', Paper, American Association of Museums annual meeting, New Orleans, June 1989.

Hilke, D D, Hennings, E and Springuel, M (1988). 'The impact of interactive computer software on visitors' exhibition experiences: a case study', *ILVS Review* 1(1), pp. 34–49.

Index

242

collaboration *see* exhibition teams

comfortable viewing zones 148

comment books 225

computers 7, 136–40
  evaluation of impact of interactive project 237–8
  principles of design 137–40
  programme examples 137
  usefulness of 136
  visitor attraction to 137–8
  working within visitor relationship 140

conceptual orientation 149

constructivism 30–4

Contemporary, The 170, 171

context, notion of 27–8, 32

Continental Puzzle 137

Cornell, Joseph 38, 42–3

Corrin, Lisa 170, 171

Craik, F I M and Lockhart, R S 233

Csikszentmihalyi, Mihaly and Rochberg-Halton, Eugene 4–5

'cumulative learning' 21

curators 15, 58
  presentation of as individual 7–8
  role 10, 11, 13, 14

Damon, William 27

deaf people
  services for 97–8

Deer Game 137

Department of Education and Science 163

Desert Explorations 136

designers 10, 11, 14

developmental theory 22–3, 24, 25

Dewey, J 31, 32

Diamond, J 79

didactic panels 202

disability culture 92–4

Disability resource directory for museums 100

disabled people 11, 91–103 *see also* visually-impaired, learning difficulties
  consultation of 96–7
  guidance on provision for 101–3
  importance of appropriate language 98–9
  and legislation 99–100
  MGC guidelines 91, 96, 100, 110
  need for improved access 95, 99, 100
  number of 95–6
  services offered 97–8
  targeting of 56, 96
  targeting of by Laing Art Gallery 157

discovery rooms 162

display cases 148

displays 80–1
  guidelines on planning ix–x

Donaldson, M 168

Earth Over Time (videodisc) 137

educators 10–15, 70–1
  impact of 14–15
  responsibilities 11–14

entry surveys 59–60

Equal Arts 157

ethnic groups
  targeting of 56–7

Eureka! 86

evaluation 12, 122, 143, 160, 215–41
  behavioural mapping 222–3, 225–6
  criteria for successful 238–9
  of display for people with learning difficulties 228–30
  formative 12, 143, 216–17, 218, 219, 238–9
  front-end analysis 12, 217
  goal clarification 217–18
  importance of 216, 219
  interviews 217, 219, 221–2, 226, 234
  of *Launch Pad* 232–4
  methodology 236–41
  need to test entire installation 219
  problems with defining exhibition success 224–5
  in process of transition 215
  questionnaires 220–1, 226
  summative 216, 237–8
  techniques 218–19, 220–3
  trends supporting re-emergence of 216

exhibition policy 109–11

exhibition producers
  imposition of learning impediments on visitors 3–4, 5

exhibition teams
  and *American Encounters* 112–16
  definition of roles 11
  inclusion of educators on 10–15
  problems 10

exhibitions
  audience-related guidelines for 110, 143
  characteristics of successful 4–5, 227
  design 22, 121
  goal clarification 112–13, 217
  planning 107–51
  problems with defining success 224–5

Printed for The Stationery Office by Hobbs The Printers of Southampton
TJ839 3/00 C4 10170